John Ogilby

and the Taste of His Times

IOHANNES OGILVIVS

Portrait of John Ogilby, c. 1660 (Lely-Faithorne) Aesop, 1665
By permission of the Folger Shakespeare Library, Washington DC, USA.

John Ogilby

and the
Taste of His Times

by

KATHERINE S. VAN EERDE

DAWSON

First published in 1976

© Katherine S Van Eerde 1976

Wm Dawson & Sons Ltd, Cannon House
Folkestone, Kent, England

British Library Cataloguing in Publication Data

Van Eerde, Katherine S
    John Ogilby and the taste of his times.
    Bibl. - Index.
    ISBN 0-7129-0690-8
    1. Title
    686.2'092'4   Z232.0
    Ogilby, John
    Printers - England - Bibliography

Printed in Great Britain
by W & J Mackay Limited, Chatham
by photo-litho

Contents

For
LOUIS BOOKER WRIGHT

A small token of a far greater friendship

Preface

It is to the Introduction that I have committed much of the explanation of my interest in John Ogilby and the paths to which that subject led me. It was, of course, my work on Wenceslaus Hollar that first introduced me to Ogilby and to a host of other persons; it was Ogilby who caught and held my attention, even before the publication of the Hollar book.

With so brief a note on the subject of this volume, I may turn to the other purpose of a preface — the expression of gratitude for favours and assistance granted. If the first paragraph was short, it will be more than compensated for by the length of the second part. Working on John Ogilby has led me to experts in various fields, to remote bookshops, to libraries in three countries, and to a succession of people who have been helpful and knowledgeable in diverse ways.

I should begin, I think, with my thanks to Muhlenberg College, which has sustained my research with a sabbatical and has again matched a Ford Foundation grant for summer study. As the College staff is primarily involved in teaching and not research, President John H. Morey and my department head, Professor John J. Reed, have had to make adjustments of considerable extent in order to accommodate my research needs. I am grateful. Once again, I have been a demanding user of nearly all departments of the Library; in particular, I should like to thank Mrs. Valborg Jepsen, who has tracked down and found so many unusual volumes through the Inter-Library Loan service. Two colleagues deserve especial notice: Professor John S. Davidson, Librarian Emeritus, for his assistance on the early part of the book, and Professor Jay H. Hartman of the English Department for his continued helpfulness, particularly on the latter part.

Without the great libraries, public and private, my work would be impossible. I am most indebted therefore to the founders of various august institutions and to their well-informed and obliging staffs. Nowadays, they must do more than supply volumes; there are the intricacies of permissions and duplication and reproduction to be handled, always, in my experience, with efficiency and good will. I owe much indeed to the Folger Shakespeare Library, its Director O. B. Hardison and its Director Emeritus Louis B.

Wright. Miss Megan Lloyd, Executive Editor, has given me invaluable help with Ogilby, as she did with Hollar; all of the Folger staff are entitled to my warmest thanks.

I wish also to extend my thanks to the Beinecke Rare Book Library of Yale University and to its Director, Louis L. Martz, for the many courtesies rendered me. To Lehigh University and to James D. Mack, Director of University Libraries there, goes my gratitude for many hours alone in the Rare Book Room, together with the opportunity to collate and cogitate undisturbed among seventeenth-century folios. Similarly, I wish to thank the Franklin and Marshall Library, Lancaster, Pennsylvania, for its assistance with one particularly obscure volume.

To the many testimonials already offered to the British Library (still the British Museum to most of us), I should like to add mine yet again. In particular, I thank the staffs of the North Library, the Students' Room and the Map Room. In the last-named, Dr. Helen Wallis and her assistants were of significant assistance. At the Guildhall I profited from a high degree of expertise and helpfulness from all members of the staff. I should like especially to thank Ralph Hyde Keeper of Prints and Drawings and James Sewell of the Guildhall Records Office for their most rewarding aid. I worked more briefly, but again with profit, at the Public Record Office and the Bodleian Library at Oxford. I am grateful also to the National Register of Archives and especially to Miss Sonia P. Anderson Assistant Keeper, Historical Manuscripts Commission.

I should like also to acknowledge the opportunity of working at the Stationers Company, where Stanley Osborne assisted me; at the Merchant Taylors Company, where Antony Walker was of considerable help; at Trinity College, Dublin, at the National Library in Dublin, and at the National Library of Scotland, where Miss Ann Young provided me with expert help. One important query that I directed to J. B. Trapp, formerly Librarian and now Director of the Warburg Institute, received prompt and lucid attention, for which I wish to render public thanks. And Mrs Victoria Moger, Librarian of the London Museum, gave critical assistance over a particular map. To the very many others who proffered essential help along the way and who cannot all be named, I offer the tribute of my memory. And in addition to the acknowledgments attached to the illustrations, I wish to thank the various libraries for granting permission to reproduce and use those invaluable aids to an understanding of what John Ogilby was doing in the latter seventeenth century.

I acknowledge with deep thanks the assistance in this work that was rendered by my receiving a Fellowship from the Guggenheim Foundation in 1971-72. A research grant from the American Philosophical Society in the spring of 1974 enabled me to do some final checking in London, and I wish to thank the Society in this place.

Mr. Ian Williams, Publishing Manager of Dawsons, has been constant in encouragement and support of this book. I hereby offer him my sincere thanks for his excellent advice and efforts in working out the complexities of a transatlantic venture.

To Mrs. Audrey Brevik, my indexer, Mrs. Dorothy Frankenfield, who aided in various ways with the reproduction of the manuscript, and particularly to Miss Mae Borger, whose skill as decipherer and typist is of the highest order, are extended my gratitude for their continued and obliging efforts. To my husband John and daughter Elizabeth go my apologies for the numerous hours devoted to Ogilby instead of to them. And to Louis B. Wright for sustained encouragement, advice and practical assistance my debt is measureless.

K.S.V.E.
Muhlenberg College
December 1, 1975

List of Illustrations

Frontispiece John Ogilby c. 1660

Introduction

The complexity of John Ogilby's life (1600-1676) is the first inducement to a study of the man. In a lifetime covering three-fourths of the seventeenth century, Ogilby served and came to know kings, statesmen and scientists. Yet his beginnings in Scotland and England were humble, and he first gained notice as a dancer — hardly a recommendation for social advancement. From his low estate as son of a man in debtor's prison, he progressed, via the dance, to performing before the King. Permanently lamed, through an accident while dancing, Ogilby became a dancing master, and proceeded also to compose interludes and to choreograph dances for plays. After early success as an entertainer, he became founder, manager and director of Dublin's first theatre under the Lord Deputy of Ireland, the Earl of Strafford. During the Civil Wars, his fortunes fell, though not quite to the depths of his late patron, the Earl. At fifty, about the age when most of his contemporaries were arranging for their funerals, Ogilby finally felt secure enough to marry, choosing a London widow of some means. His relationship with her provided Ogilby with his chief assistant and eventual heir, William Morgan, his wife's grandson.

Inevitably, as a man of masques and of the theatre, Ogilby came to know many of the literary men and the performers of his day — probably Ben Jonson, certainly James Shirley, Sir William Davenant, Joseph Ashbury and numerous others. Although throughout the seventeenth century there was a high proportion of Catholics in this group, no evidence connects Ogilby with the Old Faith. He seems equally to have no part in the Presbyterianism into which he was presumably born; in fact, he enjoyed making fun of sectaries, as he showed in his treatment of New England in *America*. He died, as he had lived, a Church of England man, and everything points to his finding that as congenial a faith as did his first monarch, James VI and I. A child of fortune in this, as in other ways, he took religion as he found it prescribed, apparently untouched by doctrinal conflicts.

In his only effort at autobiography (the Preface to *Africa,* 1670), Ogilby ignored his early life and began the story with his translations, the first of which appeared in 1649, when he was nearly fifty years old. A varied life lay behind him; ahead was a decade of political ambiguity and economic

11

hazard. His skills in dancing and the theatre were useless in the 1650's, and Ogilby then turned, with surprising mastery, to the translation of the classics — only a few, but those chiefly the great ones: Virgil and Homer, with Aesop for light relief. His clever use first of patronage, and then of lotteries, extended his readership and success. When, at seventy, he looked back on his life, it was natural that he opened his account with this period. From then on, slowly at first, his influence on his age can be traced.

John Ogilby studied the heroic epics, translated them faithfully, and included the numerous scholarly marginalia necessary to make his work respectable. But he had been an actor and impresario before becoming a translator, and he retained an interest in the depiction of a scene as well as a sense of line and design. His emphasis on picture or illustration was unusually lavish for his time. Numerous engravings ('sculps') decorated all his volumes except for the first, and were prominently noted on their title pages. Furthermore, he paid constant attention to obtaining fine paper, to using clear and harmonious type faces and to the employment of wide margins and running heads. Sometimes he included tables of contents and lists of illustrations. He used expert artists and engravers. In his last book, *Britannia,* he employed colour with considerable success. First through association with famous printers, then by obtaining a licence for his own press, Ogilby contributed to the art of fine book-making in England, a country that then lagged behind the Continent in this craft. He created or at least helped to develop a taste for such volumes among the upper classes, who were now steadily expanding their libraries and muniment rooms.

In his work on Aesop, begun in 1651 and continued, with additions and revisions, through the 1660's, Ogilby showed a taste for the political satire so characteristic of his own times and later. Far less savage than Swift or even Dryden, he nevertheless hit out at the follies of Parliament, of fanatics, of humankind generally, following Aesop's trail but, especially in the later *Aesopicks,* adding his own touch and using varied and interesting verse forms. Ogilby's own versatility, or perhaps his urge for more financial security, caused him to break off this kind of writing, to the probable detriment of his later literary reputation — but to the advantage of his pocket.

Loyalty to the new king came into vogue in 1660, and Ogilby was one of the leaders in that field. His printing and reprinting of the Coronation Procession led to his identification with the new regime and, more significantly, for him, to new offices, patents and licences, all of them lucrative. He developed and maintained good City connections. He continued to publish translations. And he gained a patent as Master of the Revels in Ireland, which enabled him to organize and nourish a successful, though modest, Irish theatre, this one the long-lived Smock Alley Theatre.

Ogilby escaped the Plague, but the Fire brought him extensive losses. From the latter disaster, he recovered as usual, however, and proceeded to become a respected London businessman, with his own press. Sensing, as he said himself, that new currents were stirring, Ogilby left verse and turned to prose. In his atlases, he invited his countrymen to engage in enterprises of expanding England's wealth and power, through trade and exploration. Ogilby presumably thought of himself, at least in later years, as an Englishman, or perhaps as a Briton, though even to long-standing friends he was always a Scot. His travel books, while often cumbrously assembled, were full of interesting stories and illustrated with fearful and wonderful sights. Just as Pope held a lifelong regard for Ogilby's *Iliad* and its great illustrations, so many a child must have had his imagination stirred as he turned the folio pages of *Africa, Asia, America, China* and *Japan,* even if the instruction gained thereby left much to be desired. Certainly, older readers like the Earl of Denbigh and probably Anthony Ashley Cooper had direct interest in *America,* the volume most appealing to Englishmen at that time. Ogilby included pages of statistics (probably as useless then as they are now) in his great travel atlases, but he also wrote in a clear and sometimes entertaining style, as when, for example, in *Africa,* he discussed the naming of the hemisphere 'America.' He rightly associated it with 'Americus Vesputius . . . who by a lucky hit' gained the honour over Columbus. In the margin, Ogilby attributed this to 'the gingle of his Name Americk with Africk, though signifying no more in English than Harry Wasp.'

The travel atlases, issued for the most part in the 1670's, reflect a new interest on the part of Ogilby, and one coming into ever greater prominence. This was the growing attraction exerted by science for almost all learned and near-learned men of the time. In his last decade, Ogilby consorted with Robert Hooke, Sir Christopher Wren, John Aubrey and Elias Ashmole, and others of the *cognoscenti* of the time. These associations were reflected in his atlases. At the beginnings of various volumes, the author-translator-publisher attempted to fit the strange continent or land he was treating into the whole world, to locate it precisely and at times to pass judgement on some of the wilder stories he printed. This new awareness, an awareness of space, of mensuration, of accuracy, of the constant use of reason presaged the next century's attitudes. Ogilby made only tentative approaches to these ideas in most of his atlases. In *Britannia,* however, his final and most formidable work, he attempted a scientific calculation of the length and conditions of the major and minor roads of England and Wales. The work was much harder and costlier than any other he had done, and he was dying as it reached completion. Ogilby left it as his chief legacy to his heirs; and, more permanently, it was a bequest to his countrymen, a book for studying, for reprinting and imitating and, for seventeenth- and eighteenth-century travellers, above all, for using.

At Ogilby's death in 1676, his pride in his nation (once again ruled by a Stuart) was high. He had served three monarchs, his loyalty never in question. He had survived one of England's most turbulent centuries. His affairs frequently failed, but he seemed always to rise further on the next attempt. No Vicar of Bray, he nevertheless took the changing measures of his times and produced what those times admired. Ephemeral and individual as is the term and definition of taste, Ogilby was certainly involved with it in the productive years of his life. It is ironical that his name came to be remembered in succeeding centuries primarily through the ridicule aimed at his verse translations of the classics by Dryden and Pope (in 'Mac-

Flecknoe' and 'The Dunciad').

There are, naturally, *lacunae* in a life of such movement in troubled times. Ogilby is invisible, or nearly so, in the 1620's and again in the latter 1640's. There is the question of how the dancer became the impresario of the Irish theatre. There is the wonder of his apparently late achievement in the world of classical scholarship. There is the marvel of his successive defeats in one career or fashion after another and the even greater marvel of his recovery from each of these. Friends of greater repute and artistry — James Shirley, Wenceslaus Hollar, Edward Sherburn — died in poverty. Ogilby died a prosperous man. Many of the questions evoked by a study of his life are attributable to a sad dearth of personal data, either autobiographical material or letters. The absence of the latter is probably occasioned by Ogilby's few family connections, and humble social status. This volume is designed to set forth the man and his life, to indicate his influence in various areas of opinion and taste, and to revive the regard in which he was held by his contemporaries.

I

A Scottish Adventurer

Long years after the event, John Aubrey was querying Ogilby about his birth date and place. Aubrey, with his insatiable curiosity for specific factual material, recorded in the 1650's that the date of John Ogilby's birth was November 17, 1600. There was no doubt about the birthplace being in Scotland, but, said Aubrey, Ogilby would not say where. By then Ogilby's name was identified with his translations of Homer, and he had adopted the conceit of saying that he wished to conceal his birthplace so that, like Homer, various places would contest for the honour of claiming him as their native son.[1] The tradition has been that the place was in or near Edinburgh, but the registers in the General Register House there, admittedly imperfect, show no Ogilby baptized in or around 1600. In the seventeenth century, the early years of those neither wellborn nor wealthy were likely to receive scant documentation, and there is generally little of fact to be discovered about such years and even less of significance. It is therefore difficult to get a sustained and clear look at the early life of John Ogilby, despite the many details reported, some of them conflicting.

Another figure, who, like Aubrey, stood somewhere between acquaintance and friend to Ogilby, was Elias Ashmole, an assiduous compiler of fact to support his endless astrological calculations. In a book of these there appear two horoscopes of Ogilby, one of which has the following words in the centre: 'Nov. 17, 1600, 4 A.M. Mr. Jo. Ogilby of Kellemeane, 10 myle north from Dundee.'[2] The specific nature of this location would argue for its accuracy against the traditional 'in the vicinity of Edinburgh.' It would also explain why no Ogilby was found in the registers of Edinburgh parishes (although their somewhat fragmentary nature must not be ignored). Dundee, some 40 miles north of Edinburgh, appears on sixteenth-century maps, but I have not found 'Kellemeane.' Its prefix indicates a not-uncommon Celtic origin: and the most likely explanation for its omission from maps is, of course, that it was a small village. Separated from the capital city by both the Firth of Forth and the Firth of Tay, Dundee's forty-mile distance would have been considered a long one in the early seventeenth century; Kellemeane must certainly have been unknown south of the Border. John Ogilby's instinct for identifying himself with the notable and

15

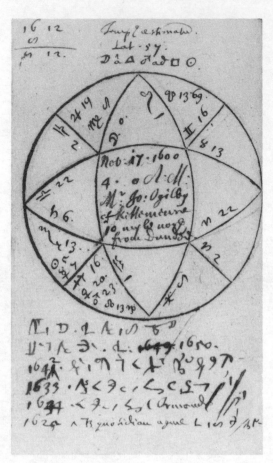

1) *Horoscope of Ogilby taken by Ashmole*
MS.ASHM.332, fol. 35 v, Bodleian Library, Oxford

successful rather than the obscure could easily have led him to say 'near Edinburgh' when asked by Southrons for his birthplace; but when he had his horoscope cast, and was told the necessity for precise and correct details to insure an accurate forecast, he might be expected to produce the long-submerged but not forgotten fact of his true birthplace.

There were, in fact, important Ogilvies — a variant for 'Ogilby' — not far from Dundee, but no direct evidence connects John Ogilby the poet-publisher with that family. The noble family of the Ogilvies of Airlie had long been established in Angus and Forfar, not far from Dundee.[3] Although some connection seems likely between John Ogilby and this family, he never claimed such a connection, and he was not the man to ignore such a tie if he knew of it. Orthography should perhaps not be cited on any side of an argument involving seventeenth-century figures, but it might be noted that John Ogilby invariably signed himself 'Ogilby' and so printed his name, whereas the public records of the Airlie family are generally of 'Ogilvies.'

John Ogilby can have spent only a few years in Scotland. It seems probable that his father moved the household south to London, in the train of the new King, sometime around or soon after the summer of 1603, when James VI and I himself arrived there. In early seventeenth-century London, the name 'Ogilby' with such variations as 'Ogilvy,' Ogilvie' and 'Ogelby' is a relatively rare one, despite the crowd of hungry Scots who then appeared in the capital. It therefore seems likely, particularly in view of later evidence, that it was the father of the future poet John Ogilby who was admitted to the Merchant Taylors Company by redemption in June 1606.[4] This entry states further that Ogilby was admitted 'at the request of Edward ap John Coen, Cryer.' His admission fee, paid to the chamberlain, was 6s.8d.

The elder Ogilby clearly commanded friends of some standing, to be admitted to the freedom of one of the great companies of the City, within three years of his Scottish monarch's coronation. Furthermore, this Ogilby's son, another John Ogilby, was admitted to the Merchant Taylors Company by patrimony on 6 July 1629, by which time his father was dead.[5] In 1654, 'the poet, John Ogilby' — in this case indisputably the subject of this work — was identified as a freeman of the Merchant Taylors Company,[6] and Ogilby made increasing use of his City connections after the Restoration of 1660. It seems likely therefore that the John Ogilby of 1629 was the same as that of 1654 and so the son of the freeman of 1606. Through much of the 1630's and some of the 1640's the future poet-printer was out of England, and during the Commonwealth records were kept with considerable laxity. It is therefore not surprising that his name does not appear in Company records in those twenty-five years.

It is Aubrey who is responsible for most of the data usually quoted on John Ogilby's early life, many items being supplied in the latter seventeenth-century, late in the life of both men.[7] Aubrey says that Ogilby came from a 'gentleman's family and bred to his grammar.'[8] It is interesting that no reference is made here to any noble or Airlie connection; but it is certain that John Ogilby knew Latin (his 'grammar') well; well enough, in fact, to revive it to good effect in middle age. On the other hand, he apparently had no Greek in his boyhood studies, which would imply that his classical education was hardly a complete one.

If it was the poet-printer's father who became a member of the Merchant Taylors Company in 1606, his prosperity was brief. According to Aubrey, the father wasted his estate and was sent to King's Bench Prison for debt sometime around 1612 or 1613. The records for that prison in the Public Record Office are scanty and unindexed. There are no lists of prisoners for this time, and in the volumes of 'Indictments Ancient'[9] I have not found the name of Ogilby in the stated years. The imprisonment gains probability, however, from further circumstantial details. As the story was filtered through some half century of memories to Aubrey's notes, the young John, then about twelve or thirteen, took over the burden of supporting himself and his mother, apparently by selling 'spangles' and 'needles.' As successful in this as in later undertakings, he even amassed a little extra money which he, or his father, adventured on an elaborate Virginia Company lottery, presumably that of 1612.

In March 1612, the Virginia Company received a charter for holding a lottery. According to a contemporary document, the lots sold for 2s.6d. apiece, and the money came in 'most of it by pettie & small somes, & by the handes of a very great & almost infinite nomber of severall persons.'[10] After considerable advertising, the draw was held at the end of June, at a special Lottery House in the West End of St. Paul's Churchyard.[11] The twelve-year-old Ogilby may have been present for the event in this bookseller's area, where his own works were to become familiar objects in a few more decades. A large first prize went to a London tailor, and one of the lesser winners was John Ogilby.[12] With the sum he won, he paid his father's debt and released him from prison.[13] Ogilby the man remembered the boy's success and in later life instituted and successfully ran several lotteries of books, the production of which were by then his chief interest and means of livelihood.[14]

Presumably, the family fortunes remained low, even after the father's release from prison. Aubrey's account states that thereafter the young Ogilby 'bound himself,' not to a master in one of the great or even lesser companies of the City, but to a dancing master, John Draper, in Gray's Inn Lane. In a life filled with enough vicissitudes and drama to rival that of a picaresque hero, this is certainly one of the most curious episodes. Clearly, the Ogilby family had not brought with them, or had already lost, any Scottish Puritan scruples against dancing. Financial stringency may also have played a part in the apprenticeship to a dancing master. It would doubtless have been a less expensive commitment than to a stationer, say, or a vintner, or, as might have been expected, in the light of his father's membership, to a merchant tailor.

The dance as art and vocation existed at varying levels in early Stuart England. The French or Italian dancing master might be laughed at and despised for his mincing, over-elegant airs. Yet, when the Court danced, or when masques, with dances, were performed in great houses, no one (except Puritans) offered to sneer at either the art or the performers. Terpsichore, the muse of the dance, had been honoured from Renaissance times;

translations on the art of dancing (from the Italian) appeared in Elizabethan England. And Sir George Buck, Master of Revels, wrote in 1612 'Of Orchestrice or the Art of Dancing,'[15] where he cited the honour accorded the dance among the Greeks, David dancing before the Lord, and various dances performed in modern courts and colleges. A further statement insisted that mastery in the area of entertainment required 'knowledge in Grammar, Rhetorick, Logicke, Philosophie, History, Musick, Mathematicks, and in other Arts.'

Although such exalted claims to the significance of the dance were being composed at about the time of Ogilby's apprenticeship to John Draper in Gray's Inn Lane, it is not to be supposed that the young man learned much of these subjects in his early years. No doubt an agile and personable youth, Ogilby served his apprenticeship successfully, and to such good effect that (presumably by giving lessons, illegal for an apprentice but tolerated), he bought out the last years of his apprenticeship from his master and set up a school of his own. One of Ogilby's own apprentices, the well-known Restoration actor John Lacy, told Aubrey decades later of Ogilby's dancing school in Black-Spread-Eagle Court. This was near the same Gray's Inn Lane where Ogilby had begun to dance;[16] established presumably in the 1620's or very early 1630's, it may have been Ogilby's first school or a later one.

It must have been clear to a youth as clever and ambitious as young John Ogilby that a dancing school would never catapult him into the world of great events, where he certainly aspired to be. That world in the 1620's centred about the Court and its King, James; his great favourite, the Marquess and later Duke of Buckingham; and somewhat to the rear, Prince Charles. For a dancer to become known within that circle it was necessary to appear in one of the theatrical companies then performing in London, and to perform in such an outstanding way as to catch the eye of young noblemen, particularly that of the favourite Buckingham. The world of dance was inextricably involved with that of the masque and the theatre, and Ogilby must have participated in some of the performances by the regular theatrical companies. The aging James doted increasingly on youth and youthful performers, and Buckingham was on the lookout for fresh faces and quick bodies to perform in some of the great masques he gave at Court and elsewhere.

The masque in James's time was designed to delight eyes, ears and mind at once, with special pleasures for the King of enjoying the capers of handsome young men, intermingled with praise of himself and spiced with wild buffoonery and bawdiness.[17] Young Prince Charles danced well, but with a dignity and reserve foreshadowing the changes he would introduce at his Court. The royal favourite, the Duke of Buckingham, however, set a more energetic style. On Twelfth Night, 1618, the Venetian Ambassador related that the King had grown angry with the dragging steps of the young dancers, who had tired at the close of a performance. To appease his master, the then Marquess of Buckingham 'immediately sprang forward, cutting a score of lofty and very minute capers with so much grace and agility that he not only appeased the ire of his angry lord, but moreover rendered himself the admiration of everybody.'[18] A youthful and energetic dancing master like John Ogilby and one, moreover, who was not ill-favoured (to judge by his portraits done in middle age), was the very kind of performer the Duke would have sought for his series of lavish and famous masques. It must have been an achievement of cherished ambition when Ogilby was selected to participate in 'the Duke of Buckingham's great masque' at Court.[19] Although it is not certain which of the several 'great' masques this was, it has in recent times been suggested that it was Ben Jonson's *The Gypsies Metamorphosed,* performed three times in August and September of 1621.[20] Certainly, Ogilby danced in one of Buckingham's famous masques; he may well have danced in several between 1621 and 1627. An examination of *The Gypsies* in some detail will serve to show the circumstances under which masques were generally presented in those years.

The Gypsies Metamorphosed, for which Buckingham paid Jonson £100, was performed in celebration of the King's gift to Buckingham of a rich estate, Burley-on-the-Hill in Rutland.[21] Buckingham, of course, played the leading role, and several other noblemen are listed among the actors. Ogilby, whose name does not appear, may have spoken a few lines, but his primary responsibility would have been in the dancing. This may not have been his first performance; in any event, he knew what was wanted. Aubrey tells the rest of the story succinctly: 'High-dancing, i.e., vaulting and cutting capers, being then in fashion, he, endeavouring to doe something extraordinary, by misfortune of a false step when he came to the ground, did spraine a veine on the inside of his leg, of which he was lame ever after.'

Whether the accident occurred in one of the gypsy dances or in the antimasque; whether it came on the night of the first performance or one of the others; how much of an interruption it caused; all these questions remain unanswered because of Ogilby's obscurity at this time. What was a momentous event for the young dancer was too unimportant to win a notice in any of the various accounts of this or other masques. Ogilby seems never to have danced again, and probably never acted after his accident. He was still able to teach dancing, and presumably turned with more vigour than ever to that activity.

It is probable that it was in these years after his misfortune that Ogilby developed from the daring performer to the master of theatrical management, whose knowledge and skill far transcended the state comprehended in the term 'dancing master.' Whether he ever studied all those arts that Sir George Buck had commended — grammar, rhetoric, philosophy and the like — cannot be presumed. What is certain is that after his accident, sometime during the 1620's and 1630's, John Ogilby became a knowledgeable theatrical manager and producer, a friend of writers and actors, and a figure who maintained useful connections with the Court.[22] Only such many-sided development could account for his appointment and success in the 1630's as Master of Revels in Ireland under the arrogant and critical Viscount Wentworth, later Earl of Strafford.

Although no records exist concerning the masque which permanently lamed Ogilby, the event was certainly not without some value for the erstwhile dancer. The Duke of Buckingham had a reputation for kindness to his servants and he seems to have recommended Ogilby to a rising courtier, Sir Ralph, later Lord Hopton. In addition, before the accident, Ogilby certainly saw and perhaps danced with Prince Charles, about whom, as the martyred king, he later wrote an epic. These various connections, slight as they may have been, proved helpful through the 1630's and again after the Restoration. Once known to some courtiers, a happy condition that his 'extraordinary' leap probably assisted in, Ogilby was not the man to let his contacts slip away, and some of these early associates remained his friends for half a century. The noblest prospect that a Scot may see, had brought John Ogilby senior and his family south. His son was to enhance those prospects considerably.

Responsive as he was to the influence of his time, Ogilby clearly appreciated the masque as a form. Even in his late teens or early twenties, the young Scot was absorbing the visual qualities of the masque; the writing of doggerel, at times vulgar, at times witty, always obsequious to the great ones; the array of characters assembled in the typical masque; the combination of words, music, dance, costume, stage effects, lighting and, last and least, plot. These early influences of the masque were evidenced in two of Ogilby's most original later works, his folio on the coronation of Charles II (*The Entertainment . . .*) and his editions of *Aesop's Fables,* especially the Masque of Apes.[23] Although the damage to his dancing career must have been disheartening, no doubt Ogilby was as resilient in this as in other adversity. It is probably his own joke that Aubrey quotes: 'He was an excellent dancing master, and never a good leg.' John Ogilby apparently never responded to the predestinarian religious influences of his native Scotland. In later years, however, he must sometimes have pondered the changes that followed his fateful leap, changes that preserved him from the life and fortunes of an obscure dancing master and brought him to a larger range of success.

Although permanently lamed, Ogilby was still in his twenties and was to live a long and active life. (Not until his seventies does he complain about his lameness.) Aubrey gives a picture of his going, after the accident, to Hopton's home in Somerset, to teach Sir Ralph's two sisters to dance. In return, apparently, Sir Ralph, a good and in time a noted soldier, taught Ogilby military science: 'to handle the pike and musket; sc. all the postures.' His lameness must have been relatively minor; it would not matter on a horse; and the dancing master apparently became knowledgeable in arms. Ogilby wrote, about this time, 'The Character of a Trooper,' an exercise in a favourite seventeenth-century genre: a character sketch, usually satirical, of some contemporary type. The trooper, or soldier, of whom Ogilby wrote was undoubtedly a new and hence intriguing specimen of mankind to the former dancing master. Aubrey speaks highly of the sketch, and tried, presumably in vain, to obtain a copy of it. It is the greater pity that it has apparently disappeared, as it seems to have been Ogilby's first attempt at formal writing. Ogilby's own skill at arms continued sufficiently for him to serve in Ireland in a 'troop of guards' in the 1630's under Wentworth and he must have found such proficiency helpful in establishing his credentials in Ireland, as the Civil Wars drew on.

These military associations make it appear worth citing various documents involving one or more men called 'Ogilby' during these dimly seen years. First, there are three letters in French written from one J. Dulbier to Secretary Conway in June 1627.[24] They deal with a Monsieur 'Ogelby,' who served as a lieutenant of a Scottish company in the service of the Prince of Mansfeld. Taken prisoner at Dunkirk, Ogilby was held for 11 months, and was, after his release, requesting some back pay. Conway's investigation of the case prompted these letters. The name occurs here as 'Oglamby' and 'Oglambie' as well as 'Ogelby' and may refer to another Ogilby and not to the former dancing master.

There is another reference to a Scottish Ogilby, this time contained in a letter from Sir Henry Martyn to the Duke of Buckingham, and written from Plymouth on 31 January 1628.[25] Some of the ships returning from the disastrous Isle of Ré expedition had been damaged or destroyed in a storm. Of those lost, one was commanded by a Captain Waters. Martyn turned over to Waters 'the *Report* [a merchant ship] of Ipswich, which shippe had a land mane, one Ogleby, a Scott, appointed Capt. of her from St. Martins, who so soone as he came to Plymouth quitting the shippe tooke his way for London and from thence procured warrant to travaile for France.' Although apparently ready to set out for France again, this Ogilby came within the circle of the Duke of Buckingham in London. There, at the heart of Court gossip and war preparations, he learned that his resignation had been too precipitate. Sir Henry Martyn reported that Ogilby, 'understanding the shippe was after the storme repayred and made fitt for service againe, came hither this weeke and tould mee your L[PP] [Buckingham, then Lord High Admiral] had commanded him downe speedily to take charge of the said shippe butt without letter or warrant.' Martyn protested the decision, claiming that Captain Waters was 'a gentleman welle qualified and a seaman, the other none, neither was hee ever heard of heere since the shippe came from the Island.' There the references to Ogilby end, with no resolution of the captaincy recorded.[26] As no real distinction was then made between land and naval warfare, it seems possible that the landsman captain of the *Report* may have been the same Ogilby who was suing for back pay as a soldier of the Mansfeld expedition. Ogilby's place in Buckingham's favour may indicate that it was indeed the injured dancing master, who, after military training under Hopton, could call on the Duke's good will for such a favour as the above.

In April of 1633, King Charles I, whose efforts were frequently bent toward reducing the rowdiness that had been characteristic of his father's court and capital, laid a charge upon his Privy Council. They were to report to the King concerning quarrels that occurred in London, including duels, or be held responsible for such omission. The King resented his ignorance of the brawling, 'though the whole Citty were full of it.'[27] It was perhaps because of this instruction that in the following month an otherwise unimportant quarrel was treated in the Privy Council in some detail.

The first of three documents involved is a petition of one John Ogilby. He was, he stated, in the Inner Temple with Robert Abercromby, Quartermaster, 'who hath long time served in the wars in Bohemia and the

Palatinate.' Several men 'in a tumultuous manner sett upon the sd Aber-cromby and tear his cloake from his back, and his ruff from his neck, en-deavoring to drive him to prison without therein any warrant.' Upon Ogilby's intervening, as he said, 'to keepe the peace, and to suppress the tumult and uprore which they had raised,' as well as to aid Abercromby, the attackers 'did riotously beat and abuse yr pet.[itioner] and with many threats and heigh [high] words' followed the two Scots. Because of their nationality, they were 'not able to wage lawe in this kingdom,' and so Ogilby asked that two of the attackers, whom he named, be brought before the Privy Council.[28]

The petition passed to the Star Chamber, which sat indistinguishably from the Privy Council at that time, and on 31 May 1633 their lordships referred its consideration to Sir Richard Shelton, the Solicitor General. He was requested to examine the parties and recommend further action.[29]

Shelton's report[30] constitutes the third and final document of the series. Ogilby had produced some witnesses, one of whom saw the attack on Aber-cromby. Furthermore, two watermen observed Ogilby and another man 'together by the ears,' but they were unwilling to say who started the trouble. The Solicitor General 'dealt privately' with one of the accused and thought for a time that he had settled the matter. He obtained from a defendant 'some money for his [Ogilby's] satisfaction, which I conceived might well have sorted with his condition and his complaint, but I find him upon such high terms that no moderate sum will content him.' So Shelton, on 15 July 1633, returned the matter to the Star Chamber for its decision, where the records tantalizingly cease.

The acquaintance of this John Ogilby with a compatriot who had long been a soldier on the Continent suggests another connection with the soldier-sailor of the 1620's. No further mention of John Ogilby appears in either Privy Council or Star Chamber records.[31] Yet this episode raises another point. Thomas Viscount Wentworth, later the Earl of Strafford, sat frequently both in Privy Council and Star Chamber at this time until his departure for Ireland in July 1633. There Wentworth became Lord Chief Deputy, and set up in Dublin a viceregal court that was a microcosm of the one in Whitehall. Ogilby followed Wentworth to Ireland within a month, to become Master of the Revels in that country.[32] It is at least plausible that, in recommending himself and his grievance to the Lords of the Privy Council, Ogilby found a patron who offered high opportunity in a different area and opened to him yet another career. Such an offer might also help to explain the 'high terms' that John Ogilby took toward any moderate settlement of his cause, demands incommensurate with his apparent position. In any event, it would be indeed unusual if, given the rarity of the name, two John Ogilbys touched Wentworth's life in the summer of 1633.

Wentworth, Charles's first minister, left an England that he considered sufficiently pacified, and proceeded to a kingdom clearly in need of organization and administration. In addition to ruling Ireland, the Lord Deputy proceeded to set up his own court in imitation of his royal master's. Dublin Castle and city were improved, and a court centre for government and patronage was established. Various direct reminders of Whitehall were introduced, and among these was the first theatre ever established in Ireland. Certainly under direct authorization from Wentworth and presumably under Ogilby's supervision, a theatre was built in St. Werburgh Street, near the Castle, sometime in the mid-1630's.[33]

Together with the physical theatre, the creation of a company of actors and musicians was a necessity, and this too became Ogilby's responsibility. He achieved it, in his own much later words, with 'great preparations and disbursements.'[34] It seems clear that Ogilby succeeded in this project partly because a severe plague in London closed theatres there from May 1636 to October 1637.[35] Certainly this factor helped the Werburgh Street, or New, Theatre to open as soon as it did, sometime in 1637.

Ogilby's connections with the Jacobean and Caroline theatrical world must have been put to considerable test in achieving the transfer of actors, some of them well known, from London to relatively isolated Dublin, under the patronage not of the King but of Wentworth. Since Ogilby had responsibility both for the theatre and for the actors, the period from 1633 to 1637 must have meant some, perhaps lengthy, residence in Dublin, supervising the theatre-building, as well as various trips to London to gather his troupe. The remaining records are inevitably partial; but they show Edward Armiger, William Cooke, William Perry and Richard Weekes acting in Dublin, either sometime during or throughout the period 1637-41, the years when the first Irish theatre came into operation.[36]

Of the plays known to have been performed during these years, there were a few by well-known, though older, playwrights: Middleton, Fletcher, Jonson. Several were anonymous, and one (*Landgartha*) was written by an Anglo-Irishman, Henry Burnell.[37] Chief dramatist and the most important writer connected with the Werburgh Street Theatre was, however, James Shirley.[38] During his presumed residence in Dublin from 1636 to 1638, Shirley wrote prologues for the plays of other men, saw a number of his own plays produced again, and wrote at least three (*Rosania; The Royal Master;* and *St. Patrick for Ireland*) that were first performed in Dublin. Ogilby himself is credited with writing a play, 'The Merchant of Dublin,' that was performed but never printed. No evidence beyond Aubrey's statement has been found for this latter claim, but it is certainly within probability. In later writings, Ogilby was to demonstrate considerable versatility in versifying and even song-making.

The success of the new theatre was probably not wholly satisfying to Ogilby's professional mind. As an appurtenance of viceregal splendor, the theatre may have performed its role successfully; but Shirley's various prefaces indicate clearly enough that the size and variety of the London audience was sadly missed. By 1638, when *The Royal Master* was first printed in London, Shirley was probably back in the capital to oversee its printing. There were mementoes, nevertheless, of the Irish stage in this first printing. The title page carried the legend 'As it was Acted in the new Theater in Dublin: and Before the Right Honorable the Lord Deputie of Ireland, in the Castle.' There was even, in the same year, a title page for the play run off for some booksellers in Ireland: 'Thomas Allot and Edmond Crooke, near the Castle in Dublin.'[39]

Shirley had been chief poet at the Phoenix or Cockpit Theatre in Drury Lane for a number of years and Ogilby, whose dancing school was not too far from that important theatre, almost certainly knew Shirley in London. Lacy, Ogilby's apprentice, apparently danced at the Cockpit, and Davenant, whom Ogilby knew, was also closely associated with that theatre.[40] Whatever the association between Shirley and Ogilby in London, it certainly developed significantly in the Dublin years. Among the commendatory verses prefaced to the first edition of *The Royal Master* was one by John Ogilby to 'His Worthy Friend the Author.' The poem has interest as the earliest piece of recorded verse by one who was to write many hundreds of rhymes. The tone at first is one of a professional workman to another:

All these thy friends subscribing to thy praise
And faire deservings, have done well, 'twill raise
Opinion in the readers, and engage
Them to peruse, what wee saw on the Stage.

Then after a bit of difficulty with rhyme and meter, the producer closes with warm, though not extravagant, praise:

The commendation's short, the Comedy
Speaks better for itself, more home; but yet
My vote must go, I say no purer wit
Did ever grace the scene, nay, it hath in't
Expressions of so new and rich a mint,
That the old poets well might wish the name
Of this new Play were added to their fame.

A decade later, in 1649, Ogilby contributed some far more polished introductory verse to Shirley's *Via ad Latinam Linguam Complanata*, in which he addressed the author as 'my much honored and learned Friend, Mr. James Shirley.'

For a short four years the Dublin theatre was operative, with Ogilby as manager and perhaps quondam playwright. According to Aubrey, he also rode in Wentworth's troop of guards and was one of his gentlemen.[41] His position seems to have been secured with his appointment, on 28 February 1637/38, as Master of the Revels in and through the Kingdom of Ireland. A warrant for this post was granted by Wentworth, now Earl of Strafford, Although apparently it was never validated by Charles I, the grant itself was acknowledged after the Restoration and was at that time used as a basis for issuance to Ogilby of a patent, similar to the warrant.[42]

This new and successful life came to an abrupt end for Ogilby with the beginning of the Irish Rebellion in October, 1641, when the disorder and tragedy in Dublin made it a truer microcosm of Whitehall than Strafford could have wished. Only one detail, given by both Aubrey and Ashmole, has come down from those days of terror in Ireland. Aubrey writes that Ogilby was nearly blown up at Rathfarnham. Not far from Dublin, Rathfarnham Castle was the residence of Sir Adam Loftus, one of the grandees of the Anglo-Irish, and a friend and confidant of Strafford. The Castle appeared a stronghold in 1641, and to it apparently there fled all those whose connections enabled them to procure the greatest safety available.[43] Even there, however, that safety was only relative. Ashmole, in the horoscope cited, relates of Ogilby: '1642 upon his birthday [November 17] he scaped blowing up with pounder [powder].' The conjunction of his birthdate and the explosion made this a memorable date, one of the few that Ogilby could later furnish Ashmole. Of his immediate moves after this incident, there is no record, but in 1644, according to the Ashmole horoscope, he entered the service, briefly or intermittently, of the Earl of Ormond, another great Irish lord. And then sometime in the mid-1640's Ogilby took himself back to England. Aubrey says he was wrecked on the homeward journey. Certainly, he found himself nearly a decade older than before his Irish adventure, penniless, patron-less and sustained only by a memory of recent honours. Strafford's impact on Ogilby's life, first elevating, then destructive, had been considerable. Not surprisingly, his Master of Revels had been a minor figure to Strafford, in whose indexed correspondence Ogilby's name does not occur.[44] John Ogilby had so far been a useful or agreeable person to various patrons, but not a personage worthy of written comment.

II

Poet & Translator

Genuine fame was to come to Ogilby through his production in the original or through translations of the Bible and the classics — the epics of Virgil and of Homer and the works of Aesop. Once involved with the world of books, whether scholarly, entertaining or semi-popular, John Ogilby was never to lose his association with it; and it is in this world that he made the chief of the reputation that is his today.

The skill and art of translation in mid-seventeenth-century England was an established one. Learning still centred on the Bible and the classics; but, as education spread to increasing numbers, it had become diluted. The educated English man of the seventeenth-century was unlikely to read Greek and Latin easily or to converse in Latin. He would know a number of useful quotations and tags in Latin. He might, given time, construe a Latin text; and sometimes he had a limited competence in Greek. Classical history, personages and mythology were still very live, as were all Biblical figures and episodes, but the speaking of Latin had become uncommon.[1] The seventeenth-century situation encouraged not only translation but varieties of translations, and many seventeenth-century readers knew enough to judge between styles of translators and to follow classical niceties when spared the drudgery of actually reading the original of a Greek or Latin classic. Schoolboys were often introduced through translations to the great works of antiquity, which later they were to study in the original.[2]

Of course, classical editions in the original, especially in Latin, were still part of seventeenth-century scholarship and learning, and Ogilby was to produce a notable volume in this field. In so doing, he pleased the group who held that the classics were debased by translation. Thomas Fuller, writing in the 1650's of the noted translator Philemon Holland, refers to this belief: 'Indeed, some decry all translators as interlopers, spoiling the trade of learning, which should be driven amongst scholars alone. Such also allege, that the best translations are works rather of industry than judgment, and (in easy authors) of faithfulness rather than industry.'[3] Yet Fuller defended the principle of good translation, and in his sketch of Holland used a pun — 'This eminent translator was translated to a better life' — that appeared about the same time in a dedicatory poem of Henry Proby to an edition of Ogilby's *Virgil*:

Yet all Translations are not Falls, for men
Say they're Translated that are gone to Heav'n.[4]

In mid-seventeenth-century England, the battle of the Ancients and Moderns was yet a generation away, and the pre-eminence of Greek and Latin writers in content, style and influence was acknowledged without question. It seemed valid therefore, not only for schoolmasters and scholars, but for many men of quality to follow the avocation of translation. In the troubled years of the middle decades, when military and political activities often became dangerous or impossible, translations could safely occupy the time of a gentleman (e.g., Sir Richard Fanshawe or John Evelyn).

When Ogilby returned penniless to England, after his successful years in Dublin as impresario and client to Strafford, he faced an admittedly bleak future. He had presumably had enough of military adventures after the Rathfarnham episode; his patron Strafford had been executed, and theatrical productions in which he had made his name were decried and even forbidden by the governments of the 1640's and 1650's. Whether from desperation, because of long-latent interest, or for some other reason, Ogilby at this point turned to the classics and to translation. On his return, sometime in the 1640's, Ogilby made his way, Aubrey says by foot, to Cambridge, from the port where he had landed, probably Bristol or Plymouth. Once there, in a Puritan stronghold, he renewed the studies of boyhood under, it is said, the tutelage of his friend James Shirley, who was at times a schoolmaster. By 1648, he was back in London, the city that was to be thereafter the centre of his activities.

In London, Ogilby renewed his associations with the Merchant Taylors Company, and it was probably thus that he met his wife. Despite the uncertain state of affairs in England, Ogilby, now approaching fifty years of age, apparently felt settled enough to marry. The Register of Baptisms, Marriages and Burials of the Parish of St. Peter-le-Poor records the marriage of 'John Oglesby & Christian Hunsdon, Widdowe' on 14 March 1649 [1650, New Style].[5] It is indicative of Ogilby's still insecure finances and of his prudence that he avoided taking a young wife from whom he might expect heirs and chose instead a not-impecunious widow who was already a grandmother and presumably about his age. Mistress Hunsdon was the widow of Thomas, a citizen and Merchant Taylor of London who 'sick of body but of perfect memory' left a will dated 29 October 1647.[6] The Hunsdons lived in Blackfriars, but there is no indication of Thomas' occupation and no mention of him in extant Merchant Taylors' records. He left everything to his 'loving wife,' who was sole executrix. Legacies, to be paid upon her remarriage or death, were designated for a son Thomas (£20), for a (presumably unmarried) daughter Ellen (£8) and for a married daughter, Elizabeth Morgan (£4).

Thomas Hunsdon's will brings into the Ogilby picture the first mention of William Morgan, a still shadowy figure, who, presumably as eldest son of

Elizabeth Morgan, received 20s. under his grandfather's will. He may already have been a child of some promise, for his bequest was double that of each of his six brothers and sisters. Hunsdon's will unfortunately fails to record the Christian name of Elizabeth Morgan's husband. Unlike the Ogilbys and the Hunsdons, there were numerous Morgans and even a number of William Morgans in the London of the later seventeenth-century. Young William, with three younger brothers in 1647, was born about 1640, or perhaps a little earlier; Christian Hunsdon, grandmother in 1647 of seven, was probably not much younger than her second husband. Her unusual name 'Christian,' a name borne also by one granddaughter, indicates a Puritan affiliation in her family, although there is no corroborative evidence on that point.[7] It was so uncommon a name that at times it appeared incorrectly in records, such as 'Catherine,' for example, when her first husband's will was proved. This event occurred, in accordance with the provisions of that will, on 4 February 1650, shortly before her remarriage, an act that necessitated payment of the stipulated legacies. From this time onwards, information about members of the Hundson family, including Thomas, the son and heir, ceases. Only the young grandson, William Morgan, played a recorded and increasingly significant role in Ogilby's story.

The parish of St. Peter-le-Poor, from which Ogilby was married, was apparently the area to which he had come from Cambridge. Once noted for the number of its poor inhabitants, it had become by Stow's time distinguished for some quite well-to-do residents. In the uncertain years of the Commonwealth, Ogilby probably had only temporary lodgings there, in this parish near the Guildhall and the Wall. Generally, his choice of lodgings was to the south and west of that area. The Hunsdon home in Blackfriars was much closer both to his former lodgings in the 1620's and to his later residences off Fleet Street than to the parish from which he was married. Whether for cheapness or privacy, or by chance, Ogilby seems often to have sought residence in a court emerging from an alley, which itself projected from a lane. A residence like this was as far removed as possible from the noise and bustle of the great London streets. If Ogilby had connections with the Phoenix or Cockpit Theatre in Drury Lane, as has been suggested, he may at times have been found farther west; he still lived within reasonable distance of his school.[8] Whitehall and Westminster, of course, must have been known to Ogilby when he danced at Court, and waited upon Hopton and other patrons. It was the City precincts however, that constituted the familiar and work-a-day ways of his life.

A few more points may be made about Mistress Hunsdon, who became Mistress Ogilby. It was presumably she who brought to her husband the capital he had so sorely lacked. He used that to produce increasingly beautiful and expensive books, to keep the sale of these in his own hands and finally to print the volumes in his own shop. Certainly, it is from his marriage that his first sustained success dates. And Christian Ogilby won the same treatment from her second husband as from her first. In Ogilby's will of 1675, he referred to his 'deare wife' and he left to her and to her grandson William Morgan all his property. There is no mention of any children born of this marriage, and from the evidence cited of Mistress Hunsdon's presumed age at marriage, it seems most unlikely. There are no further references to her in the records.[9]

His first book, however, was printed before Ogilby's marriage, and reflects the uncertainty of the times and of his own prospects. With his presumably refurbished Latin, Ogilby assembled a translation of the works of Virgil — the Eclogues, the Georgics, the Aeneid. This first book was printed by John Crook, one of two brothers who produced work of modest quality in mid- and later seventeenth-century England. John Crook had been King's Printer in Dublin in 1638-39 and, like his brother Andrew, printed a number of plays.[10] John Crook and Ogilby must have known each other in Dublin in the 1630's, and their acquaintance makes it reasonable for Ogilby to have sought out Crook with his completed manuscript. On 10 October 1648 Crook entered in the Stationers' Register, for six pence, 'a booke called Virgills Workes or Poems Translated into English verse by Mr. John Oglebe gent.[11] When the volume was printed in 1649, there was a portrait of the author done by William Marshall, an engraver of limited ability, who had supplied a portrait to the first collection of Milton's work in the same decade. Although at a later time John Ogilby stated that he had translated Virgil 'with much studie and expence,'[12] his own letter of dedication to the 1649 edition was deprecatory: 'I call it but the shadow, and cold resemblance of Virgil.' The translation, he wrote, was 'bred in phlegmatick Regions, and among people returning to their ancient barbarity [presumably Ireland].' He hoped (a hope later fulfilled) that time should 'ripen more ornament of Sculpture and Annotations.' The volume carried an 'imprimantur' [sic] even though it probably appeared after the King's execution.

Dedications, to Ogilby, as to most of his contemporaries, were matters of importance, and his choice of patron for this first volume was William Seymour, Marquess of Hertford. As no previous evidence connects the two, we may deduce that Sir Ralph, now Lord, Hopton probably was the link. Seymour and Hopton had been two of the King's chief commanders in the West during the Civil Wars just ended. If Ogilby, upon returning from Ireland, made contact with his former patron Hopton, he would have been able to meet the Marquess on some occasion. Certainly he was able to address Seymour, who, Aubrey says, 'loved him very well,' as a patron in 1648-49, at a time when the Marquess was acting as one of the most faithful and courageous friends of Charles I. Although a somewhat hazardous association at the time, Ogilby's connection with the Seymour clan was maintained through the 1650's, and no doubt aided decidedly in gaining royal favour at the Restoration.

The question arises, with this translation from Latin, and even more strongly with the later ones from Greek, of how much was Ogilby's own. Certainly, translators could be hired and translations bought, which then became the undisputed property of the purchaser. John Ogilby was to be involved in many such translations in later life, although it may be questioned whether his financial resources at this time would have permitted any such commission. Shirley may indeed have aided Ogilby in this endeavour and their close associations about 1649 are indicated by the previously mentioned dedicatory verse of Ogilby to Shirley's *Via ad Latinam Linguam*. [13] There had, of course, been a number of translations of the Aeneid into English, beginning with Caxton's, in the late fifteenth century; the last previous translation of the complete works had appeared in 1634. Any or all of these may have served to familiarize Ogilby with Virgilian content, and his introduction to the 1649 edition indicates that he was at work on a translation before leaving Ireland. How much refreshing his classical knowledge needed is uncertain, but from the time of the late 1640's Ogilby unquestionably knew enough Latin to read, understand and quote it appropriately. His familiarity was to grow, as subsequent publications showed, not only with the content of Virgil's work, but with the critical apparatus of seventeenth-century scholarship as well: Virgilian parallels with Greek writing, linguistic and textual explanations, and the historical and mythological background of the founding of Rome. Like so many other classicists, Ogilby was to feel the pull of the Trojan and Greek traditions in the story of Aeneas. This may well have led him to extend his work, later, to the Iliad and Odyssey.

Ogilby's early style has much to commend it. His translation is a straight-forward one, in acceptable iambic pentameter. An 'argument' or summary appeared before each Eclogue and Georgic, as well as before each book of the Aeneid, but the 1649 edition appeared without any critical apparatus, not even the numbering of lines. When this octavo appeared, Denham and Waller were England's exemplars of style; Ben Jonson's were the approved dicta; and French influence and the Augustan Age lay decades ahead. Against this background, Ogilby's chief virtues lay in his narrative power and lack of pretension. He used relatively few literary tricks, although alliteration and repetition occur, as the examples given below show. His rhymes are generally sound, although they fail at times. Both vigour and realism appear in his description of the swarming of bees (Georgics, Book IV):

But when thou seest a troup aspiring, flie;
Drawn from their winter quarters through the skie,
And curious hast with admiration spide
A sable Cloud through crystall Sphears to glide;
Then to sweet springs, and pleasant shades they goe,
Here oderous flowres, and beaten Milfoyle strow . . .

It is impossible not to think of contemporary allusions, in these lines written for the Aeneid in 1647 or 1648:

As oft, when a great people mutinie
Ignoble vulgar rage; stones, firebrands flye,
Furie finds arms; but if they chance to see
A grave man meriting for pietie,
All silent listning stand; he soone alaies
With words the tumult, and their passion swaies.

And finally there is a descriptive scene just before Dido and Aeneas set out on their fateful ride, which led to the storm and cave episodes:

At the Court gates, the Trojan nobles staid,
Whilst in her chamber the faire Queen delaid:
In trapping rich with gold and purple, fit,
Her proud horse stands, and champs the foming bit.
With a great troop, she guarded comes at last;
Her Tyrian habit a rich border grac'd,
Her quiver gold, gold did her haire infold,
The button of her purple vest was gold.

Such language and imagery as this, together with a narrative flow impossible to capture in short quotations, sufficed to satisfy his public; and within a few years Ogilby was known as poet and scholar to increasing numbers of Englishmen.

He turned next to Aesop, and issued his first translation of the *Fables* in 1651, versifying and paraphrasing them and 'adorning with sculptures,' to use his favourite phrase for an illustrated volume. This was dedicated to two young noblemen, the son and son-in-law of the Marquess of Hertford, his patron of the *Virgil*. John Crook's brother Andrew published this volume, which was arranged in four books, bound together but paged separately. Ogilby noted in his preface the praise that had attended his translation of Virgil, and apologized for his descent from lofty Virgilian themes to the comic strains of antiquity's greatest humourist. As an excuse for his production, he cited the poor translations so far perpetrated on that author and on the public. It is clear, however, that the 1651 edition of *Aesop* was not made directly from the original by Ogilby, since, as late as December 1653, Ashmole was seeking to discover from his horoscopes the most propitious date for Ogilby to begin the study of Greek. Possibly Ogilby worked from one of the decried translations, from a Latin version, or from a prose translation that he himself commissioned. Whatever his source for the content, he made the versification his own.

Shirley obliged with an introductory poem 'To my Worthy Friend Mr. John Ogilby,' in which he graciously combined praise of the former and the present work:

This could thy great Converse with Virgil doe,
To make old Aesop rise a Poet too.

He urged further that the next work by Ogilby should be a 'Poem, born from they [thy] own flame.' Yet another introductory verse to the *Aesop*, lengthy in this instance, came from an author with little currently to occupy his time. William D'Avenant wrote and dated his verse from the Tower, on September 30, 1651, 'to my Friend Mr. Ogilby.' He too was encouraging:

Yet in thy Verse, methinks, I Aesop see
Less bound than when his Master made him free:
So well thou fit'st the measure of his mind . . .

An outstanding feature of the *Aesop* was its illustrations. The venture on the 1649 *Virgil* had not, presumably, permitted the luxury of illustrative prints, but, on the title page of *Aesop,* Ogilby proudly announced his

31

'sculptures.' His interest in the visual elements in bookmaking — excellent quality of paper, wide margins, clear and clean type, and a profusion of prints — manifested itself early and was to continue throughout his life. The eighty-one plates were not of high artistic quality, but they added another dimension to Ogilby's work, and one that he used consistently thereafter.[14]

Ogilby experimented with varying verse forms, including the rhymed couplet, throughout his translation of *Aesop* — no doubt the easiest of classical authors to treat informally.[15] In his fable of the Doves and Hawks (Fable 20, verse 3), he wrote:

Mov'd by the Gods, the Kitish Prince proclames
War 'gainst the Turtles, and their wealthy regions;
Far more than honour, booty him inflames,
And from the North he musters feather'd legions;
*   The War grows hot,*
*   The Turtles not,*
Inur'd to battels, Camps, and fierce alarms,
Many strong houses lose by force of arms.

Ogilby seems clearly to have enjoyed versifying and elaborating on Aesop. He joined, in a semi-continuous story, fables about the same animals. And he added incidents and descriptions that made his Aesop more interesting than, even if increasingly removed in detail from, the original Greek. In the fable of the Lark and her Young (verse 1), he spent a stanza describing the location of larks' nests:

It is the sweet and early chanting Lark,
That to the Heavenly Quiresters is Clark,
And mounts the Skie as freely as a spark;
*   Yet she in haughty Towres not builds her Nest,*
Nor on the tops of lofty Cedars dwels,
Which are with all the roring winds opprest,
That Northern witches conjure up with spels;
*   But in Corn Fields her habitations found,*
*   Flanckt round with earth, six inches under ground.*

The literal descent in the last four words pulls the reader up sharply from the lyric beginning of the stanza and restores the essential realism of the Aesopic approach. A wholly different kind of descriptive passage (Fable 54, verse 2) shows the Eagle giving the Tortoise a ride in outer space:

This said, the Eagle lifts her, and her house
*   Up like a little Mouse;*
Through the cold quarters of the Stars they goe,
And Magazines of Rain, Hail, Wind, and Snow:
*   Such was their flight,*
*   They might*
See the dark Earths contracted face below,
To cast forth sullen beams, with brazen light,
Like a huge Moon, and turning on her poles
*   Dark Seas like Phoebes moles*
*   Casting a dimmer ray.*

They rowling East they view America,
Asia, and Africk; Europe next arose:
    No Map so perfect shews
How the great Midland Sea, betwixt them flows.

The vivid description is enhanced by an unsigned illustration, showing the Eagle and the Tortoise poised above the Earth, with Europe and a part of Africa visible, the Sun in the East and a crescent Moon in the West. To the student of Ogilby it presages, twenty years in advance, the series of great atlases of continents and countries of the world that he was to produce.

The writer drew most clearly on his own past experience in 'An Egyptian King and his Apes,' wherein he remarked that

Both Greece and Rome the art of Ocastrie [Orchestry, i.e., dancing]
Always esteemed, where dancing Masters be
Whose feet Historians are, and tell a History.

In Ogilby's story, European dancing masters were imported to teach the apes to dance; the latter then staged a masque, which featured some wild dancing, the description whereof must have stimulated some vivid memories in the writer of his own earlier entertainments.

In the Aesopic tradition, Ogilby emphasized the moral teaching of each fable. Loving the story for itself, however, he kept the moral short and generally pithy, unlike his successor Roger L'Estrange, whose morals subdued his fables by their length and solemnity. The fable of the Tortoise and the Frogs (Fable 53, verse 1) shows Ogilby at his most playful, with a lengthy description of the tortoise.

2) *The Eagle and the Tortoise, Aesop,*
1673
By permission of the Folger
Shakespeare Library, Washington
DC, USA

Would it not grieve one still to goe abroad,
    Yet ever be within;
To lye condemn'd to a perpetuall load,
And over-match'd with every gowtie Toad,
    And thus be hide-bound, in
        A slough
        Of proof,
    An Adamatine Skin:
    No Curase [cuirass] is more tough;
    A home Spun Iron Shirt
A Web of Maile stil on, would Gyants hurt.
    How happy are these Frogs
    That skip about the Bogs.
Some pittying God ah ease me of my Arms
    And native Farmes,
    That naked I may Swim
    Below, now on the Brim,
    Among the scallie swarms,
Searching the Bays, and Bosoms of the Lake,
And with these nymble Crokers pleasure take:
Vext at his Shell, thus the fond Tortoise spake.

After a wordy elaboration of the tortoise's experiences and his change of mind, Ogilby concludes with a moral that hardly seems in key:

Thus at home happy, oft fond Youth complain,

33

And Peace and plenty with soft Beds disdain.
But when in Forraign War death seals his eys,
His Birth place he remembers ere he dies.

Comment on the contemporary social and political scene has always been a special pleasure for paraphrasers and readers of Aesop alike. Ogilby's comment increased in scope with later editions, but even the 1651 edition reflects its own time. The Parliament of Birds (Fable 40) has perhaps the most sustained treatment (six pages) of contemporary material, of which only a small portion follows:

The Birds reduc'd thus to a Popular State,
Their King and Lords of prey ejected, sate
A frequent Parliament in th' antient wood,
There acting daily for the Nations good.
When thus the Swallow rising from the flock,
To Master Speaker, the grave Parrot, spoke.
  Great things for us, Sir, Providence hath done,
And we have through a world of danger run,
The Eagle, and the gentle Falcon are [presumably King Charles and
Prince Charles]
Destroyed or Sequester'd by happy War;
The Kitish Peers, and Bussard Lords are flown, [anti-royalist peers]
Who sate with us till we could sit alone:
Like worthy Patriots since, your speciall care
Hath settled our Militia in the aire;
All Monarch-hating Storks and Cranes, who march,
Like Sons of thunder, through Heavens Christall Arch,
When tumult calls, to beat those Widgeons down,
That vainly flock to readvance the Crown.

Ogilby's final fable told an elaborate story involving the law, perjured witnesses and false oaths. It concluded:

While Oaths and Evidence shall bear the cause,
Men of small Conscience little fear the Laws,
What Trade are you? A Witness, Sir; Draw neer,
Ther's Coyn, goe swear, what I would have you swear.

This selection on lying witnesses was sufficiently memorable to be reprinted as part of a cautionary tract on the evils of the times in 1681.[16] Ogilby's versifying abilities were probably most happily engaged in his works on *Aesop*, where heroic style and grand description were inappropriate, and a bent toward the satirical could be gratified. Aesopic verses clearly written, rhymed, and with occasional topical references, fully and cleverly illustrated, must have been among the lightest and most enjoyable reading that could justify itself as 'classical' in the seventeenth century. Ogilby's popularity in this field was attested by various later editions, and he seems particularly to have enjoyed translating that author. In the Preface to *Africa*, he wrote:

Then, being restless, though weary of tedious Versions, and such long
Journeys in Translating Greek and Latin Poets, Works asking no less than

3) *Parliament of the Birds*, Aesop, 1673

By permission of the Folger Shakespeare Library Washington DC, USA

a Mans whole life to accomplish, I betook myself to Aesop, where I found such Success, that soon I seem'd to tread Air, and walk alone, becoming also a Mythologist, not onely Paraphrasing, but a Designer of my own Fables, and at last screw'd myself up to a greater height, finishing two Heroick Poems, viz, The Ephesian Matron, and The Roman Slave.

These 'Heroick Poems' appeared in 1665, in a folio edition of *Aesop* printed by Thomas Roycroft for the author, and of excellent quality. It bears a Lely portrait of Ogilby, a title page engraved by Hollar, and a dedication to the Earl of Ossory. At the end of the fables appeared 'Androcleus or The Roman Slave' and 'The Ephesian Matron.' Both were well-known legends of antiquity, the latter having appeared in Petronius' *Satyricon*. They were lengthier, more ambitious and more original verses than the fables proper. Although for several centuries no one has said a good word for these two long poems, their contemporary reception was apparently successful. Three years later, in 1668, Roycroft printed a second folio edition of the 1665 Fables, and with them was bound the *Aesopics*. The latter collection embody some of Ogilby's most entertaining work. It was in the *Aesopics* that he became 'Designer of my own Fables,' and, while maintaining the fabulous pattern in general, inserted both original and contemporary content. Furthermore, the illustrations, as well as the situations, were portrayed in modern fashion, as witness the picture of the conventionally 'royal' swan and 'republican' stork, clad in Restoration clothing, discussing politics. The *Aesopics* were composed while Ogilby was in retreat from the Plague at Kingston-upon-Thames. In the 1665 and 1668 volumes the illustrations are lavish and attractive, the annotations full.[17]

Although Aesop may have provided Ogilby's most enjoyable versifying, it was the great classical epics on which he built his reputation. As early as 1652, Ogilby must have been planning an edition that is one of the two or three most beautiful of his entire production, the great Virgil folio of 1654. For this he commissioned prints from some of the best artists then working in England, such as Francis Cleyn, Wenceslaus Hollar and William Faithorne.[18] Ogilby, though never troubled by modesty, made an apparently valid assessment (in the Preface to *Africa*) of this volume that deserves quotation:

From a Mean Octavo, a Royal Folio flouris'd,
Adorn'd with Sculpture, and Illustrated with
Annotations, Triumphing with the affixt Emblazons,
Names, and Titles of a hundred Patrons, all bold
Assertors in Vindication of the Work, which
(whate're my Deserts) being Publish'd with that
Magnificence and Splendor, appear'd a new, and
taking Beauty, the fairest that till then the
English Press ever boasted.

Though essentially the same translation as in 1649, the folio of 1654 was a magnificent volume, both in content and appearance. The volume was dedicated to William, Marquess of Hertford, 'for discharge of my Obligation' (probably for financial assistance). With characteristic assurance, Ogilby suggested that there would not 'be much wanting in the

THE
FABLES
OF
Æ S O P.
VOLUME I.

Paraphras'd in *Verse*, Adorn'd with
Sculpture, and Illustrated with
Annotations.

By *JOHN OGILBY* Esq;
His MAJESTY's *Cosmographer*, *Geographick Printer*, and *Master of the Revels* in the Kingdom of
IRELAND.

Examples *are best* Precepts: *And a* Tale,
Adorn'd with Sculpture, *better may prevail*
To make Men lesser Beasts, than all the Store
Of tedious Volumes *vext the World before.*

The Third Edition.

LONDON,
Printed by the Author, at his House in *White-Friers*.
M. DC. LXXIII.

4) *Title page, Aesop, 1673*
By permission of the Folger
Shakespeare Library Washington DC,
USA

5) *Royal Swan and Republican Stork,*
Aesopics, *1673*
By permission of the Folger
Shakespeare Library, Washington DC,
USA

Margenta [margins] to any indifferent [impartial] Reader, for Illustration of the Poem.'

An excellent new portrait of Ogilby was included, drawn by Peter Lely and engraved by William Faithorne, with the crowned lion of Scotland shown in a seal. Facing the Ogilby portrait was another full page engraving (drawn by Francis Cleyn, engraved by Peter Lombart), this one of Virgil surrounded by various figures holding scrolls of the Mantuan's work. Next came a life of Virgil, with varieties of decorations — head-pieces, end-pieces, elaborate and often charming illustrated capital letters, the last device continuing throughout the volume. According to some of the dated cuts, the work was planned as early as 1652. A double-spread map of Aeneas's travels, engraved by Hollar in 1653, was inserted between the Georgics and the Aeneid.

Gentlemen, and even ladies, were proudly forming libraries, and Ogilby's 1654 Virgil was designed for a place of honour in such collections. In this volume, the pages themselves were beautifully set, with wide margins, most of them filled with notes. Only about twenty to twenty-five lines of actual Virgilian text appeared on a page, permitting elaborate annotations, often in Greek, in the wide margins.

The annotations are voluminous, technical and often erudite. For many of them, Ogilby relied on Joanne Ludovico de la Cerda's editions of Virgil.[19] De la Cerda, a Spanish Jesuit, produced in the seventeenth-century several elegant editions of Virgil, in which the notes and explanations (in Latin and Greek) overshadowed the text, visually and quantitatively. De la Cerda numbered his lines, and his commentaries were clearly keyed to the material being treated. His work was certainly used, and used constantly by Ogilby, who often gave credit, sometimes simply writing 'See La Cerda,' secure in the knowledge that seventeenth-century classicists could find their way to and through those volumes. In appeal to the eye, however, and in emphasis on the Virgilian text as opposed to lengthy commentary, Ogilby's page is far superior to de la Cerda's. The fact that Ogilby's text and commentaries were in English (though the latter were heavily interlarded with Latin and Greek words) obviously extended his readership considerably. Another outstanding difference was, of course, the use of numerous illustrations by Ogilby.

Other commentators as well as de la Cerda were also used by Ogilby. A quotation from Scaliger began Ogilby's volume, and probably some of Nicholas Caussin's work was used a well.[20] Some of the volumes under consideration, including de la Cerda's, were indexed. To use others, however, must have meant paging through various editions, and argues considerable familiarity with the text of all of Virgil's work. It must be a matter of speculation whether Ogilby borrowed these editions and reference books — from his schoolmaster friend Shirley, perhaps, or from a patron — or if he purchased them himself. He may, of course, have commissioned some or most of this reference work to be done by others. In any event, assiduous use was made of such compilations, and information overflowed into his notes concerning etymologies, cognate references from other classical authors, conflicting opinions on certain interpretations and the like.

mine, ita Liu. li. 10: *fubire claffem aduerfo flumine.* Ite-　A
rum lib. 45. *aduerfo Tyberi eft fubuectus.* & Symma-
chus Epift. 43. l. 3: *aduerfo amne nitendum eft.* Hero-
dotus l. 1. ita extulit, *ἀνὰ ποταμὸν ὠθέειν.* Notetur o-
biter forma *a* adagii apud Demofthene de falfa le-
gatione. *ἀλλὰ ἄντα ἀνὰ ποταμόν· ἐκείνῃ τῇ ἡμέρᾳ πάν-
τες ὅσοι, οἱ περὶ πορνείας, ἐρρύησαν λόγοι:* Sed illa die pro-
fecto omnes de impudicitia orationes, aduerfe, quod aiunt,
amne fluxerunt. Que in locum Vlpianus adnotat,
dicl prouerbium de re, quæ fit *ἐναλλὰξ ἀτάκτως*, in-
uerfim, & per confufionem.

19. *Lembum.*] *a* Dignum eft animaduerfione,　B
Lembum à Virgilio induci nauiculam fluuitialem:
cum inter maritimas naues referatur à Liuio fæpe,
ab Diodoro l. 20. à Polybio l. 1. à Thucydide l. 6.
ab Antipatro in Græco Epigram. ab Appiano libr.
4. Ciuil. vbi loquitur de Sexto Pompeio.

20. *Remigiis fubigit.* Ita in 6. *Ipfe ratem conto fubigit.*
21. *Si brachia forte remifit.*] Alcim. Auitus libr. 4.　*a* Aduerfo
Agricola oblitus fua brachia forte remifit.　　　　　　　　ane, ada g,
22. *Atq;*] *b* Hic eft, ftatim, explicatore Agel. li.　*b* Atque,
10. c. 29. idem obferuat Godefcal. lib. de Lin. Lat.　pro, ftatim.
ita Cic. 2. Leg. *fi in ius vocet; atq; eat.* Id eft, ftatim e-
at. Budæus in Comment. pag. 129: ita explicat. *Atq;*
idem effe quod *ftatim*, hoc eft, *Ideo.* Ergo in Virg.
quia remifit brachia, ideo in præceps rapitur. Ad-
dit Græcis hoc effe *κ, δή.* Quod multis firmat.
23. *In præceps.*] Seneca in Agam. *Ægifthe quid me*　*b* In præceps
rurfus in præceps rapis? & in Hip. *vadit animus in præ-*　*a* Lembus.
cepts fciens. & in Agamem. de naui quoq; loquens in
tempeftate:

　Illam debifcens Pontus in præceps rapit,
Hauritq; Eadem forma vfus Hieronym 3. in A-
mos c. 6. Plin. 2. c. 43. Velleius lib. 2.

---

　　　a Præterea tam funt Arcturi fidera nobis,
205　　Hœdorumque dies feruandi, & lucidus anguis :
　　　　Quam quibus in patriam ventofa per æquora vecti
　　　　Pontus, & oftriferi fauces tentantur Abydi.

　　　b Libra die fomnique pares vbi fecerit horas,
　　　　Et medium luci atque vmbris iam diuidet orbem:
210　　, Exercete viri tauros, ferite hordea campis,
　　　　Vfque fub extremum brumæ intractabilis imbrem.

　　　c Nec non & lini fegetem & Cereale papauer
　　　　Tempus humo tegere, & iam dudum incumbere aratris,
　　　　Dum ficca tellure licet, dum nubila pendent.

215　*d* Vere fabis fatio, tum te quoque medica putres
　　　　Accipiunt fulci, & milio venit annua cura :
　　　　Candidus auratis aperit cum cornibus annum
　　　　Taurus, & aduerfo cedens canis occidit aftro.

　　　e At fi triticeam in meffem, robuftaque farra
220　　Exercebis humum, folisque inftabis ariftis:
　　　　Ante tibi Eoæ Atlantides abfcondantur,
　　　　Gnofiaque ardentis decedat ftella coronæ,
　　　　Debita quam fulcis committas femina, quamque
　　　　Inuitæ properes anni fpem credere terræ.

225　　Multi ante occafum Maiæ cepere: fed illos
　　　　Expectata feges vanis elufit auenis.

　　　f Si vero viciamque feres, vilemque fafellum,
　　　　Ne Pelufiacæ curam afpernabere lentis;
　　　　Haud obfcura cadens mittet tibi figna Bootes.
230　　Incipe, & ad medias fementem extende pruinas.

　　　g Iccirco certis dimenfum partibus orbem
　　　　Per duodena regit mundi Sol aureus aftra.

ARGVMENTVM.

*Neceffitas Aftrologiæ. Præcepta fementis, quibus docet hordeum, linum, papauer ferenda inter
Æquinoctium Autumni, & Brumam : fabam, medicam, milium Aprili menfe : triticum, & far menfe Octobri : viciam, fafelum, lentem eodem.*

EXPLICATIO.

　a Aggreditur iam quintam partem libri huius, qua to-
ta eft de temporibus operum rufticorum. Cum hæc quarta
parte coniungit multa, quæ pertinent ad aftrologiam, nam
hæc ars neceffaria eft difcernendis temporibus operum rufticorum. Præmittit vero huic parti verfus quatuor pro proœmio, quorum fententia hæc eft, tam neceffariam effe a-
ftrologiam agricolis, quam nautis. Ergo. Nobis, quia a-

griculturam exercemus, tam funt feruanda fidera Arcturi,
hœdorum dies, anguis lucidus : quam illis, qui Pontum ten-
tant, & fauces Abydi, cum redeunt in patriam per æquora.
Vocat Abydon oftriferum propter copiam oftreorum.
　b Ab generali præmonitione contenta in proœmio, defcen-
dit ad certa quædam opera. Primo omnium conftituit tempus hordei ferendi, inter Æquinoctium Autumni quod fit
fub libra, atq; inter Brumam : fed dilatans more Poetico
fententiam, ita ait : Poftquam Libra fecerit horas dies &

　　　　　　　T 2　　　　　　　noctis

The two Extremes to this on ' each hand lies
Muffled with ftorms, fetter'd with cruel Ice.
'Twixt Cold and Heat, two more there are, th'aboads
Affign'd poor mortals by th'immortal Gods.
Athwart thefe two in ᶠ th'oblique Zodiack fhines
Whirling ftill round the twelve Celeftiall figns.
ᵍ As we the Pole to Scythian mountains raife ;
So 'tis depreft in *Libya's* Southern bayes ;
This alwaies gilds our Hemifphere, but Hell
Sees that, and Spirits which in darkneſs dwell.
Here round about the mighty Serpent glides,
And like a River the two Bears divides
With vaft infoldings ; ʰ Bears that never yet
Durſt in the Ocean bath their filver feet.
There, as they fay, either is ⁱ lafting Night,
Or gloomie fhades for ever hind'ring Light ;
Or elfe from us to them *Aurora* fpeeds,
Bringing the day, and when with panting Steeds
The Daun firft breaths on us, there Night retires,
And bluſhing kindles late Nocturnall fires :
Hence from no doubtfull figns we feafons know,
When beft to Reap, and at what time to Sow,
Or when to truft the trecherous ᵏ Sea again,
And ˡ well-rig'd Ships adventure to the Main,
Or in vaft Forefts fell well-feafon'd Pines.
Nor vainly mark fetting and rifing Signs,
Which in four quarters equall years divide.
If a Cold fhow'r makes Swains within abide,
Much may be done, which when the weather's Fair
Might take up time ; To whet the blunted fhare,
To make ᵐ a Boat, to brand the Sheep, and Mete
What Meafures make the Mountains of thy Wheat.
Thefe fharp n Forcks and Stakes, the tender Vine
Others infold with bonds of Amerine,

L   And

(e) Right and left in feveral parts of Heaven, is to be underftood in a divers N tion. If we refpect the courfe of the Sun and Stars the right is the Eaft, the left the Weft ; But the Heaven confider'd in itfelf, admits of no fuch diftinctions ; and therefore, as *Aratus* fayes, they are to be apply'd not to the form of the Heavens, but to our Pofition.

(f) He marks out the oblique Motion of the Sun through the Zodiack.

(g) As much as the Artick Pole is elevated, fo much the Antarick is depreft, this, ignorant Antiquity affign'd only for Ghofts and Hell.

(h) The leffer with his Head and Neck, the bigger with his Tail. So *Hyginus.*

(i) According to the opinion of the Epicureans, as *Turnebus* notes, who thought the Sun was diffolv'd every Night, and recompos'd the next Morning ; And therefore when the Sun left the upper Hemifphere, the nether Hemifphere could not but be dark ; elfe our Author could not be clear'd from the fufpicion of Ignorance. But upon this *Hypothefis* he ftands free, and to this moft probably *Virgil* alludes ; who loves to fprinkle his Writings with Philofophicall Readings.

(k) This time *Pliny* notes ; *The Spring, fayes he, opens the Sea to Saylors, in whofe beginning Favonius Breath foftens and mollifies the Winters rigour ; the Sun then obtaining the 25th part of Aquarius ; Intimated by the Lyrick.*

Solvitur Acris hiems grata vice veris & Favoni,
Trahuntq, ficcas machina Carinas.

This according to *Vegetius* falls about the 6th of the *Ides* of *March*, which he not unaptly calls, *The Birth-day of Navigation.*

(l) Not underftanding, as fome do, fhips of War, but Merchandize, rigg'd and trimm'd with all their tackling for Sea ; fo *La Cerda* upon the Authority of *Vitruus* ; (*lafces armate, non bellicis apparatibus inftructa, fed ornate omnibus armamentis, quibus egent ut confiftere in aquis poffint.*

(m) Others yet underftand it of hollowing Troughs for the Cattell to drink in. *La Cerda* and moft Interpreters of hollow'd Boats or *Canoa.*

In addition to the citations from standard reference works, there are a number of other notations, some of which seem clearly to be from the hand and mind of Ogilby. 'For the Reader's diversion' Sherburn's translation of Seneca's *Hippolytus* was transcribed (p. 124, n. [i]). And Ogilby seems to have been more than ordinarily interested in bees, as he cites the Countess of Kent on a portion of the 'Georgics' (p. 139), and describes how 'Mr. Butler' had experimented with the queen bee (p. 143, n. [s]). And again, on the breeding of bees, Ogilby writes: 'The great prejudice which the Commonwealth of Literature hath received by the loss of the Papers of the most Learned Searcher into Nature, Dr. Harvey, upon Insects, can never be enough deplor'd' (p. 147, n [s]).

Other quotations, from Sandys' translation of Ovid's *Metamorphoses* (p. 167, n. [2]), from Scaliger (*passim*), from Camden (p. 180, n. [o]) show wide acquaintance with contemporary or somewhat earlier writers. The familiar tone enters again in the mention of 'a very antient fair Manuscript, preserv'd by the Honour of our time, Mr. Selden' (p. 198, n. [b]). When controversies over points occur, Ogilby notes these and generally chooses a side, sometimes opting for common sense (p. 51, n.[n]). In commenting on the lines

> . . . *the Fatal Hour*
> *Of Death to stay, is not in Turnus power,*

the editor noted, 'And so they use to speak who are obstinately whirl'd away into danger, for they deny that they can avoyd it' (p. 454, n. [g]). It seems evident that, while the translation was beautifully printed and ornamented, and the English clear and straightforward, the notes themselves (an impressive sight on almost every page) repaid study, not only for the student and scholar but for the man — or woman — of letters who was interested in contemporary poetry or original editorial comment.

The 1654 Virgil was printed by Thomas Warren 'for the Author' and copies were to be obtained at his [the Author's] house in King's Head Court within Shoe Lane. This seems to be an early attempt by Ogilby to secure the rights and hence the profits of his work for himself rather than for a professional bookseller. His ability to insert those words 'for the Author' and his address on the title page came as the result of some hard and successful work. To subsidize the printing of his work, and so to obtain its profits, or royalties, he undertook to gain subscriptions, i.e., sufficient advances from patrons to ensure all or a considerable part of the printing costs of the edition. He communicated with former patrons and must have asked their aid in securing yet others, aided, no doubt, by his previously successful works. No advertisement or 'proposals' for the 1654 edition remain extant, as they do for some other of his enterprises. From the hundred patrons mentioned by Ogilby, however, enough money was collected in the early 1650's to pay for the lavish illustrations 'of the most famous Artists' and to provide for paper and printing costs. In one corner or section of the illustration commissioned, the name, the title and arms of the subscriber appeared, and constituted a satisfying reward to the person so immortalized, as the continuing success of this policy indicated.[21]

8) *Cleyn-Hollar Illustration*, Virgil, *1654*
In the possession of the Author

The names of the hundred patrons assembled by Ogilby for this 1654 edition of Virgil provide an impressive tribute, not only to his own economic acumen, but to the conditions of his times. Lavish tombs and elaborate funerals were out of style during the Commonwealth; ostentation of any sort (save religious piety) was suspect. But classical learning was irreproachable; and to have one's name, title, armorial bearings and various honours displayed on an engraving, set in a book together with some hundred other dignitaries — such display might fit well to the taste even of the Protector and of his secretary of state, Milton. Although neither of these men is represented, Edward Bysshe, Garter King of Arms under the Commonwealth, commissioned a plate. And the names of many of the great men of the old order appeared: the Marquess and Marchioness of Hertford, the Earl and Countess of Winchilsea, the Earl and Countess of Carnarvon (each of these with separate plates dedicated to them). Other mighty names appeared: the Earls of Carbery and Down; the second Earl of Strafford (whose plate was one of the most elaborate and fantastic in the volume); Henry Howard, second son of the Earl of Arundel; James Ogilvie, Earl of Arley [Airlie]; and the Earl of Ossory, one of the many friends from Ireland. Among those not of the nobility, but familiar from other activities were Elias Ashmole, the antiquarian; Edward Sherburn, the poet; Thomas Stanley, whose path was to join closely with Ogilby before long; Sir Anthony Ashley Cooper, later Earl of Shaftesbury; and Dorothy Osborne, the letter-writer. Obviously, Ogilby did not solicit each contributor himself. Some of these patrons, for various reasons, enlisted relatives and friends; also, to reiterate, these were days when display of a more common sort was frowned upon. Nevertheless, the collection of contributors to Ogilby's opulent Virgil in themselves constitute part of its magnificence and munificence. For a newcomer on the classical scene, penniless just a decade earlier, to have produced the 1654 Virgil remains a remarkable achievement.

Just four years later, in 1658, Ogilby brought out a similar volume, equally beautiful. It was another folio Virgil, but this time in Latin and without annotations. Again printed 'for the Author,' this volume was done by Thomas Roycroft, who produced a number of expensive, important and handsome editions of the classics in the later seventeenth-century. Ogilby's portrait, the Lely-Faithorne, again appeared as frontispiece. Facing him was a full-page cut of Virgil portrayed with a variety of his literary creations. About three-fourths of the number of hundred subscribers for the 1654 Virgil took pages in this folio as well.[22] In these closing years of the Protectorate, Ogilby felt it safe to dedicate the 1658 volume to William Wentworth, second Earl of Strafford, and son of his old patron, and to include a full-page illustration in his honour. In the Latin dedication, Ogilby referred with pride to his former service with the first Earl. This edition of Virgil in the original, the only such classical work in the original that Ogilby produced, certainly added a scholarly dimension to his reputation; likewise, his continued public association with a large number of distinguished gentlemen signalled his growing importance in the world of books and publishers.

Ogilby must have begun working diligently at Greek well before the appearance of the folios of Virgil's works. Numbers of scholars and theologians taught themselves Greek, Hebrew and other ancient tongues in the Renaissance, sometimes well after youth. There were fewer autodidacts in the seventeenth-century, but Hobbes came to Euclid at forty and worked at becoming a mathematician, though not wholly satisfactorily. Ogilby seems to belong in such a category. Surely he never knew Greek to the extent that he did Latin; but also surely he learned to read it in his fifties, and was able to handle much of the existing scholarly minutiae of annotations, emendations and correspondences involving the great Latin and the great Greek epics.[23] At seventy years of age (again from the 'Preface' to *Africa*, 1670), Ogilby looked back to this period and reviewed his progress.

I betook myself [during the Civil Wars] to something of Literature, in
which, till then, altogether a Stranger . . . And first Rallying my new
rais'd Forces, a small and inconsiderable parcel of Latin, I undertook . . .
the Reducing into our Native Language . . . of . . . Virgil.

Yet this, he realized, meant only that he was a good translator — 'one that had dabled well in anothers Helicon.' Ambition led him on, and Ogilby's later assessment of his Aesop venture was much higher than it had been in 1651:

The most Antient and Wisest of the Grecian Sages, who first led us
through a Vocal Forest, where Beasts also spake, and Birds sat Chanting
in every Tree, Notes for Men to follow: Aesop the Prince of Mythologists
became my Quarry, on his plain Song I Descanted, on his short and pithy
Sayings, Paraphras'd, raising my voice to such a height, that I took my
degree amongst the Minor Poets.

Next, 'with Sails a Trip, and swoln with the Breath of a general Applause,' Ogilby set out 'to discover Greece.' His intent, he said in 1670, was not only to translate Homer but to learn how to compose an epic of his own, of which more will appear later. He gives no specific details of the troubles inherent in mastering the Homeric language and accompanying scholarly paraphernalia beyond saying that his work meant 'much Cost and Labor.' In 1660, the Restoration year, *Homer His Iliads* appeared, in iambic pentameter, 'Adorn'd with Sculpture, and illustrated with annotations.' This volume was printed by Roycroft, with the usual opulence, and was dedicated, like so many others at that time, to the returned monarch, Charles II. A volume of over 500 pages, the work was formidable with the trappings of seventeenth-century scholarship. Ogilby included a 'Life of Homer,' composed primarily of quotations and speculations, and gave three folio pages to listing previous editions of Homer's works. Annotations had proliferated, both in number and complexity, ranging from a simple identification of the muse Calliope to a trilingual comment on the word 'cuts.' As the Greek and Latin are generally translated, it appears that Ogilby was still addressing the intelligent and informed reader, but not necessarily one who was classically educated. Some of the marginalia are formidable in their minute detail. The illustrations remain elaborate and lavish in scale, many showing they were commissioned by subscribers. In 1660 the translator, fully emerged as entrepreneur, again announced on the title page that copies were 'to be had at the Authors House in Kingshead Court within Shoe Lane.'

For over a decade now, Ogilby had been translating and versifying; in the *Iliad* and later in the *Odyssey* his pace and force show signs of lagging. Style in an epic is a cumulative force. An epic is not meant to be read in a sitting or two, and excerpts are misleading. A selection from one dramatic moment — when Andromache learns of Hector's death — may show how Ogilby can sustain interest when he reports on action, but is somewhat overpowered by words in the descriptions preceding and following:

> . . . *Andromache not yet*
> *Heard how her Lord remaind without the Gate:*
> *In private She beguild the tedious Houres,*
> *Working a curious Web with gaudy Flowres,*
> *And bade her Damsells get a Bath 'gainst Night,*
> *To cheer her Lord, returning from the Fight;* . . .
>
> *When from the Tower She heard a dismall Yell:*
> *Down from her trembling Hands her Shuttle fell,*
>   *And thus She said: Straight two of You prepare*
> *To waite on Us; my Mothers Voice I hear:*
> *What means this dolefull Cry? I fain would know;*
> *My Heart beats high; Ah, Me! I scarce can goe:* . . .
>
>   *This said, like one distracted out She flew,*
> *Trembling with Fear, attended on by Two:*
> *When to the Tower She came and gather'd Throng,*
> *And looking down saw Hector drag'd along.*
>
> *There by remorsless Steeds before the Walls,*
> *Her Spirits suffocated, down She falls;*
> *Off flyes her Veile, and regall Ornament,*
> *And Crown which Venus did to her present* . . .[24]

The only complete predecessor of this complete *Iliad* in English was that of Chapman (1598-1611); the next person after Ogilby to attempt a complete translation was Thomas Hobbes (1675-76). Ogilby's translation is closer to the Greek than Chapman's or Hobbes', and his use of couplets may have influenced Pope's translation (1715), as his work as a whole certainly did.[25] With the publication of the *Iliad*, Ogilby's reputation as a translator of classical works became widely established. He followed the *Iliad* with a translation of the *Odyssey* (*Homer His Odysses Translated, Adorn'd with Sculpture, and Illustrated with Annotations*) in 1665, again printed by Thomas Roycroft, and 'for the Author.' The Lely portrait was used, and the printing, margins, annotations (many in Greek) and footnotes were as impressive as in the *Iliad*. Small and full-page illustrations were scattered throughout, and numerous plates bore the names of distinguished personages. The volume as a whole was dedicated to the Duke of Ormond, a patron and acquaintance from the years spent in Ireland.

By 1665, when the *Odyssey* was published, the author-translator had become a royal official — Master of His Majesty's Revels in the Kingdom of Ireland. The new volume reflects his new and useful court connections, with its inclusion of a page certifying his copyright of his work for fifteen years from the date (25 May 1665) of the document. Ogilby described the *Odyssey* as 'the most Ancient and Best Piece of Moral and Political Learnning,' indicating that by this time he may have been thinking somewhat less in literary and more in political terms of his work.

Thomas Hobbes, as stated above, was to make the next English translation of the *Iliad* and *Odyssey*. In his preface to the latter work (1675), he wrote a critique of epic style that corresponded in feeling to Ogilby's own and was responded to appreciatively by Dryden (1700). Hobbes noted, among other things, that women, who love poetry, often were ill-prepared to read the classics in the original and so welcomed translation. He spoke for natural order and 'contexture' in style 'as a torch in the night shows a man the stops and unevenness in his way.' At the close of his preface, Hobbes asked himself a series of questions, which he at once answered. Why write the translation? Nothing else to do. Why publish it? To distract adversaries from revealing their stupidity in criticizing his more serious writings. And finally — 'But why without Annotations? Because I had no hope to do it better than it is already done by Mr. Ogilby.' This judgment, made in 1675, a decade after John Ogilby's *Odyssey* and fifteen years after his *Iliad,* was in all probability concurred in by the majority of cultivated readers at that time and for some years thereafter.

His reputation as translator of classics apparently assured by the early sixties, John Ogilby had already moved to endeavours in other fields. One of these established his connection, tenuous as that seems to be, with a handsome two-volume folio edition of the Bible. The publishing of Bibles in the seventeenth century was, of course, a steady activity, and by 1660 the King James version had become the one familiar to the majority of Englishmen. While at Cambridge, Ogilby may well have come to know John Field. Field had been successively Printer to Parliament and then to Cromwell. In 1655, he became Printer to the strongly Puritan Cambridge University, and obtained, with Henry Hills, a copyright to print the Bible. In the 1650's, he and Hills printed six editions, in which a contemporary claimed to have discovered some 20,000 errors.[26]

'Ogilby's Bible,' as it came to be called, can be so designated because of two factors, the first certain, the second deducible. Certainly Ogilby found or commissioned suitable illustrations for the Bible, and noted on the title page that the work was 'illustrated with Chorographical Sculps' by him. And secondly, he presumably obtained either plates for or copies of folio sheets, printed by Field, which the latter was willing to sell. Field's readiness to sell and Ogilby's eagerness to buy may have derived from the same source: the Restoration. A Puritan copyright was unlikely to survive the return of the Stuarts, and Field may have been glad for a buyer of some of his more expensive stock. On the other hand, Ogilby, a Scot and apparently always an accredited royalist, was eager to make the strongest assault upon his returning monarch's consciousness. The *Iliad* was coming to press just in time for a royal dedication, and a magnificent Bible, similarly dedicated, would enhance the translator's steadily growing reputation. Ogilby may in fact have been planning such a work for some time, as the earliest Hollar illustration in his 1660 Bible is dated 1656.

In the *Africa* Preface, Ogilby was explicit about his responsibility for the entire work: 'I thought it also Religious, and the part of a good Christian, to do something for Gods sake, to adorn in like manner, with Ornamental Accomplishments, the Holy Bible, which by my own sole Conduct, proper Cost and Charges, at last appear'd the largest and fairest Edition that was ever yet set forth in any Vulgar Tongue.' Aubrey was equally enthusiastic, and echoes the very phrasing: 'As if by a prophetique spirit, forseeing the restauration of King Charles IId, and also the want there might be of Church Bibles, he printed the fairest impression, and the most correct of English Bibles, in royall and imperiall paper, that ever was yet done.' The size and weight of the two volumes made it a ceremonial rather than a devotional object. But institutions were interested in such a showpiece, and the vitality and hopefulness characteristic of Restoration times made this a singularly clever choice for such a production. Ogilby was indeed sensitive to the opportunities that the situation presented.

The first volume, which extends through the Book of Job, bears the 1611 dedication to James I and the prefatory 'Translators to the Reader.' Then comes a list of the books of the Old Testament, the Apocrypha and the New Testament, followed by six maps, unsigned. The book is printed with full margins and annotations, though Ogilby claims credit for no more than the illustrations. The second volume is dated 1659, and does *not* contain the claim about Ogilby's illustrations. At the conclusion of Volume II is a statement that John Field printed it.

The binding and rebinding of books in various materials, and the creation of extra-illustrated volumes were characteristics of Bibles even more than of other books in the seventeenth-century.[27] Copies of 'Ogilby's Bible,' which became among the most expensive of English books in the seventeenth century (see below), vary in what they contain. For example, the copy in the National Library at Edinburgh has the Apocrypha removed and a metrical version of the Psalms included, as well as various other, later changes. The volumes in the British Museum were dedicated to Charles II in a delightful visual fashion. The words run: 'To. . . Charles II . . . This Edition of the Holy Bible . . . Dedicates your Sacred Majesties Most Humble, Obedient and Loyall Subject John Ogilby,' and the last eight words retire gracefully in small print to the right-hand side of the page, giving the effect of a low bow. Facing the title page in this copy is an engraving of the royal arms by Hollar; a double-page spread of Adam and Eve in the Garden by Lombart is included: and there are, again by Hollar, maps of the Holy Land (dated 1657), with dotted lines, presumably to show roads, plates of vessels of the Temple and the Ark of the Covenant (dated 1656), and some very well-drawn though much reworked views of Solomon's Temple (dated 1657, 1659 and 1660). A fold-in map of Jerusalem, almost twice the size of a double page, copied by Hollar from Villalpandi and dated 1660, is the only engraving in the second volume of the British Library copy.[28] It may have been a copy of this 'rich-adorned

Bible' that Charles II received at his Restoration, and to whose principles he promised fidelity.[29]

The *Iliad* and the Bible, both dedicated to Charles II, were impressive volumes. They must have been influential in obtaining for Ogilby the opportunity to write and print the several editions of *The Entertainment . . . of Charles II* in 1661 and 1662. As this will be treated at length in Chapter III, only a few words are required here. This became the commemorative record of the new monarch's coronation, comparable to and probably more admired and influential than Harrison's *Archs of Triumph* (1603) in honour of James I. Certainly Ogilby's *Entertainment* had more significance than Gregory King's ill-timed work on James II's coronation, which he had ready only in 1688. *The Entertainment* (1662) is a noble folio, the making of which cost Ogilby considerable trouble as well as effort, but which also confirmed him in royal favour, and became a much quoted and memorable volume.

Among the Thomason Tracts in the British Library[30] is a sheet of the ephemeral sort that must have flooded London in these years. Dated 1661, it bears a cut of Charles II by P. Willemsen, and under it the following verses by 'John Ogil' [the remaining two letters have been cut off]:

The Second Charles, Heir of the Royal Martyr;
Who for Religion, and his Subjects Charter
Spent the best Blood, that unjust sword e're dyed,
Since the rude Souldier pierc'd Our Saviour's Side
Who such a Father had'st, art such a Son,
Redeem Thy People, and assume Thy Own.

The extravagant imagery and pervasive religious tone, like that in the *Eikon Basilike,* was not, in those early years of the Restoration, uncommon, and these lines are in fact from Ogilby's own epic — an abortive project, to be considered later. There may have been other such tributes to the monarch by Ogilby, as there certainly were by other writers, in broadsheets too fragile to last for three centuries. Alone, that kind of tribute would scarcely have been noticed. Joined with his impressive folios, such homage to the new monarch was not to be ignored.

Scarcely less important than the contents of the books he produced were the methods by which the ingenious but sometimes impecunious author financed his works. There is no evidence as to how his first book — the translation of the works of Virgil — was financed. Although there was a dedication to a noble patron, expensive illustrations and annotations were lacking; it was, presumably, a publisher's venture. With the success of the *Virgil*, Ogilby was encouraged to continue, and his popular *Aesop,* two years later, was illustrated, had introductory poems from well-known figures, and showed much greater ease in composition and verse.

As noted earlier (pp. 39 ff.), Ogilby solicited patrons for his illustrations, once he became known as an author. By the time of his third volume, the folio *Virgil* of 1654, Ogilby was well launched into the subscription business in selling books, and his success in that pursuit was considerable.[31] The receipt of substantial advances enabled him to control the printing and some of the sales of his books. By 1654, he apparently kept some of his stock for sale at his own house, and probably before 1670 set up his own press there. He also undertook, with distinct success, standing-lotteries of his own books on numerous occasions.

One further means of raising funds commended itself to John Ogilby — a less usual way than those described above. This was his practice of presenting his volumes to various bodies, with the implicit understanding that there should be a monetary grant in return. How many volumes he presented in this way, and how many failed to produce financial recompense it is impossible to say. Some positive evidence remains.

In 1654, John Ogilby delivered to the Merchant Taylors Company, of which he was a member, the volumes of his *Virgil* and *Aesop,* 'very fairly bound.' For this he received £13.6s.8d.[32] In 1660, he presented his Bible to the House of Commons for their use. Commons voted to accept the volumes and asked the Lord Treasurer to pay £50 to Ogilby. The Treasurer objected that the money must come from the Privy Seal, and he had no warrant to pay £50 for such a purpose. There, with a less energetic author, the matter might have rested. Ogilby, however, petitioned the King;[33] he also petitioned the Clerk of the House, who supported his claim;[34] and a warrant finally came from Hampton Court for the Treasurer to pay the £50 from the Privy Seal to Ogilby. In addition, the Clerk of the Signet was directed to pay him £200 for various works presented to the King.[35] In later years, Ogilby was to continue the policy of presenting a book or books to groups or institutions, often eliciting a sum of money with the thanks returned.

The troublesome question of copyright — unclear, complex and variable at the best of times — was made more difficult during the Interregnum. And, of course, if a work or works became popular, the problem was magnified further. John Ogilby faced copyright difficulties throughout his life, difficulties that grew as his popularity increased. The printing rights to Ogilby's first two volumes — the 1649 *Virgil* and 1651 *Aesop* — were vested in the Crook brothers, who had published them. In 1665, when Ogilby's name had become quite well known, Andrew Crook brought out a second edition of the 1649 *Virgil*. It is a meaner volume than the first edition, more crowded in type and margins, and apparently produced without revision or addition. It is hard to imagine that the poet-translator was pleased with the appearance of such a volume, and it may be presumed that he therefore bought from the Crooks the copyright to his *Aesop,* which Thomas Roycroft then very handsomely printed 'for the Author' in 1665 and again in 1668. A second edition of the *Aesopics* was printed in 1673 and in a copy at the Folger Shakespeare Library is bound with the *Fables of Aesop,* which are designated as 'the Third Edition.'[36] In the separate title pages, John Ogilby is called by his full royal title (see Chapter IV); both pages say 'Printed by the Author, at his House in White-Friers' and bear the date 1673. Only the first part has a Table of Contents. The *Aesopics* is dedicated to Charles FitzRoy, Earl of Southampton, a bastard son of Charles II. Another 'third edition' so called, was printed in 1675, in two volumes, 'Adorn'd with 160 copper sculptures and Illustrated with Annotations.' It falls far short of the 1665 and 1668 editions, with reworked and poor cuts, and with the annotations placed all together at the beginning of the first volume. It may have been a pirated edition. It was printed for T. Basset, R. Clevel and R. Chiswill and dedicated, like the 1673 edition, to the Earl of Southampton. Presumably, by then, even a poor edition of 'Ogilby's *Aesop*' would find buyers. The confusion attendant on the differing descriptions of editions reflects clearly the state in which printers, booksellers and authors subsisted.

By coincidence, in the same year (1675) that the last edition of *Aesop* appeared, another edition of Ogilby's *Virgil* did so likewise. This was a distinct improvement on the second Crook edition. A new translation (perhaps commissioned rather than made by Ogilby), it was a much fuller, smoother and more embroidered story, with elaborate annotations, and illustrated with some unsigned and not very impressive cuts. It was printed by the author, for Peter Parker and Thomas Guy, and dedicated to Mary, elder daughter of the Duke of York and the future Queen of England. It is easy to imagine Ogilby, in the 1670's walking through his by-then-crowded workshop, remembering and examining his earlier editions, deciding in the light of current tastes what works might be reissued profitably, and then selecting some new patrons to whom to dedicate the volumes. Some ventures were doubtless more happy than others. Both the *Iliad* and the *Odyssey* were reissued in 1669, and an elaborate *Iliad* again in 1670. Ogilby's Bible was still on sale, at high prices, late in the century, but whether some of these copies were reprints or simply well-preserved stock is impossible to say.

Although Irish records are notably imperfect, it is not surprising to find John Crook, again King's Printer in Dublin, issuing Ogilby's *Works of Virgil* in 1666, and sometime after that a listing of O'Gilby's translation of Homer in two volumes in large paper.[37] There may well have been other editions of Ogilby's works printed in that city

Ogilby's work as translator and poet brought him the first sure sense of influence and prestige. He devoted his energies to find useful patrons and soliciting subscribers, to the skill of translating and versifying, and to the annotating of verses and commissioning of illustrations for Virgil, Homer, Aesop and the Bible. If one wonders why Ovid, with his attractions for the visually minded, or Juvenal, full of satirical emphasis, escaped his attention, it seems likely, as Ogilby suggested in 1670, that he yielded to the shift of interest from the quiet of the study to the governance of growing areas of the world, a shift that was beginning to absorb Englishmen in the later seventeenth century. In the 1670's he turned to prose and began his great series of world atlases (to be treated in Chapter VI).

III

Restoration: Royal Favour & Advancement

For Ogilby, as for so many others, the Restoration of Charles II was a climactic event. Through the patronage of the Duke of Buckingham and later of the Earl of Strafford, Ogilby came to know the early Stuart Court and courtiers. It is likely that he had seen and perhaps performed before Charles I; and Ogilby's associations with the Marquess of Worcester in the 1640's, at a time when that nobleman was one of the King's most loyal servants, make it possible that there were contacts near the end of Charles's life. Certainly by 1660, Ogilby had already begun an epic poem — the *Carolies* — based upon the life and martyrdom of Charles; he had apparently completed it by 1666, when it was destroyed by a stroke of fate, kinder to the cause of literature than to Ogilby, that was the Great Fire.

The years 1660-1662 were filled with renewed royal contacts for John Ogilby, in whom genuine loyalty and desire for advancement joined to create an intensive activity. His *Iliad,* just nearing completion in 1660, was dedicated to the new monarch; so were at least some copies of his sumptuous illustrated Bible, produced in the same year. One broadside survives, dated 1661, extolling the Restoration and the martyred Charles I. Ogilby likewise was in contact with a number of courtiers, and made numerous requests for privileges connected both with his publishing and with the Irish theatre. The most significant and long-lived of his efforts, however, would seem to be the creation of his two major editions of *The Relation of His Majestie's Entertainment Passing through the City of London, To His Coronation: with a Description of the Triumphal Arches, and Solemnity,* in 1661 and 1662.

The outpouring of affection for the long-deprived young monarch was one of the most genuine popular phenomena of seventeenth-century England. With it went a renewed dedication to the idea of monarchy itself, coupled with a remarkable tendency to bury the memory of Charles I's transgressions under a mound of idealizing and even idolatrous writings. Into these varying emotions John Ogilby entered sympathetically and contributed something of his own. The Common Council of London, in planning its homage, had created a special committee to celebrate the coronation. That committee in turn appointed Ogilby, already a citizen, and freeman of a great company, to write the 'poeticall parts' of the great Coronation procession honouring Charles. His designation as 'poet' in 1654, when he presented the Merchant Taylors Company with copies of his works, was repeated in one of the pertinent documents still extant concerning the procession; it seems apparent that his classical reputation was responsible for the honour done him in this selection. Ogilby himself, of course, was busy soliciting royal favour directly, but the opportunity to write the script and later to publish the magnificent record of the Coronation pageant was probably at least as important for his advancement as any personal approach to the King.

Two days before the procession, which took place on 22 April 1661, the Council bade the Chamberlain pay Ogilby £50 'for the present.' The receipt, shown on the reverse of the warrant, discloses that the money was collected the same day.[1] Nearly three months later, on 6 July 1661, a complementary warrant was issued, again to the Chamberlain:

You are desired to pay unto Mr. John Ogleby [sic] the poett imployed for the composeing of the Speeches Songs and Inscriptions against the said solemnity the summe of ffifty pounds as a gratuity for his care and pennes [pains] taken therein.[2]

This warrant was not receipted until 18 August, and appears to constitute the final payment (£100 in all) to the 'poet' of the ceremonies.

At least one of the volumes, and perhaps several, had a special dedicatory page just after the title page. One copy, with a 1661 date, bore the statement:

To the right honourable the Lord Mayor, Court of Aldermen, Committee for the Coronation, and the Rest of the Worthy Members of this honourable City.[3]

There are other specific references in this volume to the City. Various City companies and trained bands were stationed in appropriate places, and in St. Paul's Churchyard the children of Christ's Hospital (reportedly 1100 of them), 'a numerous Testimony of the Charity of this Honourable City,' sang a hymn. Ogilby's account concludes, 'But this being the Limit of the Citie's Liberty, must be so likewise of our Description.' This edition, or perhaps a particular issue, must have been prepared for distribution to City patrons, and so emphasizes the City aspect of the procession.

By this time, Ogilby's work, demanding and many-faceted as it was, required a reliable and permanent assistant. This the emerging businessman was apparently able to find in his young step-grandson. William Morgan is clearly identified in later years as citizen and freeman of the Clockmakers Company, and there are a number of Morgans active in that company: for example, a Thomas Morgan was chosen Clerk in 1652, and another Morgan (Christian name not given) was Beadle in 1641.[4] Records in the middle decades of the century are notably less full than later. If William Morgan was apprenticed, the most likely entry is the one dated 6 May 1650, when someone of that name was made apprentice to Lionel Wythe for eight years.[5] On the other hand, this young relation of

Ogilby may not have served an apprenticeship at all, but rather have purchased his freedom or obtained it through patrimony. Certainly, he practiced clockmaking, if at all, for a very few years. It seems more probable that, like his grandfather, he found membership in a City company — any City company — vital for conducting business, and chose to join one where he had relatives. Although the Clockmakers were a minor Company, membership therein sufficed for a creditable standing, and in later years William Morgan became somewhat active in Company affairs.

The first evidence of Morgan's assistance to Ogilby comes in a warrant dated 18 July 1661, just twelve days after the second warrant for payment to Ogilby himself. The Committee in charge of Coronation preparations authorized the Chamberlain to pay Morgan 'for attending and doing business for Mr. Ogleby the poett the summe of nine pounds and tenn shilling.' On the fifteenth of August, the sum was discharged; and in a list of 'Bills paid' this is confirmed, for Morgan's 'paines and Attendance on the said bussines.'[6] According to extant records, the young man received only about one-tenth as much as his grandfather; nevertheless, it was a substantial sum. Their co-operation was to grow, to prove useful to both men and finally to shape Morgan's own life and career.

The tradition of London celebrating the coronation of a new king or queen was well established. Elizabeth's progress through the City, filled with pageantry and song, and enhanced by the monarch's lively participation, occurred the day before her coronation in January 1559.[7] The Corporation of London arranged for a record of the procession to be made and published; one edition appeared in 1559, another in 1604. For James's progress, postponed by the plague till March 1604, the Corporation established a select committee of sixteen, and Ben Jonson and Thomas Dekker shared the major responsibility for the written part of that entertainment.[8] Stephen Harrison, an architect and carpenter, published the illustrated account known as *Archs of Triumph* in 1604, and Dekker and Jonson likewise left their records, *The Magnificent Entertainment . . .* and *Part of the Entertainment . . .*

James made it clear that he did not enjoy this or later processions through London, and his son, far more austere, never countenanced one.[9] Charles agreed to make a passage, but seized on one excuse after another to postpone and finally to cancel the event. He did make a great progress through Edinburgh in June 1633, the published account of which was called *The Entertainment of the High and Mighty Monarch Charles . . . into his Ancient and Royall City of Edinburgh.* Both in 1604 and in 1633, the progress of the monarch was marked by arches, at which points various entertainments were presented; this device was continued by Ogilby.

The entertainment in the progresses was necessarily of an episodic nature, with only the monarch and his train viewing the entire presentation, and most observers seeing at best one single scene. Ben Jonson set forth his own principles, which seem to have been the prevailing ones, underlying the construction of the pageants: 'The nature and property of these Devices being to present always some one entire body or figure, consisting of distinct members, and each of these expressing itself in their own active

50

sphere, yet all with that general harmony so connexed and disposed, as no one little part can be missing to the illustration of the whole.' The symbols, he went on, were not to be simple or obvious 'but a mixed character, partaking somewhat of all.' Nor should they, as in a puppet show, be identified in a simple-minded way by such a legend as 'This is a Dog,' or 'This is a Hare,' but rather 'without cloud or obscurity, declare themselves to the sharp and learned.' The common viewer was dismissed summarily: 'For the multitude, no doubt but their grounded judgments did gaze, said it was fine, and were satisfied.' Under such circumstances, the elements of plot and character development were neglected, and instead a theme or themes were emphasized. Actually, however, lavish visual and sometimes aural aspects constituted the heart of the presentations. For sixteenth- and seventeenth-century writers, the authors of antiquity, figures from mythology and types of moral allegory were, of course, prime elements to be used in composition. All these were present in Ogilby's text. Because of the circumstances of Charles II's accession, however, there was a significant theme available to Ogilby that had been absent in 1559 and 1604 — the theme of restoration. Allied to this were the corollaries of the return of peace and prosperity, the righting of injustice, and the triumph of the monarch, God's representative, over the forces of rebellion. Ogilby's text, in reflecting this content, achieved more coherence than earlier versions of coronation pageants, although it lacks the facility and sweep of some of Jonson's lines. In addition, Ogilby had the drive and the good fortune to be able to publish the entire work himself, thereby consolidating and enhancing his fame.

Certainly, Ogilby had at his disposal the records of previous processions — the 1559 progress of Elizabeth and the various reports of James's 'entertainment,' all of which were printed or reprinted in 1604. He kept to the essential pattern of a procession interrupted at intervals by a pageant or show; and some of the stops, though not all, occurred at places where, in 1559 or 1604, various representations had been presented. There had been five pageants for Elizabeth and seven for James. Ogilby staged only four, but as with the other entertainments, there were numerous displays and speeches along the way. In 1661, the representation and praise of Parliament, present in both the earlier pageantries, was significantly omitted.

In most ways, however, Ogilby presented a series of performances similar in tone and spirit to those of 1559 and 1604. Like Elizabeth's pageants, those for Charles II were erected solely by Londoners. Like James's procession, his grandson's was marked by triumphal arches. English or Latin were the languages used throughout all the ceremonies for speeches, inscriptions and placards, usually with translations from Latin given at the time or made for the printed version. Children were used in all the pageantry, generally from the City schools, and a variety of music was performed, commonly designated as 'noise,' and interspersed into each entertainment. The civic theme was strongly emphasized in the two Stuart accounts, and Ogilby adopted the term 'Entertainment' that Dekker and Jonson had used. His misspelling of 'Saint Dunstones' in his first edition, later changed to 'Dunstans,' may have reflected his reading of the Elizabethan account, where it is so written. Although Harrison in *Archs of Triumph* (1604) claimed that no one had printed a processional account before, he was obviously incorrect, and the three sets of records, dated 1559, 1604 and 1661-62, form a similar and interconnected set of statements.

The two basic texts of Ogilby's *Entertainment* (1661 and 1662) differ markedly, but both are alike in being fuller than earlier records, and the 1662 edition is more lavishly illustrated. Ogilby made considerable use of the themes of Rebellion subdued and Restoration triumphant. And his account, situated in time between the First and Second Dutch Wars and foreshadowing England's search for and growing dominance of world trade, emphasized constantly the anticipated growth, in conjunction with the return of the monarchy, of unprecedented commerce and prosperity.

Ogilby's concern, from the inception of his labours, was that he should have exclusive rights to the publication of the story of the procession.[11] Although his 1661 editions appeared without illustrations, engravers for the later volumes must have been commissioned and perhaps already at work in that year. The 1662 folios contain not only the depiction of the great coronation procession signed by Hollar (with some work by others), but numerous other engravings. Nevertheless, conception outstripped execution, and even these later volumes have a number of abortive illustrations, with legend and positioning, but without the drawing. What was unfulfilled, however, was essentially background, not contemporary, material, and Ogilby's volumes were so comprehensive on coronation procession and procedure as to constitute a valuable reference work for nearly two centuries. His debt to previous accounts was more than repaid by his endeavours in 1661 and 1662.

Although for the bibliographer there are three editions of the 1661 *Entertainment,* they are essentially alike in text. They read like an extensive news account of Charles's procession: where he stopped; what was said, sung and performed; and, very briefly at the end, the names of some of those responsible for the performances. These volumes, without illustrations but with varieties of type and margin, read quickly and easily and convey with clarity the sense of the City's welcome. Ogilby supplied and printed some extra materials, probably for inclusion in the volumes presented to or purchased by important City officials. An example would be the volume referred to containing a page of dedication to the Lord Mayor and Aldermen and other city officials (see page 49). It continues, in a direct statement to these gentlemen,

> *'The Relation of this Solemnity and of what, in pursuit of their Commands, He undertook, and hath compleated, is Humbly Dedicated, by Their Most Obedient Servant, John Ogilby.'*[12]

At the close of the text there is appended the list of the nine aldermen and fifteen commoners who constituted the committee in charge of the coronation festivities. Their activities in raising money, railing the streets and adorning the houses and windows with rich tapestries are fully noted, as are the oration and the gift of Sir William Wilde, Recorder of London.

A detailed examination of the two texts is probably the most meaningful way of distinguishing the two basic editions. The 1661 text is of interest in two particulars: its choice of themes, as reflecting the interest and hopes of Londoners in the Restoration; and its prose, essentially Ogilby's, and the most original, together with the *Aesopics,* of his versifications. For Londoners there was especial significance in the sight of their aldermen appearing before a triumphal arch in Cheapside. The companies of the City with trophies and ornaments stood on one side, the trained bands on the other. Later, the City's charity was attested to by the performance of the children of Christ's Hospital (Ogilby sets their number at '1100,' presumably having added an extra digit at the beginning or the end of the figure). These lads sang hymns, and one of their number made an oration to the King. Of more general interest than just to Londoners, however, were the four pageants composed by Ogilby, and to these he gave most of his descriptive space. The four themes that he chose to treat in his four arches were: first, Rebellion vanquished by Monarchy and Loyalty; next, the naval might of England; then, the return of Concord; and, lastly, the coming of Prosperity. In the first and second there was considerable liveliness of invention and execution exhibited. The performance at the first arch began with Rebellion, a woman, attended by confusion and mounted on a hydra. A painting over the arch showed Usurpation retreating before the king, exhibiting many heads, 'one particularly shooting out of his Shoulder, like Cromwell's.' Quotations from Virgil and Horace appeared in various places, and a device used by Ben Jonson in 1604, was adopted: 'S.P.Q.L.' with 'Londinensis' substituted for the familiar 'Senatus Populusque *Romanus.*' After some spirited battle music from trumpets and drummers, Rebellion made a vigorous speech to the King:

. . .

The Names of Princes are inscrib'd on Flowr's,
And Wither with them! . . .
I am Hell's Daughter, Satan's Eldest Childe,
When I first cry'd, the Pow'rs of Darkness smil'd,
And my Glad Father, Thundring at my Birth,
Unhing'd the Poles, and shook the fixed Earth.

. . . Great Cities are my Sphear:
I Sorc'ry use, and hag Men in their Beds,
With Common-wealths and Rotas fill their Heads,
Making the Vulgar in Fanatique Swarms
Court Civil War, and dote on Horrid Arms;
'Twas I, who, in the late unnatural Broils,
Engag'd three Kingdoms, and two Wealthy Isles:
I hope, at last, to march with Flags unfurl'd,
And tread down Monarchy through all the World.

To which Monarchy, another lady, but of much less vivid language and personality, made a brief answer, in part as follows:

To Hell, foul Fiend, shrink from this glorious Light,
And hide thy Head in Everlasting Night.

And all Confess, whilst they in you [the King] are Blest,
I, Monarchy, of Governments am Best.

With this somewhat qualified expression of the value of monarchy in his ears, Charles II then passed on to the East India House in Leadenhall Street. Here an entertainment was presented, the report of which appears in some, but not all of the 1662 folios. It was not of Ogilby's composition, as he makes scrupulously clear in a marginal note,[16] but it must have been one of the most interesting sights of the day, with two blackamoors attending a young man in Indian habit, and a camel bearing another youth who scattered jewels, spices and silks among the spectators. The two young men were sons of Sir Richard Ford, of the East India Company, and the speech of one alluded to 'the encroaching Holland's Rival Force' and concluded with that proud boast of sixteenth-century Spain, which was to become Britain's by the eighteenth-century: 'That we never see The Sun set on Your Crown, or Dignity' (p.10).

The second arch was devoted to naval matters and showed Father Thames, who had appeared in the 1604 pageant as well. Included in this entertainment were paintings of Neptune and Mars, quotations from Virgil and a representation of Charles I showing his fleet to the Prince of Wales, the present monarch. Other figures were depicted as well, and music was played at this spot (Cornhill) continuously until Charles II's arrival. The *pièce de résistance* of the second pageant, however, centred about the deck of a ship on which three seamen were represented. They sang a lengthy and jolly chantey that must have delighted the listening citizens, one of Ogilby's liveliest pieces of verse. It began:

In that fluctuating Sphear,
* Where stout Ships, and smaller Barks*
Are toss'd like Balls, or feather'd Corks,
* When Briny Waves to Mountains swell,*
Which dimming oft Heavn's glittring Sparks,
* Then descending low as Hell;*
*   Through this Crowd,*
*   In a Cloud,*
By a strange and unknown Spell,
*   We newly Landing,*
*   Got this Standing,*
All Merry Boys, and Loyal,
*   Our Pockets full of Pay*
*   This Triumphal Day,*
To make of our skil a Tryal,
* Of our little little skil:*
* Let none then take it ill,*
We must have no Denyal.

The second verse described the vicissitudes of the sailor's life:

We, who have rais'd, and laid the Poles,

Plough'd Frozen Seas, and scalding Billows,
Now stiff with Cold, then scorch'd on Coals,
Ships our Cradles, Decks our Pillows;

. . .

Through Gibraltar's contracted Mouth,

. . .

Or Baltick Waves bound up in Ice,
Or Magellan as Cold, though South . . .

And in the third verse, Ogilby inserted a vigorous description, no doubt calculated to stir the hearts both of burgesses and apprentices, of England's naval efforts at sea:

We, who so often bang'd the Turk,
*   Our Broad-sides speaking Thunder,*
Made Belgium strike, and proud Dunkirk,
*   Who liv'd by Prize, and Plunder,*
And routed the Sebastian Shirk;
*   We paid their Poops, and painted Beaks,*
*   Clean'sd before and eft their Decks,*
*   Till their Scuppers ran with Gore,*
Whilst in as fast salt-Water breaks . . .

After Father Thames had made a dignified speech, noting London's place as a centre for import and export and commenting on the Royal Navy through which 'You Alone the wat'ry World command,' the seamen returned in an even lengthier performance.

*   . . . Wee'll not care a fig*
For France, for France, the Netherlands, nor Spain;
*   The Turk, who looks so big,*
*   We'll whip him like a Gig*
*   About the Mediterrane*
*   His Gallies all sunk, or ta'ne.*

*   Wee'll seize on their Goods, and their Monies,*
*   Those Algier Sharks*
*   That Plunder Ships, & Barks,*
*   Algier, Sally, and Tunis,*
*   We'll give them such Toasts*
*   To the Barbary-Coasts,*
*   Shall drive them to Harbour, like Conies.*

After further boastful lines about the devastation the English Navy would wreak, the seamen then put off their hoods and drank a toast to the King. Next they fell on their knees

*   T'our Royal Admiral,*
A Health for his Preservation,
*   Dear James, the Duke of York,*
*   Till our Heels grow light as Cork,*

The second Glory of our Nation.
Tantara ran tan tan
Tan tara rantan tara
To the Royal Pair-a . . .

The theme of Concord, which Ogilby undoubtedly felt to be a major one in his production, produced actually his most flaccid and derivative pageant. Numerous figures representing Virtues, a concord of twenty-four violins, and elaborate appurtenances to the great arch all combined to give only a static performance. There was indeed a man in a purple gown, 'like a Citizen of London, presenting the King with an oaken Garland' (p. 23), and in the midst of the arch a curtain was drawn, when the King approached, and several women entertained him with a song. It is notable chiefly for a conscious use of alliteration — one of Ogilby's few literary tricks, and rarely used at that. The theme of the next arch, prosperity, is foreshadowed in part of the song:

Peace, and Concord, never poor,
Will make with Wealth this City shine,
  Ships freight with Spice, and Golden Ore,
Your Fields with Honey, Milk, and Wine,
  To supply our Neighbours Store.

The theme of Concord itself is directly treated at the close with reference to the royal arms:

Your Sacred Brow the blushing Rose,
And Virgin Lilly twin'd inclose!
The Caledonian Thistle-down
Combine with these t'adorn Your Crown!
No Discord in th' Hibernian Harp!
Naught in our Duty flat, or sharp!
But all conspire, that You, as Best,
May 'bove all other Kings be Blest.

There was music, vocal and instrumental down Ludgate Hill, across Fleet Bridge and past Fleet Conduit. Near White Friars, on Fleet Street, stood the fourth arch, with a Latin legend to the increase of prosperity, erected by 'S.P.Q.L.' again. In this final presentation there were numerous figures, living and painted, and much music. Only one speech, and that relatively brief, was given. Then, at Temple Bar, where one of Ben Jonson's notable presentations had been staged, there was a brief view of a park with animals 'both Tame, and Savage.' Rather hastily, however, Ogilby's account concluded, 'But this being the Limit of the Citie's Liberty, must be so likewise of our Description' (p. 32).

No doubt there was pressure to finish the account quickly and get the manuscript into print. In a brief addendum to the account, in which Ogilby gave credit to a number of those who participated in the arrangements, he noted that the arrangers 'performed all to Admiration, and, considering the Shortness of the Warning, much beyond what could have been imagined.' The Surveyor of the City, with another who wished to remain anonymous, had devised the arches, and Matthew Lock, Composer in Ordinary to the King, had composed all the music. The other names, of painters, carpenters, carvers and so on, are apparently those of City men, all of whom worked under the Council's direction. As noted earlier, Ogilby received at least £100 for his part in the ceremonies; his return from the editions of the *Entertainment* cannot be calculated.

For the 1662 text, Ogilby had secured illustrations, chief among them being the magnificent set of plates of the processional (all but the fourth by Wenceslaus Hollar). In addition to providing a valuable record of the officials in attendance and their order, the illustration indicates how long a time the procession must have taken to make its way from Tower Hill to Whitehall, with most of its members on foot and the horses no doubt proceeding at the slowest pace. David Loggan provided plates of the four arches, but showed only one side of each, and often the description in the text cannot be followed in the pictorial representation. Nowhere is any indication of the crowd itself given. Scattered throughout the 1662 folio are numerous cuts of ancient coins, indicating the growing interest in their collection and study. Ogilby's acquaintance with Ashmole, who knew and was soon to inherit the Tradescant collection, may have been responsible for the reproduction of so many of these items. Some, indeed, are described, but the space provided for the engraving remains blank — an omission probably attributable to publication pressures. Different illustrations appear in different folios, apparently according to the wish of the buyer: a frontispiece portrait of Ogilby; the royal arms, engraved by Hollar; various portraits (some later than 1662) of Charles II; and the plate of the coronation in Westminster Abbey by Hollar.

The 1662 text, very different from the editions of 1661, was probably prepared with a different market in mind. Ogilby's task in regard to the procession was to prepare 'the poetic part.' His own enterprise urged him on to publication of the story of the procession. Finding that an obviously successful venture, he planned, almost at once (the Hollar procession is dated '1661'), to expand his work. Whereas the original text was essentially clear and descriptive and intended to please the City officials who had commissioned Ogilby's services, the 1662 edition was probably designed as a showpiece for the ample purses and growing libraries of the nobility and gentry of England. In addition to the illustrations, it is a vastly expanded volume (165 pages on the procession, as against 32 in 1661). Although the folios vary in size, those of 1662 are quite large (43, 48 cm.) and are printed on paper of excellent quality, generally exceeding the editions of 1661 in both regards.

The content is strikingly different in 1662 from that of 1661, again in accord with the presumed new audience. Although much less clear in description, the 1662 text abounds with classical references and quotations, both in Greek and Latin, and with the translations from those tongues. The story of the royal procession through London is quite lost in surrounding embellishments, which often stray so far from the original point as to lose contact with it completely. Virgil, Statius, Ovid, Livy, Silius Italicus, Anacreon and many other classical writers appear, with greater or less relevance. Citations of 'Mr. Ross's' translations of Silius Italicus, 'Mr. Stanley's' of various Greek poets, and Drayton's *Poly-olbion* show Ogilby's acquaintance with the writings of his own times. As an account of the coronation procession, the 1662 text is confusingly organized, although by diligent search the original text can be found, submerged but hardly changed. As a work pretentiously stuffed with classical quotations and elaborations (when possible, cited from Ogilby's own translations), enlarged with illustrations and handsomely printed, the 1662 volume became an acquisition that would be a matter of pride or a source of ostentation, although it might never be read save in small portions. The omission of the East India scene in some of the 1662 texts is curious, explicable perhaps because, as he had stated, it was not Ogilby's own work. One further piece of information appeared in 1662 (p. 183) concerning the procession, that models of coronation medals, both in gold and in silver, were flung to the people during Charles's passage.

In passing from the texts to the production of editions of *The Entertainment,* many curious problems appear. One of the most complicated is the addendum in the 1662 editions dealing with the coronation itself. As Ogilby wrote, in his brief 1661 account, he was charged with describing only the reception and events in the City of London; and, at Temple Bar, he closed his story. When, however, he foresaw the opportunities inherent in a larger and more opulent volume, he realized that, without the report of the Coronation ceremony, his work would be incomplete. Thereupon, he apparently turned to his friend Elias Ashmole, Windsor Herald, who obligingly produced an account of 'The Solemne Rites and Ceremonies performed on the Day of the Coronation' [23 April 1661].

Ashmole's voluminous notes contain materials relating to his involvement with the festivities of the coronation.[14] His account of the event, illustrated by Hollar's fine plate, is that of a person intimately and knowledgeably concerned with all aspects of it. He deals with details of the individuals present, the robes worn, and the actions performed. The work proceeds through the story of the coronation ceremony, including even the prayers and anthems used, and the dinner served to the King and his nobles in Westminster Hall. The sudden eruption of thunder and lightning, occurring at the end of the feast, is noted, which 'some sort of people were apt to interpret as ominous, and ill-boding.' With the reassurance that in antiquity this was a favourable sign, the description ends. Its inclusion with Ogilby's story of the coronation procession unquestionably rounded out the 1662 text, and made it a more comprehensive account than any of the 1661 editions.

Unfortunately, however, the Ashmole portion also created problems of its own, problems involving the licensing or copyright of printed material; a conflict between personalities, and some rivalry within the hierarchy of the College of Arms. The pirating of books was a menace that faced Ogilby both as author and as publisher. He was clearly aware of the problem and he was especially anxious to protect his rights in the valuable property of the coronation account. Even before his first, 1661, text appeared, Ogilby had petitioned the King for the exclusive right of publication of the coronation progress, for which he had been commissioned to write 'the poetical part.'[15] That this was granted appears from the royal licence prefaced to the 1661 edition and signed by Edward Nicholas. Dated from Whitehall, 11 April 1661, it indicated that, already at this time, plans for the more elaborate edition of 1662 were well developed. Inasmuch, said the licence, as the commissioners had

appointed our Trusty and Well-beloved John Ogilby, Gent., for the Conduct of the Poetical part thereof, consisting in Speeches, Emblemes, Mottoes, and Inscriptions, which he intends to set forth in a large Treatise, and Represent in Sculpture; Our will and pleasure is, That no Person, or Persons whatsoever, do presume to Print, or publish the said Treatise, or any relation whatsoever, of the said Solemnitie, or Sculpture, in any size, or Book, or Pamphlet, in any Volume whatsoever, concerning the same, without the Consent of the said John Ogilby, as they will answer the contrary at their perill.

Ogilby's personal concern may have been for the pirating of his prose and illustrations, but he emphasized the possible dangers to the King in any unauthorized version of the coronation. In the introduction to the 1661 text, he wrote: 'To the intent, that the Ingenious may be instructed, the Malevolent silenced, and Misinformations prevented, it is thought fit to publish a perfect Description of the Solemnity.' This theme appeared also in his petition for the copyright, designed, he said, 'to prevent the false relations, which, if not prohibited, will be made of it, to the disadvantage of so great a solennity [*sic*].'

In fact, the haste with which the first, incomplete edition was produced is amply explained by a notice that appears in at least one of the 1661 texts:[16]

By reason of some fictitious Printed Papers of the Manner of His Majestie's intended Proceeding through London, on Monday the two and twentieth of this instant April, lately spread abroad; it is thought fit, for better Satisfaction, to Publish this Copy of that, which is by Authority appointed.

Ogilby's commission from the City to describe London's entertainment for the coronation was clearly set forth, and with a royal licence in addition, his account was wholly and solely legitimate. Not so was Ashmole's record of the coronation proceedings. Whether Ashmole as Herald wished to make his own record or whether Ogilby persuaded him to write a supplementary and complementary report on the actual coronation cannot be ascertained. It is clear, however, that Ashmole had taken no precautions to safeguard his work, a fact that precipitated a number of events. Ashmole's brief treatise was actually printed with his name and title (Windsor Herald), on the title page of his work, and this presumably was available, to be bound with Ogilby's 1661 text, just after the date of the coronation.[17] The problem that occurred at this point involved Sir Edward Walker, Garter King of Arms, and Ashmole's superior in the College of Arms. Sir Edward was a testy and suspicious old gentleman, who had just succeeded in wresting the Garter Kingship from Sir Edward Bysshe, the incumbent of that office under Parliament and Cromwell. Bysshe, by one of the minor miracles of the Restoration, managed to retain office in the College of Arms (Clarenceux), and it was he who in 1661 had signed the grant authorizing the style of Ashmole's arms and had noted at the time 'the greate and good affection which I beare unto the said Elias Ashmole.'[18] This friendship may have irritated Walker, or he may simply have acted imperiously as usual to maintain his prerogative. Furthermore, he apparently at some point wrote his own account of the coronation, which, however, was not published until 1820. At any rate, Sir Edward must have complained to the King about Ashmole's published and signed work. For, at the conclusion of the licence 'To our Trusty and Wellbeloved Ogilby,' granting him the right to publish an illustrated volume, the King refers to Walker's inherent jurisdiction over the description of the coronation. The licence states that the 'whole Ceremonie and proceedings were principally drawn up and Ordered' by Walker — a statement open to challenge on the basis of some notes of Ashmole.[19] It is further stated that Sir Edward had assisted Ogilby in his own preparations. Consequently, the latter was to publish nothing that had not been 'viewed, corrected and approved' by Walker, 'who is best able to Judge what is proper to bee published and what not.'[20] Annoying as this may have been, Ogilby knew how to recognize authority and come to terms with it. The Ashmole text was submitted to the Garter King, who made revisions in it (the copy, presumably one of those still extant in the Guildhall), and the later, revised issues bore Walker's imprimatur, dated 13 June 1662.[21] No doubt both negotiation and financial recompense were required to gain the Garter King's approval of the Ashmole text for inclusion in Ogilby's publication. A further change, and one reflective of Walker's petty nature, is the omission of Ashmole's name and title from subsequent publications of his account. This latter fact long concealed Ashmole's part in the composition of the *Entertainment*.

Ogilby's printed work prior to 1661 had been confined to translations from the classics and to elaborations upon them. With the *Entertainments* of 1661 and 1662, he turned to prose and to descriptive and narrative writing. Although the purchasers of the *Entertainment* may have known Ogilby's name or already had some of his works, this venture toward a more popular taste and away from the classics seems to foreshadow his later work, that from 1670 onwards. Certainly it appears that Ogilby anticipated considerable profit from his City commission, and that he exploited every possible advantage in producing the volume. The many issues and editions of the *Entertainment* testify to his success.

His plan, as has been stated, to write and print a handsome, illustrated folio of the coronation was early developed (March 1661), and he perceived the necessity for obtaining a royal monopoly. Alert as ever to prevailing opinion and practices, however, Ogilby quickly realized that such a licence would not prevent unauthorized accounts from circulating, and apparently at least one did so. Thereupon, he immediately prepared to issue a preliminary edition, without cuts, to establish his primacy in the field. He announced, in the *Mercurius Publicus* for April 11-18, 'There is now in the

Press (to be published the beginning of this next week) a Relation of His Majesty's Entertainment.' It has been suggested that the first copies of the first edition may have gone to press on the day of issue (11 April 1661) of the royal monopoly and may have appeared on the very day of the coronation itself.[22] As Ogilby was the author of the speeches and in close touch with the architects, carpenters and musicians for the procession, he was uniquely qualified to anticipate the event in printing. His direct involvement with the manuscript probably explains why he permitted Richard Marriott, the bookseller, to handle the 1661 editions, printed by Thomas Roycroft, who had brought out a number of Ogilby's finely produced translations.

The policy of seizing the auspicious moment was obviously successful, despite the many signs of haste in the early editions. Bibliographical evidence indicates that a second edition was on the press almost as the first was being run off. Yet another edition appeared in 1661, with present tenses changed to the past, and some additional material, describing certain changes that had been made just before the procession.[23] With these three editions, Ogilby had made effective his dominance of the reportage of the coronation — certainly the greatest event to occur in England in the first half of the 1660's. His control extended even to maintaining Ashmole's account (though without the author's name) in his own work. The remainder of 1661 and early 1662 must have been filled for Ogilby with making new arrangements, with the illustrations from Loggan and Hollar to oversee, the selection and reproduction of coins to organize and the elaborate classical allusions to select and incorporate, albeit awkwardly, in the great edition of 1662.

For this edition, therefore, Ogilby turned again to his former publisher, Roycroft, although keeping in his own hands the lucrative sale of such works ('to be had at the Authors House in Kings-Head Court within Shoe Lane'). The difficulty with Sir Edward Walker was resolved, certainly by the time of the imprimatur date of 13 June 1662, and probably soon thereafter the elaborate folio would have been available. Later in 1662, the *Kingdoms Intelligencer* for 3—10 November advertised the volume as being for sale by Richard Marriott and Thomas Dring. Ogilby, having reaped the benefits of nearly six months of the sale of his book, was now apparently prepared to turn it over to established booksellers. He had, as will appear later, a new Irish venture in hand that would preclude his giving first-hand attention to work in London. The copyright remained in Ogilby's name, however, and in May 1665 he petitioned for its renewal, along with a monopoly for printing other volumes of his own. In the same month, Charles II granted this renewal, to last for fifteen more years.

So successful was this particular publishing venture that, when a new coronation, that for James II, was imminent, nearly a decade after Ogilby's death, another edition was issued. William Morgan, Ogilby's stepgrandson, who had been associated in the planning and execution of the City's entertainment, published in 1685 an edition entitled 'The Kings Coronation . . . the Cavalcade . . . from the Tower to Whitehall.' He kept Ogilby's name (with 'Esquire' added) as author, and included Ashmole's account, together with Walker's imprimatur. The text is sharply reduced in size from the 1662 version, and would have been useful chiefly as a guide to coronation procedure. No illustrations appear in any copies I have seen, but some were available, and are advertised at the beginning of the text. They included the four triumphal arches and the interior view of Westminster Abbey at the coronation. These were sold by Morgan at his house, 'Done on Copper, and propper to be added to this Book.'

The entire situation regarding the publishing, printing and sale of books was in a state of considerable confusion during the Commonwealth and early Restoration days. Ogilby's work as author had begun in 1649, the year of Charles I's execution. A time followed when the nominal head of all institutions in church and state had been removed, and the actual authority varied, was sometimes absent altogether, and often unclear. This situation affected the London world of books and bookmaking, as it did so much else. In the relatively free atmosphere of the 1650's, Ogilby had composed a number of his most significant works and began to produce and sell them as well. During this time, when City records decreased in number, when City offices were left vacant and old-established restrictions were ignored, it was possible for an enterprising newcomer to make his name by energy and talent. With the Restoration, however, the old machinery returned to operation, records expanded, patronage and commissioned work increased, and apprentices were bound in some numbers again. For Ogilby this would presumably have meant, at best, extended negotiations with the Stationers Company, of which he was not a member, if he wished to pursue his newly developing career.

Various devices were being created and extended in 1661 and 1662 to regularize some of the situations left by two decades of civil war and interregnum. One was the *ad hoc* licence or patent, available from the new king's plenary power, to adjust all sorts of problems. The patent rolls and signet books reflect the inordinate number of petitioners who were striving for adjustment, recompense or gain in these early days of the Restoration. Among the first in line was Ogilby, now 60 years of age, who had won royal attention by his dedications of impressive folios to Charles II and of course by his production of various versions of the *Entertainment*. To safeguard his previous operations and protect the extension of future ones, Ogilby from 1660 on was constantly petitioning the King, generally with success, for rights and grants connected with books, with the theatre in Ireland and with personal titles.

A patent of 21 January 1661 shows Ogilby's success in having procured royal attention.[25] Described as 'gentleman,' he had petitioned to be allowed to use a new kind of 'letter and character' devised and used at the Louvre in France. The petitioner's aim was to print in Greek and Latin characters a series of mathematical works by ancient authors, a number of whom were specified, such as Euclid, Archimedes, Ptolemy and Proclus. This was granted for a period of thirty-one years, though the process was not exclusively confined to Ogilby. The petition must have been drafted at the close of 1660, when, with the production of the *Iliad* and the Bible behind him, the would-be printer-publisher was striking about, looking for further works, still in the classical domain, with which to catch attention. Shortly thereafter came the invitation from the City Council to write the script for the coronation procession, a task that Ogilby manoeuvered into a considerable success. Apparently in consequence of this, the project for printing mathematical works was dropped, as new areas now opened wherein to exploit royal favour.

One of these areas came as an echo from a world long past. At about the time that Ogilby was requesting a monopoly on printing the *Entertainment,* he moved to re-establish himself in a profession that he had left some two decades earlier, that of the theatre. In so doing he joined issue with an old friend, Sir William Davenant, who was likewise seeking preferment at this time. Davenant, after release from the Tower, had not only survived the Cromwellian regime but had been active during it as producer of musical dramas — the closest approach to professional theatrical entertainment in the 1650's. When the Restoration came, Davenant obtained a patent for erecting one of two theatres in London, the other to be operated by Thomas Killigrew.[26] Davenant had had such a patent under Charles I, and it was reasonable to ask for its renewal. Not satisfied with this, however, he extended his request to Ireland. In November 1660, Charles II granted him a patent as Master of the Revels in Ireland and the right to erect the only theatre in Dublin.

News of Davenant's successful suit aroused Ogilby, involved though he was in other pursuits, to assert his own prior rights in regard to Ireland. There exists an undated petition of his for the office, which probably followed very closely in time the grant to Davenant. He specifically recalled past events and referred to the Davenant grant as an injury:

. . . *Yor petitioner had a graunt from the Right Honorable Thomas Earle of Strafford then Lieutenant of Ireland for the enjoying and executing the place and office of the Master of the Revells of that kingdome which after his great preparations and disbursements in building a new Theatre, stocking and bringing over a Company of Actors and Musitians and setting them in Dublin fell to utter rueine by the Calamities of those times to the utter undoeing (by the Damage of Two Thousand pounds att lest) of your petitioner.*[27]

Later in the petition Ogilby indicated knowledge of his rival's suit for this office, asking that his request be granted, 'notwithstanding Sr William Davenets [*sic*] pretences.'[28]

As early as March 1661 there is evidence that Ogilby had succeeded in his petition, in the record of a grant to him as Master of the Revels in Ireland.[29] The office, described as 'new erected,' was granted for life, and with all the fees appertaining to it that belonged to the same office in England. The licence further gave Ogilby the right to build a new theatre in Dublin and elsewhere in Ireland, and permitted him 'to represent Comedyes, Tragedyes and Operas and other Enterludes decent & not obnoxious.' This was a true monopoly, as no others were permitted to stage such performances unless accredited by Ogilby. The actual patent, dated 8 May 1661, revealed still more details.[30] It began with a historical exposition, stating that Ogilby had had a licence dated from Dublin on 28 February 1637 [New Style, 1638], appointing him Master of Revels in Ireland; that he had built a public theatre 'at his owne greate cost and charges as we are informed'; and that he had produced plays so blamelessly that 'those recreatons [*sic*] formerly obnoxious were made inoffensive'; and finally that that theatre was now in ruins. In consequence of the foregoing, Charles II now established the office of Master of the Revels in Ireland, as the previous licence from Strafford was considered not to have been a true predecessor, the Viceroy exercising derived, not absolute, royal powers. The King granted this title, 'reposing especiall trust and confidence in the loyalties, integrities and abilities of the said John Ogilby,' to him or to his deputy. The patent reiterated the right to build one or more theatres where the patentee wished, a right that was made transmissible to Ogilby's heirs and assigns. And finally, 'common players as shall presume to act any stage plays or enterludes' must obtain a licence from the new Master, in order to perform.

With his reputation in the world of books so recently enhanced by the success of the *Entertainment,* there must have been a distinct element of hazard for Ogilby in the decision to leave the metropolis of London for the provincial barrenness of Dublin.[31] He had turned over, as stated above, the remainder of the now-finished, opulent 1662 edition of the *Entertainment* to professional booksellers; and within that edition there appeared not only Charles II's licence or copyright but also Walker's imprimatur. Ogilby could therefore confidently expect that with it in print, as well as his translations, his name would not quickly be forgotten. And so, exhibiting that zest for new undertakings that was to remain with him to the end of his life, he now, in his early sixties, started a new chapter with his second Irish venture.

One of the first efforts Ogilby undertook after securing his patent, must have been the search for capital to rebuild his theatre. Presumably in the 1630's Strafford's lordly munificence had provided most if not all of the funds. No such sponsor now stood behind the newly created Master of the Revels. Anthony à Wood estimates that the new theatre cost about £2000.[32] Although Ogilby may have put up part of this money the greater part would have to have been supplied by someone of real wealth. Presumably through his friend James Shirley and possibly through others, Ogilby found the patron he was seeking in Thomas Stanley, Esq., of Cumberloe, Herts. (See Chapter V for further details.) Stanley, who was a patron of poets and a minor one himself, apparently was searching for an entrée into the world of the arts for his son and heir, Thomas, junior. The father supplied capital, the son was to share the repute and profits of the Dublin theatre, and Ogilby was to contribute expertise. Thomas Stanley, senior, however, proved a shrewd bargainer. Not only was his son to share in the profits; he must be made co-patentee in the new office. Ogilby therefore sought for and secured a new patent on 7 September 1661 for himself and 'Thomas Stanley, Gent., jointly, to be by them held and enjoyed for and dureing their natural lives, and ye life of ye longer liver of them.'[33] This second patent, though necessary for financial reasons, must have been a less than welcome expedient for Ogilby. He apparently cherished his original grant, the one naming him alone, and for some time, despite various orders, held on to it, as well as to the newer one. Finally, however, on 21 April 1663, the second patent was enrolled in the Irish Chancery Rolls, and the original patent at last relinquished.[34] Since the young Stanley was not born until 1650, both negotiations and any activities involving him in the 1660's must have been carried on through the agency of his well-known father.

Not without one final triumph did the new Master of Revels set out for his second stay in Ireland. He obtained yet another royal office, Master of the Royal Imprimeries, or King's Printer (see Chapter V), and undoubtedly exploited this title in conjunction with his imports of fine paper and in maintaining Continental contacts. Then, presumably in the summer of 1662, Ogilby embarked for Ireland, probably accompanied by his young relative and assistant, William Morgan. It is likely that the redoubtable Mistress Ogilby remained in London to watch over his continuing interests there, and that Ogilby made frequent trips between the two countries in the next four or five years.

Ogilby's fortunes were for a time to be bound fairly closely to a new patron, the newly-appointed Lord Lieutenant of Ireland, James Butler, first Duke of Ormonde. A decade younger than Ogilby, Ormonde had served in Ireland under Strafford in the 1630's, and had probably shared a long acquaintance with his new theatre manager. As a patron of the arts and premier peer of Ireland, he must have had considerable interest in Ogilby, and it was of course reciprocated. The capital city to which these two men returned after an absence of about two decades was still a small town of perhaps 30,000 to 35,000 inhabitants. The Lord Lieutenant in his castle remained the centre of government, patronage and cultural life, in a far more concentrated fashion than did the King in London, and the circle for whom Ogilby was to entertain was limited. Nevertheless, the Dublin of the 1660's was a livelier and more cosmopolitan place than it had been under Strafford.

The former Werburgh Street Theatre, which was so near the Castle, had been thoroughly destroyed. Ogilby sought another site for his new theatre, and found it in Smock Alley, to the north instead of to the west of the Castle. If he accompanied Ormonde to Ireland in July of 1662, he must have moved rapidly, for the new theatre opened, according to custom, in the autumn — October, 1662. It has been estimated that the theatre was about 55 feet wide by 110 feet deep, and that it was far larger than Davenant's London building in Lincoln's Inn Fields. It was close in size to Killigrew's modern Theatre Royal in Covent Garden, a theatre, however, that was not to open till 1663. The Smock Alley theatre had a pit containing rows of benches covered with cloth. Three tiers of galleries rose behind and around the pit, with boxes built on the lowest gallery. A proscenium arch and curtain divided the fore-stage from the rear, and within the latter were the flats and other scene sets needed. The lighting consisting of a series of oil lamps sunk in a long pit, served as 'footlights,' and candelabra were placed along the galleries, in front of the proscenium

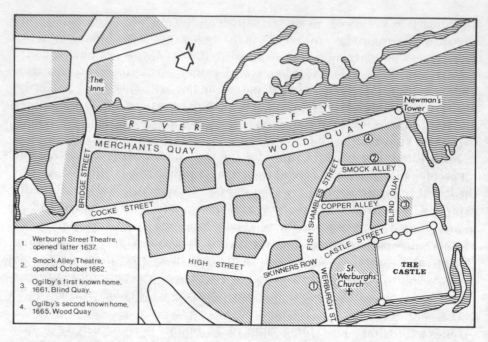

9) *Ogilby's Dublin*
Drawn by Derek R Harris

1. Werburgh Street Theatre, opened latter 1637.
2. Smock Alley Theatre, opened October 1662.
3. Ogilby's first known home, 1661, Blind Quay.
4. Ogilby's second known home, 1665, Wood Quay

and behind it. As performances began in the late afternoon and some natural light may also have been available, the lighting arrangements seem effective as well as relatively elaborate.[35]

In this first of the new Restoration theatres, then, the innovation of movable scenery occurred, in an outpost of British society, rather than in London itself. Once the fabric of his theatre was complete, Ogilby had two other major concerns. One was the recruitment of actors and actresses; the other was the assembling of plays — both those old favourites so long in retirement and others of newer vogue, French in tone and Augustan in style. Assembling a troupe of actors was a task he had undertaken once before, in the 1630's. Then, however, Ogilby had been much closer to the theatrical world than he was now. Furthermore, the aridity of the theatrical scene under Puritan dominance, despite amateur performances and Davenant's ventures with opera, must have reduced significantly the numbers of actors available to a manager-producer. Nevertheless, Ogilby assembled a company, only a few names of which can be established as early as 1662 and 1663. One was Joseph Ashbury, apparently a novice, but a man destined for a significant theatrical role in Dublin. Another was the more experienced John Richards, whose appearance was to cause considerable turmoil. Then there was Nicholas Calvert, a former strolling player, and two less well-known men, William Moore and a Mr. Yeoghny. Whether any women acted in Dublin at this time is unrecorded, nor are any names given other than the five above, although there must have been other actors in Dublin in the early 1660's.[36]

Ashbury's skill, whatever his origins, seems quickly to have become marked and he was to reappear prominently in the later story of Ogilby's theatrical ventures. A skirmish over Richards' services was an amusing counter by Ogilby for Davenant's attempt at becoming Irish Master of Revels. Richards, one of Davenant's troupe, and a brother-in-law of

66

Ashbury, was enticed to Ireland by Ogilby, no doubt for substantial reward. Despairing, apparently, of regaining Richards' services by additional inducements, Davenant moved, as Ogilby had done earlier, to obtain redress through royal intervention. Richards was ordered by Charles II to return from Ireland to rejoin his original company.[37]

Although only a few actors' names are extant from the early years of the 1660's, the Smock Alley Theatre must have counted a growing number of troupers. The first recorded play, John Fletcher's *Wit Without Money,* was performed on 18 October 1662, although the scenery was not yet ready.[38] The Fletcher play may well have been one of those acted decades earlier in the Werburgh Street theatre and presented again in Smock Alley as a standard favourite. Other well-known plays were also presented in these early seasons: Jonson's *Volpone,* and the *Othello* of Shakespeare. But new tides of taste were flowing from the Continent to London, and they crossed the Irish Sea with producer and players to Dublin. In 1663, an English translation of Corneille's *Pompey* was presented in Dublin and somewhat later still a version of Corneille's *Nicomède* was given there.[39] No doubt other French plays in translation appeared, and new vogues in theatre continued to develop in Dublin as in London.

In fact, with the Lord Lieutenant's arrival in the summer of 1662, Dublin began to grow in numbers and sophistication. New houses, new societies, the establishment of St. Stephen's Green and a doubling in population in twenty years: these and other factors brought wealth and society fit to support a theatre and to appear to justify Ogilby's gamble in leaving his bookish world to return to the livelier one of the theatre. There was a literary circle gathered around Mrs. Katherine Philips, 'the Matchless Orinda,' as well as a number of culturally minded members of the nobility, many connected through birth or marriage to the Lord Lieutenant, the Duke of Ormonde. There were also some noble relations of the powerful Earl of Cork, and various high officials serving in Ormonde's entourage, numbers of whom ordered books from abroad, wrote poems and letters to each other (some of them extant), and enjoyed the theatre. For many of these various interconnected groups, Ogilby's theatre was a focus for social and cultural activity, as some scattered references show. Outstanding among Dublin's *cognoscenti* was Roger Boyle, fifth son of the Earl of Cork, and the first Earl of Orrery.[40] Boyle, who knew both Ireland and France well, was one of the able politician-soldiers who could serve and win favour under both Lord Protector Cromwell and King Charles II. He was known as a friend of Suckling and Davenant, and John Ogilby was certainly in the fringes of his acquaintance. Pursuant to a purported request of Charles II, Boyle composed (in Dublin) a tragicomedy in the French manner, in rhyme of ten feet. Charles approved it, and Orrery composed another, sending both to London.[41] The first experiment was not presented in London until 1664, but it was performed in Dublin in October 1662, at the Earl's home at Thomas Court. It is likely that Ogilby's actors were co-opted for the performance of the play, which was called by the two titles of *Altemera* or *The Generall.* This 'first' performance of a play in the heroic mode might have been expected to add to Dublin's theatrical distinction; however, the town, the clientele and the cultural climate were apparently too provincial to sustain permanently what might have become a healthy theatrical heritage. Nevertheless, the 1662-63 season in Dublin was an intriguing one. As early as 19 October, 1662, Mrs. Philips wrote, 'We have a new Play-house here, which in my Opinion is much finer than D'Avenant's; but the Scenes are not yet made. I saw there Yesterday *Wit without Money,* which as far as I can judge was indifferently well acted.' By November of 1662, Ogilby's new scenery was in place, and Mrs. Philips wrote to London, in early December, 'We have plays here in the newest mode, and not ill acted.'[42] In the following month (January 1663), Col. Edward Cooke, a high official in Dublin, wrote to Whitehall that 'Mr. Ogilby gets money apace, and his actors reputation.'[43]

Mrs. Philips' own ambitious translation of Corneille's *Pompey* was a triumph for Ogilby and his new theatre. Having finished it sometime in late 1662, 'Orinda' was persuaded to offer it for its première in Dublin rather than in London, and it became the spectacle of the season, with the Duke of Ormonde and others of quality in attendance. It was presented on 10 February 1662/63. The Earl of Roscommon obliged with an opening eighteen couplets, praising guests and especially the author. Then the play began, with verses in the new style of heroic writing, the first Restoration exhibition of a French play translated into English. Since Ogilby was no doubt producer and possibly stage manager as well, it is not surprising that after each act there was a song and after several of the acts there were dances. One, 'an Antick dance of Gypsies,' may well have brought an echo to Ogilby's mind from half a century before, when the Duke of Buckingham produced his Masque of Gypsies. Just before the epilogue, there was a 'grand masque . . . made (as well as the other Dances and Tunes to them) by Mr. John Ogilby.'[44] Clearly, the years of translating and bookselling had not destroyed that earlier skill in music and dancing that had characterized the young dancing master of Jacobean times. Through this production of *Pompey,* Ogilby's theatre in Dublin scored another first over the London stage. Oblique references to other plays indicate that current London hits were brought to Dublin in the spring of 1663, for example Sir Samuel Tuke's *The Adventures of Five Hours* and Cowley's *The Cutter of Coleman Street.*[45] Mrs. Philips, whose correspondence and reading were both comprehensive, left an amusing complaint that Tuke's *Adventures* 'was snatch'd from me for Mr. Ogilby, to have it acted here, almost before I had read it over.' A friend of Mrs. Philips was Sir Nicholas Armourer, Captain of the King's Regiment of Guards and an important official. He wrote doggerel and was a decidedly spirited elderly gentleman. In May of 1663, he decided to entertain his soldiers by paying for a performance by 'Mr. Ogilby and his comedians.'[46] The references to Ogilby and to the Smock Alley Theatre in these early 1660's are tantalizingly brief, as in these instances, but they testify to the vitality and influence of this new venture in Dublin's somewhat limited cultural life.

Ogilby and his company clearly had a successful first year. They were supported by Lord Deputy, nobility, intelligentsia and even by the populace. The theatrical company created innovations in staging and presented new styles in plays. According to Mrs. Philips, however, discords began to develop by the summer. On 3 June 1663, she wrote in discouraged fashion about the printing of her play *Pompey,* adding that 'the Players fell out about it here.' Shortly thereafter, in an undated letter, written before 15 July of that year, she wrote again: 'The Players disband apace, and I am afraid you will shortly see a Farce, or a Puppet-show at London, call'd *Ireland in ridicule*; wherein all the Plays will be repeated, and the Actors themselves acted in Burlesque.[47] It seems likely that the Smock Alley Theatre, like those in London, closed for the summer. Such a procedure in this and the next few years would have permitted annual summer visits to London by Ogilby and Morgan, visits that would enable them to maintain ties in the publishing world, to renew contacts with actors, and, most important of all, to be seen and heard in the purlieus of Whitehall.

Little more in fact remains to tie Ogilby with Ireland. He resided near his theatre on Blind Quay, in 1664; in the next year he moved to a larger house on Wood Quay.[48] It is doubtful that he ever remained away from London for a whole year, or that he removed his true residence to Dublin. Certainly by 1665 and 1666, his base was again in London. Morgan as Deputy Master of the Revels and later Joseph Ashbury seem to have been charged with actually conducting the affairs of the theatre in Dublin. As the years passed, Wycherley, Shadwell, Addison, Etherege, Dryden, Cibber and other well-known names were added to the repertory of the Dublin stage. But Ogilby's own connections appear to have been confined to obtaining the title of Master of the Revels; to building, establishing and staffing the theatre; and to encouraging some of the new aspects of theatrical history to occur in Dublin in the first part of the 1660's. Certainly by 1665, he had abandoned his gamble on Ireland and the theatre there, and had returned, now and finally, to the world of books.

IV

Patrons & Friends

Patronage and friendship were closely intermingled in the seventeenth century. One's betters might be persuaded to make one's fortune; equals could bestow and might equally ask favours; and from inferiors there were constant petitions, many of which were acted upon as duty, pity or sense of fitness might dictate. Within the circle of Ogilby's friends and acquaintances, then, the concept of patronage would never be forgotten; but it was regarded as within the normal context of the times.

One aspect of patronage was indeed not associated with friendship, and perhaps that should be first considered, as an aspect that would have occurred first to someone of the seventeenth-century. It involves the question of royal and semi-royal patronage — the search for the almost limitless sources of riches, power and prestige that the Stuarts and Stuart favourites offered their protegés. Ogilby had considerable experience of such favour, an experience that extended over a long life. The search for patronage probably brought his father south to London. By his late teens or early twenties, the young dancing-master had already advanced some distance along the enticing path to royal recognition and favour. To have danced in the Duke of Buckingham's 'great masque' was to have danced before King James and probably in company with both Prince Charles and the Duke. Ogilby's skill and energy might have carried him far in the music-loving court of Charles I had it not been for his extravagant and fateful leap.

Not given to resignation, however, Ogilby, even after this accident, probably pursued his relations with Buckingham, a patron generous to his followers. To be in touch with Buckingham in the 1620's was to have contacts with Charles I; and it is significant that the great epic projected and written by Ogilby (the 'Carolies') had that monarch as its subject. For a time after his accident, Ogilby apparently retired to the country with Sir Ralph Hopton; then he was recommended, perhaps by the King, who forever cherished his memories of Buckingham, to the Earl of Strafford early in the 1630's. By joining the Earl's household in Ireland, Ogilby again was able to enjoy viceregal patronage.

To this point Ogilby had only his services to offer — as dancer, as dancing-master, as theatre manager, perhaps as trooper, or as secretary, if varying accounts be believed. After the débâcle in Ireland, Ogilby returned to an England in disorder. He then prepared to offer potential patrons something of less personal but more permanent value than services — the dedications of his forthcoming books. The first of these dedications, that for the *Virgil* of 1649, was, significantly enough, offered to the Marquess of Hertford, one of the King's most faithful servants and a companion even to Charles's death.

During the kingless 1650's, Ogilby dedicated his various works to impeccably royalist peers, but by 1660 a royal patron was again available. Among the many works showering upon the returned Charles II, Ogilby's contributions were impressive. In 1660, the elaborate, illustrated translation of the *Iliad* was ready; Ogilby dedicated it, with flourishes, to the new king. The insertion of a dedicatory page to Charles into a royal folio two-volume edition of the Bible was another striking gesture, especially in view of the monarch's solemn public avowal of his devotion to that book. It may be recalled that Aubrey spoke of this as 'the fairest impression, and the most correct of English Bibles, in royall and imperial paper, that ever yet was done.' Then came Ogilby's selection as writer for the City's offering of a coronation celebration. His subsequent elaborations on that effort, all dedicated to Charles, bore subsidiary dedications to additional figures in certain volumes. Before the appearance of the folio (1662) *Entertainment,* his cultivation of the monarch had already produced recognition; now Ogilby was prepared to offer his monarch varied services. His prize was continued royal patronage and not one but several royal titles.

From the time of his appointment as Master of the King's Revels in Ireland until he became Royal Cartographer (later Royal Cosmographer), a title conferred near the end of his life, Ogilby was a steady petitioner for and recipient of royal favour. In this, as in other ways, however, he remained on the fringes of power and fame. He was known to the King, probably had audiences with him, and certainly had friends at Whitehall. There is, in fact, a graphic picture of Ogilby presenting a list of subscribers to *Britannia* to Charles II, who had often expressed interest in the work. The picture appeared an an edition after Ogilby's death, however, and may be only an imaginary representation. Some earlier works may indeed have been proffered by hand from author/translator to monarch. On the whole, Ogilby, who was sixty-years old at Charles's restoration and no sharer in his exile, was hardly qualified by birth, nature or activity to become a courtier. As a Scotsman, however, and one of undoubted loyalty, as a writer and a gifted suitor, he stood on the outer circle of Charles's acquaintances. His relationship to the King was cherished by Ogilby; the King, in return, clearly regarded Ogilby with some respect and was prepared to grant him titles and privileges so long as they did not involve financial outlay.

Beyond royal and viceregal patronage, it is possible to distinguish four and possibly five circles (some of them intertwined) of friends and patrons in Ogilby's life. Among the high nobility, Buckingham and Strafford have already been mentioned. As indicated above, Ogilby turned to royalist peers when he first wrote and dedicated books. The 1649 *Virgil* dedication to Hertford was reiterated in the beautiful folio *Virgil* of 1654, and the

10) *Ogilby presenting his Subscription List for* Britannia *to the King and Queen, From Morgan's map of London, 1682*
The Museum of London

1651 *Aesop* bore a joint dedicatory tribute to Hertford's son and son-in-law. A statement in the 1658 *Virgil* was addressed to William, Second Earl of Strafford, with a reminder of Ogilby's service to the first Earl.

Removed to Ireland again in the 1660's, Ogilby followed faithfully the path of tribute to the nearest great man. The Duke of Ormonde, Lord Lieutenant of Ireland, had been with the first Strafford in Ireland, and had been known to Ogilby then. The nobleman had, in fact, lived in Drury Lane in the 1620's and may have encountered Ogilby as dancing-master and man-about-the-theatre in those years. Ormonde was the object of the fulsome dedication of the folio edition of the *Odyssey* in 1665, an edition that must have been worked on extensively in the Smock Alley years. Ormonde was naturally, as viceregal representative, the chief patron of Ireland's second theatre. The ties therefore to the Butler family, of which the Duke was head, were probably warm and genuine. Furthermore, Ogilby dedicated his 1665 *Aesop* to the Earl of Ossory, eldest son of the Duke of Ormonde. Ossory died before his father, leaving behind a reputation not only as a soldier and sailor but as a musician, linguist and friend of John Evelyn. Ogilby's dedication to him, in spite of convention, suggests some of the devotion with which he regarded the Butler family.

Less generous and more obviously self-seeking were the dedications of the *Aesopics* (1668) and a second edition of 1673 to Charles FitzRoy, Earl of Southampton, and one of Charles II's bastards. Of similar nature was the tribute to Mary, later to become Queen of England, in the dedication to the 1675 edition of *Virgil*, just a year before Ogilby's death. Not to be forgotten also was the ingenious device of the many minor dedications to those who might be enlisted as patrons of illustrations. Ogilby developed this type of dedication into a techique that could bring substantial advances as well as final payments, provided the good faith of the projector was maintained, as his was. The hundred or so nobles, gentlemen and ladies who contributed to the *Virgil* of 1654 and to successive Ogilby volumes, count as minor and often faithful patrons, although in most instances they were not friends or even acquaintances.

The next two groups constitute friends rather than patrons and include theatrical associates and men of letters. They also include quondam critics or rivals. Because of his long career in the theatrical world, Ogilby, though never of the Tribe of Ben, may have known Jonson and danced in one or more of his masques. Certainly he also knew and used Jonson's work on the coronation of James I. Much closer in age to Ogilby and certainly to be classed as a friend was James Shirley, dramatist, courtier, contributor to the Werburgh Street Theatre, and, in difficult years, schoolmaster. By 1649, each had published a book, and Ogilby wrote complimentary verses for Shirley's work. Shirley obliged with even more strongly commendatory lines to Ogilby's *Aesop* two years later (see Chapter II). It has been variously suggested that Shirley translated for Ogilby and that a teacher in his school, David Whitford, taught Ogilby Greek. Without assurance as to detail, it is clear that the two men were close associates through the 1630's and for parts of the next twenty years. Though Shirley died in need, never recovering his fortunes, as Ogilby did several times, his reputation as writer and dramatist has survived at a moderate level. Together with Ogilby, he achieved the derision of Dryden in 'MacFlecknoe.'

So far as evidence goes, Ogilby and Shirley seem always to have been friendly. Relations with Davenant were more complex. Sir William, playwright and courtier of Charles I, must also have known Ogilby in prewar times. He was unable to achieve the welcome insignificance of Shirley and Ogilby in the Interregnum, however, and spent some time in the Tower from which, tradition avers, the influence of Milton freed him. It was from this uneasy abode that Davenant wrote a long set of verses for the same volume of Ogilby for which Shirley had written, Davenant's verses expressing the conventional phrases of esteem of the time. After his release, Sir William, cautiously exploiting the Protector's love of music and his own abilities in that line, was able to circumvent the Puritan prohibition against theatres by creating and staging a form of opera. Whether or not Ogilby ever saw 'The Siege of Rhodes,' he must have been aware, though busy now with translating, of some slight activity in theatrical matters. After the Restoration, swift though Ogilby was to join the swarm of royal petitioners, he apparently failed to consider his former theatrical monopoly of Ireland until reminded of it by Davenant's successful licence to hold that very monopoly there. Once reminded, Ogilby made a case for himself and won, and with it won Davenant's enmity. The rift widened when Ogilby enticed to Smock Alley in Dublin an experienced player (a rare find in those days) from Davenant's London troupe. The king's support, granted to Davenant in this instance, probably marks the peak of bitterness between the two producers.

As writers, the two men can hardly be compared; they wrote different types of literature, for different audiences. As producers, however, they may well have been fairly matched, as Ogilby's ability to steal a player indicates. Although Ogilby was a choreographer and certainly knew music to some extent, he does not appear directly with Henry Lawes or other musicians of the time, who were friends of Davenant. The higher social standing of Sir William undoubtedly aided in making and maintaining his name in history, as well as in such pedestrian matters as preserving correspondence and references. It is probable that, had it been *Sir* John Ogilby, there would have been a larger number of dedications, allusions and extant documents referring to him than now exist. As a widow, Lady Davenant lived in Lincoln's Inn Fields, not too far from Ogilby's last home in Whitefriars. Since Davenant and Ogilby must have known each other fairly well, it is curious that so few extant records tie the two men together.

Killigrew and Betterton must also have been known to Ogilby, the former as one who, like Davenant, quickly moved to form a company after the Restoration, the latter as a young apprentice. Killigrew's London theatre was close in size to that opened by Ogilby a season earlier in Dublin (in the autumn of 1662). Surely there was exchange of ideas concerning various innovations of the Restoration among these manager-producers. It was to Killigrew that Orrory offered his play, the *Altemera* or *The Generall,* after its first presentation in Dublin. And it was to Killigrew's patent as Master of the King's Comedians that Ogilby's heir Morgan later referred when seeking an elaboration of his own patent.[1] The associations of Killigrew, Davenant and Ogilby were probably frequent, even from early Stuart times. Ogilby's relations with Killigrew, however, seem never to have involved the rivalry that later affected his dealings with Davenant. Betterton, a young actor under Davenant, would have known Ogilby's name and been aware of the enticement to Ireland of one of his company, followed by the actor's enforced return. His recollections, at the end of a long life, barely touch Davenant, however, and do not mention Ogilby. His description of early life as a player would be applicable to the conditions for Ogilby's actors as well: 'When I was a young player under Sir William Davenant, we were under a much better Discipline, we were obliged to make our Study our Business, which our young Men do not think it their duty now to do.'[2]

The Thomas Stanleys, father and son, present a number of problems in their relations with Ogilby. Sir Thomas, connected by birth and marriage with many of the early Caroline poets and men of letters (e.g., the prolific Sandys family and Stanley's first cousin, Edward Sherburn), was himself an excellent scholar. He must have known Ogilby's translations of the classics and his 1658 Latin version of the *Aeneid*. Furthermore, Stanley was a friend of both Shirley and Ogilby, adding a human link to the professional. In fact, as early as 1649, Stanley as well as Ogilby had contributed commendatory verses to Shirley's *Via ad Latinam Linguam*. Stanley's own early work was elegiac, pastoral, romantic: derivative from many sources. His tastes changed somewhat with increasing age, and with his marriage to an heiress. He turned in the mid-1650's to philosophy and to translations from Greek, though not to the epics. These translations were known to Ogilby, who frequently annotated his Homeric presentations with lengthy quotations from Stanley's *Anacreon* and *Aeschylus*. Stanley's manuscript of 'A Register of Friends,' which includes tributes to Lovelace, Shirley and Sherburn, fails to include one to Ogilby, who was perhaps considered an acquaintance rather than a friend.[3]

If, as seems likely, Ogilby lacked enough capital to build the second (Smock Alley) theatre in Dublin, he presumably turned to the now wealthy Stanley, who had become a patron of the arts. Inevitably, the two men must have met over the arrangements whereby Stanley's young son and heir, another Thomas, became a co-patentee with Ogilby in the monopoly of the Irish Restoration theatre. Thomas Stanley the younger, about twelve years of age at the time of the patent, followed his parent's example as a precocious scholar, and is even noted as a translator of Latin histories.[4] But whether through early death or for some other reason the young Thomas did not become a figure in the Irish theatre, as his father had apparently planned. Ogilby's kinsman, Morgan, and the leading Dublin actor, Joseph Ashbury, were the men left in charge of Smock Alley when Ogilby finally departed from Ireland. Although there are tantalizing omissions, as, for example, the precise considerations offered by Stanley to have his son made co-patentee with Ogilby, the story indicates something of how well known the Scotsman must have been in Restoration England. To Sir Thomas Stanley, Ogilby was a business associate, at least. For many other men of letters, the evidence of connections with Ogilby is less substantial, but still intriguing.

Ogilby's involvement with the theatre and also with belles-lettres was so long-lived and at times so intensive that his acquaintance probably extended from Ben Jonson all the way to Dryden and Jacob Tonson. Certainly he knew Mrs. Katherine Philips and worked with her in theatrical productions in Ireland. He lived near Shadwell in London and appears to have been in Ireland (1663-64) at the same time as that writer. The Shadwells had Irish connections and were clients, as was Ogilby, of the Duke of Ormonde.[5] In the small world of the Dublin theatre, if not before, Ogilby and Shadwell must have had numerous contacts. Thus, when Dryden, in response to Shadwell's criticisms, launched his vitriolic and highly influential 'MacFlecknoe,' it was no doubt natural for Ogilby's name to occur to him in conjunction with Shadwell's. Dryden himself lived near Ogilby in London and made use of some of his work. Once launched on his survey of Shadwell's pernicious ways, however, Dryden extended his acidulous comments to Ogilby and to Shirley, among many others. Thomas Hobbes, on the other hand, spoke with genuine admiration of Ogilby's editions of Homer.

Although no direct evidence connects Ogilby and Milton, they certainly had a mutual acquaintance in Davenant. And Edward Phillips, Milton's nephew and student, was warm in Ogilby's praise, speaking more highly of him, than of Sherburn and Stanley, and rating him above Shirley. For Phillips, Ogilby was 'one of the prodigies of our age, producing from so late an initiation into literature so many large and learned volumes, as well in verse as in prose.'[6] One may debate, of course, if this judgement reflected Milton's own. Numerous other literary figures must have been known to Ogilby and have known him, by reputation and writings if not personally: Sherburn, Elkanah Settle, John Evelyn. One royalist, Sir John Berkenhead, who knew so many of the figures familiar to Ogilby — Hobbes, Dryden, Hopton, Mrs. Phillips, Stanley — appears to have had no direct connections with him.[7] The cross-currents of translating, political writing, publishing, loyalty to the Stuarts and long-time involvement in the arts — all of them common both to Berkenhead and to Ogilby — indicate, however, that they may well have made contact with each other more than once. The accumulation of direct and indirect evidence reveals that John Ogilby, by name, by reputation or in person, must have been a familiar figure in the literary world of much of the seventeenth century.

As he moved from writer/translator to publisher, Ogilby came to know, as acquaintances and fellow-workers, a wide range of men, including members of the Stationers' Company, and a number of subsidiary figures such as booksellers, illustrators and some minor printers. These were men nearer to himself in station than were the patrons, great and small, in his life. One of the Crook brothers, John, published (1649) the first book of John Ogilby, then an unknown; and much later in life the Crooks still held copyright of some of Ogilby's work. Presumably, they had a number of contacts over those years. As soon as he was able to do so, however, Ogilby turned to the far more distinguished publisher Roycroft to issue his translations, and eventually, probably about 1670, he began to print his own works. Throughout many of these years, from at least 1660, his chief assistant appears to have been William Morgan, his step-grandson and heir. Morgan, also a member of a City company, after assisting in the work of creating the *Entertainment,* then spent some time with Ogilby in Ireland and perhaps stayed on after his relation's departure to keep the theatre in order. By the time that Ogilby set up his own firm, Morgan was a trusted and confidential assistant. From the autobiography of Gregory King, it would appear that there was some rivalry between the two younger men for Ogilby's favour. The latter gave King commissions and probably some useful introductions. His business and titles, however, were eventually left to Morgan, his kinsman. According to King, some debts of Ogilby to him were not honoured by Morgan after 1676, when Ogilby died.

Ogilby used many of the well-known illustrators of his day, as he perceived early the extra cachet that his 'sculps' gave to his works. Wenceslaus Hollar, William Faithorne and David Loggan are only some of the many men Ogilby knew, commissioned work from and, in certain instances, probably exploited.[8] He would have known many, probably most, of the booksellers around St. Paul's, some from early boyhood. Assuredly, they knew him and stocked his books in quantity.[9]

Another category of people known, though more formally, to Ogilby, consists of those associated with various institutions. His presentation of an elaborate version of the Bible to the House of Commons in 1659 would have involved negotiations with the Clerk and probably with certain M.P.'s. Furthermore, in the City, Ogilby was well known to some members of his company, the Merchant Taylors. He presented, in 1654, to the Company his translation of Virgil and his Aesop 'very fairely bound,' and was requited 'for his encouragement, being a member of this Company' the sum of £13.6s.8d.[10] This gift, and his recognition by the Company, may well have been instrumental in his selection as writer of 'the poeticall part' of the City's celebration in honour of Charles II's coronation. This accolade, certainly one of the outstanding events in Ogilby's career, involved him directly with the King's musician, with actors, dancers and singers, with carpenters, joiners and masons, and of course with the Lord Mayor and Aldermen of London. The latter group heartily approved his work and rewarded it financially.

Other associations in the City were no doubt developed during these years, the chief evidence of which was to appear after the Great Fire (see Chapter VII for further details). Ogilby was then appointed as one of the assistant surveyors for the new City of London, destined to rise, in the phrase of the day, like a phoenix from the ashes. The work would bring him, along with Morgan and King, into regular (weekly or more frequent) contact with Robert Hooke and Christopher Wren, among others, and would make Ogilby respected and known, though not necessarily personally, to the ubiquitous chroniclers Pepys and Evelyn.

A final grouping could be made for those who wrote, more or less at length, about John Ogilby the man, and about his career. Their judgements appear in various places throughout these chapters, and form the basis of most later comment. Among his contemporaries was John Aubrey, who spoke of his friend's 'excellent inventive and prudentiall witt,' and deemed him 'master of so good addresse' that he could always recover from adversity. Further, he 'never failed in any thing he ever undertooke but allwayes went through with profits and honour.'[11] To Anthony à Wood, Ogilby was 'a prodigy in that part of learning which he profess'd,' and he echoed much of Aubrey's account, sometimes in the same words.[12] Elias Ashmole, the antiquary, knew Ogilby as early as 1653 and listed a number of events in his friend's life gleaned for use in casting horoscopes. The two men worked together on the 1661 *Entertainment,* although Ashmole's profit from the book was probably cancelled by the hostility of his chief, Sir Edward Walker, Garter King at Arms. In 1671 and 1672, Ashmole was acting as friendly agent between Ogilby and the Earl of Denbigh in regard to the production and perhaps the selling of one or more of Ogilby's folios.[13] He may well have done this service on other occasions as well, a testimony of the good relations that must have subsisted between the two men.

In retrospect, it seems clear that Ogilby was an assiduous and successful suitor, ready to supply service as well as to offer homage through the printed page. That patrons at times became friends with their clients is not surprising; in the patronage-filled years of the Restoration, numbers of men in both groups met, dined and corresponded on relatively equal terms. Toward the end of his life, at least, Ogilby certainly was on such terms with some of his patrons. On the whole, however, he seems to have been a man with many acquaintances and no really close friends. His Scottish birth, the extraordinary vicissitudes of his life and his late marriage probably combined to make him an independent spirit. In a formal age his lack of family and school ties — the best sources for familiar letters and enduring friendships — must have isolated him further and reduced potential evidence concerning him; probably his closest friend was his step-grandson, William Morgan, his confidential assistant from 1660 on and his heir. One can glimpse Ogilby, through various records, limping about the coffee houses of Stuart London, cheerfully meeting and greeting the great and near great of his time, learning the news of the day and sometimes making it. He was respected and admired. Of intimacy, however, of deep regard for him, of strong affection, no traces remain.

V

Printer and Publisher

At the centre of his contemporary reputation stands the story of Ogilby's work as printer and publisher, particularly as regards the content and style of the great atlases that he produced in those capacities. Although his first tentative ventures into publishing began in the 1650's, it was only in later years that they gained real strength. From 1670 when the first atlas, *Africa,* appeared, John Ogilby became well established as a publisher-printer. And his work for the remainder of his life was significantly to affect the interests and form the taste of influential readers and men of affairs. Leaving the world of the quiet study for subjects pondered in the counting rooms of merchants, the Council chambers at Whitehall and even the coffee houses, Ogilby shifted his attention and drew with him the minds of many Englishmen. His projection of a series of atlases covering the world was grandiose, and he nearly succeeded in the entire venture. He failed to cover Europe, but even that regrettable omission is lessened as Europe was familiar territory, both from travel and from books, to many readers. Ogilby did, however, produce atlases with the titles *Africa, Asia, America, Japan, China* (to be more specifically treated in Chapter VI). These were areas of increasing concern to Englishmen, who had thriving colonies along the Eastern seaboard of North America; who had, under Cromwell, added Jamaica to earlier Caribbean holdings; who became possessed of Tangier in North Africa upon Charles II's marriage with Catherine of Braganza. The atlases of Ogilby spoke to those for whom trade to the Levant was already important and for whom Asia and Africa beckoned as hazardous but rewarding areas for greater contacts. Ogilby's appeal to these instincts, through word and picture, was a culmination of his efforts to impress the intelligent reading public of England. His rewards, both in money and prestige, were considerable. His final volume in this series, *Britannia,* finished and produced just a year before his death, is a special case, and will be treated in Chapter VII.

John Ogilby's emergence as a publisher, bookseller and eventual printer was a gradual one, probably influenced by the upheaval of the times in which this aspect of his career began. In general, the printing of books was controlled by the Stationers' Company, by royal licensing for special projects, by various acts of censorship, and by constant supervision (sometimes through an authority as august as Star Chamber) of all publications and the publishers thereof.[1]

All printed books were supposed to be listed in the Register kept by the Stationers' Company, a Register still extant, and in the Company's possession. The notations in the Register follow a generally chronological order, and are listed by the publisher (or stationer) who enrolled the work he was presenting. It is therefore necessary, in working with the seventeenth-century record, either to know who published a particular book or to read through the entries for all the years concerned. The Register, like most other City records that I have seen, was much less carefully kept in the 1640's and 1650's than at other periods in that century. It is clear that during the Interregnum numbers of books were published without being recorded, and even published by men with no connection with the Stationers' Company. Also noticeable is the sharp increase in sermons and devotional literature satisfying to Puritans under the Commonwealth; so is the increased amount of publication of the classics.

John Ogilby's first ventures into the world of books were, as noted above, concerned with the classics. And his first publishers were the Crook brothers, members of the Stationers' Company, and one of them at least an acquaintance from the days in Ireland under Strafford. By 1654, however, Ogilby acted to take advantage of the unsettled conditions characterizing the publishing area. His success in gaining ever greater influence over the making and selling of his productions is logically attributable to the breakdown of the Stationers' control and to the relaxation of censorship. Especially in the realm of the classics, where Ogilby began, it might have been assumed that censorship could safely be omitted. Ogilby made many a satirical comment in his *Aesop* and particularly in his *Aesopics*. Evelyn published one of the books of Lucretius (in 1651), though referring warily to the radical ideas of that classicist. Ogilby's entry into publishing may well have been assisted by the increase in capital available to him after his marriage in 1650 with the former Mistress Hunsdon. As stated before (Chapter II), Ogilby early envisaged the creation of a fine Virgil folio, and its appearance in 1654 was a notable event in book production. Furthermore, although the volume was printed by Thomas Warren, it was done so 'for the Author,' not for a publisher. And the title page sent prospective purchasers to the author's house in King's Head Court, a small alley 'within Shoe Lane,' which wound itself in crooked fashion north from Fleet Street toward Holborn. Ogilby was still there in the 1660's, and it was probably his chief residence after his marriage. It is likely that he expanded it from a place of lodging, to include storage space for books and eventually, a printing establishment and shop. The many patrons from whom Ogilby secured contributions for the illustrations undoubtedly provided much of the capital that he needed. This capital in turn enabled him to escape the expensive association with a middleman-publisher, even as the unsettled legal aspects of the 1650's permitted him to avoid prosecution by the Stationers for such publication.

His Latin *Virgil* (1658) was again printed 'for the Author,' although the printer this time was Thomas Roycroft, one of the few outstanding printers still working during the Commonwealth. Again, Ogilby presumably financed himself and avoided a publisher by the successful policy of selling dedicatory illustrations. Naturally, with each impressive folio, his prestige, and presumably his purchasers, increased. The 1660 Bible and the *Iliad*, the former somewhat mysteriously passed on from John Field to Ogilby, the latter printed again by Roycroft, were projected before and finished at just about the time of the Restoration. *The Bible* and the *Iliad* marked the last volumes that Ogilby could produce without reckoning with a revived Stationers' Company, a system of censorship, and, eventually, with Sir Roger L'Estrange, by 1663 'Surveyor of the Imprimery' and a ferocious censor.

Aubrey remarks that Ogilby retired to Kingston-upon-Thames 'during the sickness,' presumably the Plague of 1665. This town, on the border of Surrey, was both safely in the country and yet near London. Ogilby, still in his prime, took work along and composed his *Aesopics* in this retreat. He was wise to flee, presumably with his family. The registers of St. Bride's in Fleet Street record a number of deaths in King's Head Alley (or Court) and Shoe Lane during the Plague period.[2]

An abortive project, but apparently one whose loss was much regretted by Ogilby, was his epic poem, the 'Carolies,' on the life and death of the Martyr King, Charles I. This 'long intended Edifice, my own great Fabrick,' was composed in twelve books, some almost completed at the time of the Great Fire. Presumably, all copies were swept away in the conflagration, save for a few lines that had appeared as a single-sheet pamphlet in 1661. These eight lines are quoted at length in the Preface to *Africa* and may be judged among Ogilby's worst. The first of them follow:

Mirror of Princes! Charles, the Royal Martyr,
Who for Religion, and His Subjects Charter,
Spent the best Blood Injustice Sword e're dy'd,
Since the rude Souldier Pierc'd our Saviours side . . .

It seems indisputable that Ogilby's epic energy was dissipating even during the translation of the Odyssey; it is unlikely that his intent, to spend the rest of his life refining the 'Carolies,' would have repaid the effort. The Great Fire destroyed much of his past and all of his projected work; but it set him on a new and most fruitful venture — the atlases — that would absorb him for the decade remaining until his death.

Meanwhile, there was the protection of his books from rapacious editors and booksellers to be arranged. The return of the King restored many areas of public life to the order, or constriction, that had characterized them under the previous Stuart monarch. With a legitimate ruler on the throne, patents, companies, monopolies: all resumed their former legitimacy, were renewed, or, in many instances, were newly instituted. Ogilby's publishing ventures, therefore, were distinctly affected by the Restoration. He was, of course, in the happy condition of having dedicated his *Iliad* and Bible to the newly restored monarch. Furthermore, his production of the story of the King's coronation procession through London kept him in public view and certainly appealed to the Court. It was therefore an advantageous time for Ogilby to consolidate his independent position as publisher. Instead of making an effort to join in partnership with a Stationer, he moved directly to obtaining royal licences — in essence, copyrights — for his published work, past and projected. A series of documents, remain, no doubt only part of the whole, which attest to Ogilby's pursuit of royal favour and his varied successes in gaining privileges in the world of book publishing.

Ogilby's opulent Bible, presented both to King and to Commons, led to a command for him to supply copies of it for the royal chapel, closet, library and council chamber. He was to be remunerated for this to the sum of £200.[3] In August 1661, he petitioned the King to prohibit for ten years the right of anyone to print a folio Bible like his, and to commend his edition to all churches and chapels. This edifying request Ogilby hoped to justify by producing a polyglot Bible, a project that apparently never passed beyond a paper proposal.[4]

A petition undated, but presumably from about the spring of 1665, requests in effect a copyright on all Ogilby's published work so far, enumerating these volumes, for the forthcoming fifteen years. The petition reads:

Your petitioner at his great charge, labour and expense of time (being the work of 20ty yeares) haveing [sic] printed and published the severall Bookes being very faire volumes adorned with Sculpture (vizt) Virgill translated, Homers Iliads, Esop paraphrased, and your Maty's Entertainment in passing thru the Citie of London and Coronation, and lately Homers Odysses after the same manner, and his former Esop with additions and annotations in folio.

Your Petitioner therefore humbly prayes that your Majesty would be gratiously pleased (according to the use and custom of forreigne Princes for the encouragement of Authors) to prohibitt all persons whatsoever for the space of fifteen years, without license and permission of your petitioner, his heires, executors or assigns, etc.[5] [from pirating these works].

In his references to the 'forreigne Princes,' Ogilby would apparently be appealing to practices familiar to Charles through the latter's enforced foreign travels; in fact, however, even in England special grants or monopolies of printing certain works had long been royal prerogatives. For Ogilby it was a convenient method — the royal grant — of bypassing the harassing regulations of the Stationers' Company designed to prevent outsiders from printing and publishing. A warrant granting this petition follows it immediately.[6] It is dated at Whitehall, 25 May 1665, and describes Ogilby as 'Master of Our Revels in Our Kingdom of Ireland.' The signer is Arlington.[7]

Two years later (20 March 1666/67), in response to another request from 'Our Trusty, Etc., John Ogilby, Esq.,' a royal warrant, again signed by Arlington, referred to the aforesaid copyright (then called 'sole priviledge and immunity'). It stated that Ogilby had 'humbly' sought further copyrights on 'Homers Workes in ye Originall adorned with Sculps [never published and presumably not even begun], a Second Collection of Aesops Fables paraphrased, adorned with Sculps, the Embassy of the Netherlands East India Company to the Emperor of China with Sculps and an Octavia Virgill in English without Sculps heretofore by him printed.' The King granted this, by extending the above-requested copyright for fifteen years. Significantly, as in the earlier warrant, the last section read, 'Whereof the Wardens and Company of Stationers of Our City of London are to take particular notice that due obedience bee given to this Our Royall Command.'[8] It seems apparent that the Stationers were resisting the flow of books published by one not of their number. Ogilby's recourse, a step that others had used in the past, was to produce a royal warrant. After the Restoration, with a legitimate king again in power, the warrant unquestionably took precedence over a Company's general monopoly.

A petition of Ogilby, undated, but written shortly after the Fire, is charged with intriguing detail and reveals, in the almost intimate way in which the writer details his distresses, the relatively informal relationship that must have existed between his monarch and himself. The petition begins with a review of Ogilby's previous work and its total destruction:

Your petitioner for above 20 years past hath with great paines and study, and with great charges, composed, printed and set forth Severall Bookes with Sculpts in a more noble & heroick way, then hath heretofore beene done in England, and now when hee was in some hope to have reaped the fruit of his soe long paines & charges — by the late unhappy and lamentable fire (which consumed all his whole reserved Stock of Bookes to the vallew of upwards of 3000 £) hee was frustrated of all, to his utter undoing.

The preceding sentence clearly shows that Ogilby by this time was maintaining stocks of his books for sale ('all his whole reserved Stock'), no doubt in his own home and print shop. Even allowing for the customary human overstatement of losses, the sum he mentions — £3,000 — is an impressive one to have amassed in book stocks by 1666. After the Fire, he says in the Preface to *Africa,* he was worth only £5. He may have been one of those ill-fated booksellers who stored their volumes in the vault of Old St. Paul's and then, through checking too soon, created a draught that destroyed their otherwise safe volumes.

Ogilby's only remaining hope, the petition continued, was the assistance of the great personages and patrons who had formerly assisted him. He acknowledged the King's 'gratious acceptation of most' of his former works [one thinks of the picture of Ogilby presenting *Britannia* to Their Majesties, possibly an act performed on more than one occasion, with other volumes]. And, in conclusion, the petitioner asked a licence to import 10,000 reams of 'printing paper from France (where it is onely to bee had) in such vessells as hee can procure . . . custome free.'[9] The privilege of importing fine French paper for his impressive folios, and of doing it tax free, was probably granted, and the petition was to be successfully repeated in later years in connection with *Britannia.*

Yet another petition of Ogilby at this time (also undated) recalls the

King's granting the copyright of his works for fifteen years. It adds: 'Now your Petitioner's whole Stock being consumed in the late Dismall conflagration, he humbly praies, that ye books following (now in the presse)' be granted that former copyright. He lists once again Homer in the original (a project that seems never to have seriously advanced), a second edition of Aesop, paraphrased, with illustrations, the Embassy to China, illustrated, and an octavo Virgil in English without illustrations, formerly printed by him (possibly the 1649 edition with publication rights purchased by now from John Crook).[19]

It is likely that the above mentioned petition was granted, but a much more comprehensive copyright was being prepared (no doubt at Ogilby's request) during this time. It appeared in a warrant dated 1 November 1669, under the signet and sign manual at Whitehall, and was affixed to the introductory material of *Africa* (first of the great atlases), following the dedication.[11] This patent recapitulated the earlier warrants of 1665 and 1667. Ogilby's new request was for the sole privilege (copyright) of printing a description of the whole world (his series of atlases) in several volumes, with illustrations. The copyright was granted, on both text and 'sculptures' for the following fifteen years.

In the following year (June 1670), a warrant was issued, permitting John Ogilby, described as 'Esquire,' 'to import 20000 [*sic*] Reames of Royall or other sort of paper custom free within the space of five years next ensuing the date hereof by 4000 Reames each year for which the said farmers [customs collectors] are to have allowance made them upon their Accounts.'[12] The importation of high quality, extra-sized paper was, of course, an essential in Ogilby's continuing book production. Paper-making in England lagged over a century behind that in France. Ogilby's licence, not only to import such paper in quantity but to escape the import tax, was a valuable favour conferred by Charles.

In welcome contrast to the official aridity of these petitions and warrants is Gregory King's account of Ogilby and his printing establishment, describing a period when King was a very young man, and Ogilby his elderly, well-to-do, prominent employer. King, later Lancaster Herald, wrote the memoir in his old age in the third person, and its accuracy may be impugned in places. Furthermore, he was a character whose exalted judgement of himself necessarily rendered a somewhat patronizing view of the lesser figures surrounding him. Nevertheless, his picture is a valuable and sustained account of the activities and some of the personalities of the 'printery' of John Ogilby, probably sometime in the 1670's. King, after having been clerk to Dugdale, and others, made his way to London to seek his fortune. Among others there, he visited Hollar, 'ye Eminent Gentleman in his way for Etching, who recomended [*sic*] him to Mr. Ogilby to manage his Undertaking' [presumably, some aspect of Ogilby's business].

According to King, Ogilby at this time was printing not only his own works, for which he had a royal licence, but others as well, in conjunction with some member of other of the Stationers' Company:

Mr. Ogilby, having the King's License to print all things of his own Com-

posing or Translating, kept a Press in his house, and under the Name of
Leyburn or some other Master Printer, did also Print any other Works,
and was at that time printing Sir Peter Leicester's Antiquities of Cheshire,
wherein some old Seals being to be engraved, Mr. King made his first at-
tempt in Etching upon them and performd [sic] them to Satisfaction.[13]

King describes further how he 'reduced' some etchings from Ogilby's folio
Aesop to an octavo one. He claims also that he did some of the 'Sculps in
the History of Asia, Vol. 1, which was then printing at Mr. Ogilby's, being
a Translation from De Meurs's Dutch Impression at Amsterdam; Africa,
America, the two China's and Japan being printed before.'[14] King assures
his readers that 'Mr. Ogilby was very sensible of Mr. King's great assistance
to him, and was very kind to him on all occasions, allowing him a musick
master to teach him to play on ye violin.' This somewhat uncharacteristic
generosity from a hard-headed Scot was reinforced, according to King's account, by Ogilby inviting King to join with him in a renewed Patent for the
title of Royal Cosmographer. King, however, says he declined the
proposition. It was, in truth, about this period that Ogilby did indeed get a
renewed patent, but with his kinsman, William Morgan, not Gregory King,
included in its reversion. It seems likely that between these two young men,
King and Morgan, there was rivalry for the attention and favour of the
well-to-do old publisher. The ties of kinship won out, and it is probable
that in old age Gregory King remembered a more flattering version of the
situation than had occurred. One other piece of evidence indicates that ill
will existed between King and Morgan. The former writes of 'Mr. Ogilby's
dying above [£]100 in his debt, whereof he never got one farthing.' The
debt, if indeed incurred by Ogilby, would presumably have been for work
done by King on the *Britannia* (see Chapter VII). Since Morgan was
Ogilby's heir, it was he whom King was accusing of non-payment in this
autobiographical memoir written many years later.[15]

Ogilby used a variety of devices to aid the sales of his books: lotteries,
subscription lists, advertisements. His employment of the first of these,
though an incomplete story, is one of his most original and presumably successful operations. Lotteries had apparently begun in England in the sixteenth-century, and the curiously learned John Minsheu had actually
created a lottery of his books in the early seventeenth-century.[16] Generally,
however, the lottery was held by a company and was in aid of a colony or of
some other worthy national purpose. The young John Ogilby had participated successfully in the lottery held by the Stationers' Company to aid
the establishment of the Virginia Plantation, sometime around 1612-14.
His winning was too important a piece of good luck to be forgotten,
although his memory had to lie dormant during the long years of Puritan
dominance.

Shortly after the Restoration, the device was resumed, and a lottery was
begun on behalf of impecunious royalist officers. That may have been instrumental in rousing Ogilby's interest in organizing such an activity on his
own behalf. At any rate, back from Dublin (whether temporarily or permanently is unclear), in the spring of 1665, John Ogilby concluded that he
had sufficient stock to open 'a standing Lottery of Books.' He obtained a

licence from the Duke of York. The procedure was as follows. Ogilby announced a sizeable collection of books: 'very large, fair, and special volumes, all of his own designment and composure, at vast expence, labour, and study of twenty years; the like impressions never before exhibited in the English Tongue.'[17] There were 500 copies of his 1665 *Aesop* offered and 225 of the *Entertainment*; the price for a ticket was 40s. (or £2).[18] The element of chance, an appreciation of which is still evident in the modern British character,[19] was what Ogilby appealed to, although he tried (as will appear shortly) to indicate that almost everyone who bought a ticket would receive something of value.

Alas for his first venture. The draw was set for 10 May 1665, and the Plague had already made its dread presence very clear. Despite the growing sickness through the summer, however, the office for distribution of prizes was kept open until late July. It was apparently possible to claim one's prizes throughout the winter following, for in February 1665/6, Pepys wrote: 'Thence to the Change, and from my stationer's thereabouts carried home by coach two books of Ogilby's, his *Aesop* and *Coronacion,* which fell to my lot at his lottery; cost me 4 1. [£4; Pepys must have bought two tickets at 20s. each], besides the binding.' The latter item, the binding, may have been done by Ogilby or by John Cade, Pepys's regular stationer. During these months, Pepys, who by now disposed of considerable personal sums, was buying for his home, plate, prints, furnishing, and, of course, books. That Ogilby had touched his fancy is clear not only from the lots he purchased, but from an earlier *Aesop* of Ogilby that he had bought and from which he read to his wife.[20]

The 1665 lottery opened again fully in April 1666, 'whither people repaired daily for their Prizes, and continued open untill the Fire.'[21] The double blow to the printer-publisher, first the Plague and then the Fire, must have proved nearly calamitous. Ogilby claimed variously that he had lost all but £5 in the Fire, or, in another instance, two-thirds of his stock. He insisted, however, that only six of the original prizes of his first lottery were not distributed.

Ogilby's resilience to disaster, which by now was becoming notorious, led him to undertake a second lottery in 1668.[22] The propositions were designed to entice even those reluctant to trust to the whims of chance. No concessions were made to the buyer of a single 5s. lot. For someone more intrepid, however, willing to part with 25s., Ogilby promised a prize of greater value than the money, 'if such his bad fortune be that he draws all Blanks.' And, lastly, if anyone should invest 40s. for eight lots, he would receive nine. Should all of these be blanks, he might nevertheless have his choice among the two volumes of Homer; the two *Aesops*; *China*; or *Virgil*.

The lots themselves were listed, by numbers, and with prices given for different volumes. The Bible led the list, valued at £25. *Virgil* and the *Iliad* were £5 each, the *Odyssey* £4, *Aesop* £3, *China* £4, the *Entertainment* £2. There were differences in some of the editions, of course, depending upon size and illustrations. Taken as a group, however, the listing and pricing of Ogilby's work at this stage show an impressive and expensive output of published material.

About the success of this (1668) lottery there is conflicting evidence. Encouraged by various patrons, Ogilby reprinted his former editions, thus indicating that some, at least, of his stock had escaped the fury of the Fire. The *London Gazette* of 11 May 1668 reported the new lottery, stating that the draw would be held on 25 May, a Monday, at the Old Theatre, between Lincoln's Inn Fields and Vere Street.[23] One week previous to the lottery, the books might be viewed and lots could be purchased. Ten days later, Ogilby announced that so many 'adventurers' had appeared, that the draw was postponed until 2 June 1668. In fact, however, the prices were apparently too high for a London still recovering from the twin blows of Plague and Fire, and Ogilby was forced to reduce the subscription price (the lottery ticket) from 40s. (£2) to 5s., adding further blanks among the slips to maintain some kind of balance. He offered special prizes to any who took five or more tickets; and he announced 3,368 prizes ranging in value from £51 to £3.[24]

Whether the draw of 2 June was again postponed, or whether the 1668 lottery continued into the following year, as the first one had done, is not clear. On 11 February 1668/9, however, the *London Gazette* carried another item:

Mr. Ogleby's Lottery-Books will be delivered on Monday the First of March.
next, at the Black Boy against St. Dunstan's Church in Fleet-street, and
continue as before, Mondays, Wednesdays, and Fridays from 9 to 12 in
the forenoon, and from 2 to 5 in the afternoon. The conclusion of the said
Lottery will be opened on Thursday the 11th of the same moneth at the
Coffee-House in Pinners-Hall in Broadstreet.[25]

For lotteries to be successful, there must be advertisements or 'Propositions,' as they were often called. The success of the 1665 and 1668 lotteries led Ogilby to the publication of a 'Proposal' on 10 May 1669 that included not only what he projected but a considerable amount of information on his past.[26] It began with a brief survey of Ogilby's earlier lottery operations:

Whereas Mr. Ogilby Erected a Standing Lottery of Books of his own Com-
posure, which were lately Drawn to the general Satisfaction of all, by
which Low-rated Vendition [Sale], or New Whole-Sale of High-pric'd
Volumns, he hath not onaly [sic] Recruited his Loss by Fire, and His Purse
with a competency of gain, but also by his fair and ingenious Dealing, got
a handsom Stock of Reputation; Whereby enabled, encouraged, and still
covetous of Fame, and having likewise by a long habit contracted a
Necessity of retired Endeavors, he is forced for his Divertisement as well as
Profit, to prosecute whilest he hath vigour and abilities, the Business of
the Pen.

His losses from the Fire made good, his Irish adventures now apparently concluded, Ogilby was preparing to shift his attention and efforts toward a new and, he expected, lucrative endeavor. He was planning to begin his last, great project, the printing of atlases of the world; the idea clearly fascinated him, and dwarfed all his previous activities. He continued in the 'Proposal':[27]

And as at first stooping at no small Game, he [Ogilby] fell upon Virgil,
Prince of Latine, and on Homer, Prince of all Poets, then, thought Bold
Undertakings, and almost impossible to be rendred in our Modern Dress,
and Mode of English Language; He now in like manner resolves to over-
come, breaking through all Difficulties, a far greater and higher Design
looking down on Pernassus, Greek and Latine Paper-Kingdoms.

Those 'Paper-Kingdoms' had brought Ogilby fame and considerable fortune; yet now he could contemn them when he regarded the new worlds he
envisaged:

. . . girding himself couragiously for no less than the Conquest of the
whole World, making the Terrestrial Globe his Quarry, by a New and Ac-
curate Description of its four Quarters, viz., Europe, Asia, Africk, and
America, and teaching them English, [he determined to] bring home in
triumph illustrated with large Maps, and embellished with various Sculp-
tures of their Several Concerns, adorning with their most Famous Cities,
and other Rarities and new Remarks, the product of our later Discoveries.

Ogilby's rather unusual scheme was to proceed from the unknown to the
known: 'Africa, though not remotest, yet furthest from our Acquaintance,
the Author intends to be the First Volumn.' Then were to come America
and Asia. His plans for Europe (the only part he never actually executed)
were complex: 'Europe, that hath been most Surveyed, of which much is to
be said that hath not yet been Collected by an English Author, he designs to
be his Fourth and Fifth Volumn; the last, but not the least [i.e., Vol. V] in
our Concerns, will onely contain the Business of Great Britain, or our
English Monarchy.'

These five volumes might be secured with an immediate deposit of 20s.,
with an additional 20s. for each of the five atlases, as it was printed (a total
of £6 in all). Anyone with enough faith to advance £5 at once would get
'one perfect set more, that is, Six for Five.' And Ogilby attested that the
work was really worth £20 and that 'the like Volumns' sold in Holland for
£30. It sounds as if already he had in mind and in hand much of the
material he meant to use, the laws of copyright being non-existent not only
in England but elsewhere as well. The first volume was promised by Easter
Term 1670 (*Africa* appeared in that year), and subscribers might pay John
Cade, the bookbinder, or at 'Mr. Ogilby's office' at Black Boy [in or near
Fleet Street] against St. Dunstan's Church.

Among the books included in the 1668 lottery had been the volume *An*
Embassy from New Batavia, to the Emperor of China. It was the successful
reception accorded this book that, together with other considerations,
determined Ogilby 'to carry on in the same way hereafter, the whole
Business of my Pen.'[28] That decision, in which he persevered, led to his
prospectus for a standing lottery of all his works, designed to assist in the
production of *Britannia*. These 'Proposals,' elaborately set forth, clearly
and beautifully printed, and even illustrated, show the care and expertise
lavished by Ogilby on advertising for subscribers. They were printed after,
but probably not long after, the appearance of *America* in November
1671. (This last lottery will be discussed at length in Chapter VII).

Gregory King, not one to slight his own achievements, claimed that he was involved in Ogilby's lottery (probably the last large 'Proposals'). King, speaking of himself in the third person, said that he had 'contrived and assisted at [the lottery] in the managing thereof.' Further, he continued, 'he also framed for Mr. Ogilby a lesser Lottery of Books for Bristol fair at St. James tide 1673 which turned to good account, Mr. King managing it there.'[29]

Ogilby used the device of the lottery in yet another money-making scheme. As Master of the Revels in Ireland, he claimed the right to licence lotteries in that kingdom.[30] A single-sheet licence remains, granted by Ogilby to an unnamed licensee, to hold a 'Wheel of Fortune' plate lottery in Dublin who has written at the bottom of the sheet: 'My Shop is in Christ Church yard under the 4 Corts [Courts].'[31] It seems likely that Ogilby issued more than one such licence, and perhaps collected fees over a number of years, though the ephemeral nature of the lottery ticket has apparently destroyed all except this sheet.

Certainly, as a natural publicist, Ogilby used all the techniques of advertising his work that were available to him: dedications, subscriptions, patents, lotteries. He was accustomed to detail his various works in any petition he wrote, and was no doubt gratified to see the rehearsal of his achievements stated in the licences or patents that he received. When he affixed to his edition of *Africa* (1670) a patent speaking of forthcoming volumes of his projected worldwide atlas, it conveniently served as an advertisement. When, ten years or so after the Restoration, regular book catalogues began to be issued, Ogilby became a constant advertiser. Some of his notices are brief, others lengthy and specific. He advertised in the *Mercurius Librarius* and also in the 'Catalogue of Books' in 1670. From that date until 1711, there were numerous advertisements concerning Ogilby's many works constantly before the book-buying public of later Stuart England. When Ogilby began his most complicated endeavour (research for and publication of *Britannia*), he sent representatives to booksellers in cities other than London to publicize that volume.[22]

A significant aspect of his schemes for financing publications was Ogilby's practice of soliciting subscriptions, begun, as described earlier, with his 1654 *Virgil* and continued for most of the rest of his works.[33] His success in this area applied to both the 1654 and 1658 editions of the Latin poet. It was exhibited not only in the records of one hundred patrons' names in 1654, but in his maintaining three-fourths of these as contributors again in 1658, and in adding another twenty-five patrons in the latter volume to take the place of those who had dropped out. The appeals for these early subscriptions appear to have been lost, but those for his next classical venture — that upon Homer — remain.[34] As usual, Ogilby first identified himself with his previous work (Virgil and Aesop). Then, estimating the cost of his Greek translations at nearly £5,000, he proposed that the illustrative plates be engraved with the names, arms and titles of the subscribers, as had been done in the *Virgils*. The *Iliad* and *Odyssey* were promised, to those purchasing a plate, for £12, with £5 down, £5 upon receipt of the *Iliad*, and 40s. when the *Odyssey* was ready. For those wishing to buy the volumes but unwilling or unable to afford a plate, the cost for the complete Homer was reduced to £6: £2 upon subscribing, and £2 upon receipt of each book. Should anyone bring in five subscribers or take five subscriptions, he would receive an extra set. As yet, apparently, still relatively unknown, Ogilby gave the names and addresses of three printers (including Roycroft) where subscribers might enrol, if they were 'such . . . as know not the Author nor his dwelling.' In due course, both volumes appeared, filled with elaborately worked plates and dedications. For his *Aesops,* his edition of the Bible and for the *Entertainment,* Ogilby did not follow the practice of using (or apparently of soliciting) dedicatory plates. His proposals for subscribing to the atlases were, however, set forth in enticing terms, both substantive and financial. They were designed to attract a wider audience than the classical volumes; and so, combined as they were with the lottery scheme, the atlases were generally offered on their contents alone, without vanity's lure of a personalized plate.

Both in his search for subscribers to a world atlas and in his publication of the components, Ogilby had a close rival in Richard Blome. Shortly after Ogilby's 10 May 1669 'Proposal', Blome published *A Geographical Description of the Four Parts of the World,* drawn from a French work. The *Description* contained a proposal for further works on geography and related matters, and Blome followed the Ogilby pattern of printing plates with names and honours of the nobility and gentry who subscribed. And, in fact, in 1673, while Ogilby was somewhat desperately angling for more money for his own great survey (see Chapter VII), Blome published *Britannia, or a Geographical Description of England, Scotland and Ireland,* using the very title Ogilby had announced. Roycroft, Ogilby's sometime publisher and printer, was used by Blome for the latter work, of which some elaborately extra-illustrated copies remain. The challenge of a rival writer, working so close in subject matter and in time to his own final publications, must have made Ogilby's last years uneasy. He was the King's Cosmographer; he had his own press by this time (the 1670's); and he was a known and respected figure in the City. Yet Blome and Blome's work, both of which were generally successful, were surely a trial for Ogilby and indicate the freedom permitted to writers when no copyright laws existed.

Subscriptions, lotteries, advertisements were all adjuncts, of course, to the main business of publishing and printing books. Ogilby's specific operations in that area must be deduced from various indirect evidence. Although he, very early, saw the advantages to holding the rights of publication to his own works, he never became a Stationer and he certainly had constantly to work at amassing the capital required for producing his lavish volumes. When, in the early 1660's, he gained royal favour and the equivalent of a copyright to his own books, he might have been expected to settle into publishing. He allowed himself, however, to be distracted by a second theatrical venture. His success in becoming Master of the King's Revels in Ireland, although a notable honour for him and presumably a cultural service to Dublin, retarded his development as a London publisher. Nevertheless, during the years 1662-69 (during which time Clark says Ogilby was residing at least partly in Ireland), two issues of the *En-*

tertainment appeared, a folio of the *Odyssey*, two different folios of *Aesop* and the *Embassy to China*. Toward the end of the 1660's, upon his final return from Ireland, Ogilby, now about seventy, set up his own printing shop, and thereafter produced his own books and some others as well. In addition to printing the great atlases, he presumably reprinted earlier volumes so extensively during the 1670's that lotteries of his books continued after his death, and Dryden (in 'MacFlecknoe') could remark on the numerous volumes of Ogilby, Shirley and Heywood that, with Shadwell, 'almost chok'd the way.'[35] Sir Roger L'Estrange, at about this time, in commenting on the surfeit of books and translations, wrote of

the selling of Translations, so Dog-Cheap, that every Sot knows now as much as would formerly have made a Passable Doctor, and every Nasty Groom and Roguy Lacquay is grown as familiar with Homer, Virgil, Ovid, as if 'twere Robin the Devil; The Seven Champions; or a piece of George Withers.[36]

The title of Master of the Royal Imprimerie, or King's Printer, which Ogilby had obtained shortly after the Restoration, appears to have been a relatively empty honour. No doubt it assisted in adding dignity to his petitions, such as those for the importation of special paper, and it looked imposing in dedications and on title pages. In no actual sense, however, does Ogilby seem to have been the King's Printer, and he had no part of the censorship office, which L'Estrange jealously guarded.

The Stationers Register for the 1660's and 1670's shows some of the complexities of printing rights (copyrights) during these years without illuminating any principles governing such rights. Presumably, as Ogilby advanced in royal favour, scholarly reputation and personal wealth, he printed his own works without challenge, thanks to his royal licences. He may, also, have made arrangements with some of his early publishers to buy out their interest in his first books (see Chapter II, pp. 46 ff, and *passim*). Nevertheless, in 1675, the widow of John Crook, Ogilby's first publisher, was selling to a Stationer 'all the Right . . . to one book or Coppy Entituled Virgills Works or Poems translated into English Verse by John Ogilby Esq.'[37] This apparent speculation in copyrights continued for at least another century, and a lucrative copyright might be divided into numerous shares.[38]

A final subject that must be treated in the story of Ogilby as printer-publisher deals with the evanescent figure of William Morgan.

The relationship between the elderly and the young man seems to have been a happy as well as productive one; in fact, the only relative (although not one by tie of blood) with whom Ogilby could associate himself was apparently William Morgan, and their connection lasted until the elder's death. The two men worked together first — and closely — in the production of *The Entertainment*; for this Ogilby procured both recognition and pay for his young kinsman's part. Then Morgan must have gone to Ireland, either with Ogilby, or to take his place on that island, during the decade of the 1660's, when the new Master of Revels must have been travelling back and forth fairly often. Ogilby had Morgan made Deputy Master of Revels by patent, and apparently the two worked as closely in the theatrical business as in publishing. After Ogilby's death, it was Morgan and Ashbury who ran the Smock Alley Theatre for some (undetermined) years. Described as an 'assistant' to Ogilby, Morgan also was mentioned in Ogilby's patent as Royal Cosmographer. In the 1670's, as Ogilby grew older, Morgan's role in business affairs undoubtedly increased. It seems likely that for a time he met a rival in the able and ambitious young Gregory King. But, as usual in the seventeenth-century, ties of kinship prevailed over all others, and it was Morgan who was designated (after Mrs. Ogilby) as the printer's heir.

If, as believed, Mrs. Ogilby died a year after her husband, Morgan must have assumed almost at once the responsibility for continuing Ogilby's manifold works. There were two major areas: the printing and publishing of Ogilby's works, and the running of the Smock Alley Theatre in Dublin. Certainly, Morgan finished the printing and promotion of the *Road Maps*. He also must have continued selling off stock already printed, and issuing new, if the market called for it. In time it became 'Mr. Morgan's maps' that the advertisements spoke of, but Ogilby's name remained attached to the other works he had translated or written. As Morgan's house was less expensive than Ogilby's, so his acumen (with one exception) seems also to have been inferior. He was content to follow his grandfather's policies, but not to extend or elaborate upon them. He remained a figure of minor importance in London. Toward the end of the 1670's, Morgan was apparently a person of sufficient prominence in the Clockmakers Company to be appointed as a steward for the annual feast on more than one occasion. This was, apparently, an 'honour' that he was content to escape, for he pleaded business or 'could not bee mett with by the Beadle' on these occasions.[39] Association with the Company had no doubt been useful to him, but there is no record of his participating in Company activities.

In the matter of the Irish theatre, Morgan showed himself somewhat more aggressive. He must have been travelling back and forth between England and Ireland fairly regularly from the time of the Restoration,[40] and he apparently decided it worthwhile to obtain a patent in his own name as Master of Revels in the Kingdom of Ireland. In an undated petition, written sometime after Ogilby's death in 1676, Morgan spoke of helping his 'Unkle' in building the Dublin theatre and in organizing the company there. As Deputy of the Master of Revels, he had 'been at very great Charge to maintain and uphold a Company of good actors who still continue at the Theatre in Dublin.' The petition mentioned also the debt still owed by Ogilby in Ireland (presumably for building the theatre), and asked that a new patent be granted Morgan, which should exclude Stanley.[41]

Presumably, the complexity of operating the Dublin theatre led to a new arrangement when the patent was finally issued. The warrant granting the request was dated 28 November 1683, and described Morgan as 'Gentleman and Our Cosmographer.'[42] Morgan was associated in this patent with Joseph Ashbury, resident actor-manager at Smock Alley, and with his son Charles Ashbury. The Duke of Ormonde, Lord Lieutenant of Ireland, had approved the arrangement before the patent was granted.

Although the two Ashburys were fully associated with Morgan in the exercise of the office of Master of Revels, and no doubt handled the running of the theatre, it was to Morgan, his heirs, executors and assigns only that it was granted 'to enjoy the benefit of the Theatre already built . . . and to Erect and build One or more Theatre or Theatres . . .' [an act never performed]. Whatever revenue accrued from the Dublin theatre, after expenses, would seem to have been Morgan's to enjoy, without interference from the Ashburys. In yet one more document from this time, dated 20 January 1683, there was granted by Morgan a power of attorney to his 'loveing friend Edward Corker of Dublin, Esquire' to relinquish the Ogilby patent, as, presumably, Morgan now had the new copy of his own.[43] This last document indicates the kind of arrangement that Morgan — and earlier Ogilby — must have had in order to carry on the business operation of the theatre (as distinct from theatrical operations, which were in Ashbury's hands) when not actually resident in the city or even in the country where it was situated. Some responsible man of business in Dublin, or perhaps a lawyer, would have looked after business affairs on the spot, and considerable trust must have been reposed in him. That Mr. Corker was Morgan's 'loving friend' suggests a circle of friends in Dublin, outside the members of the theatre proper, but their names have generally been rendered invisible by time.

The will of William Morgan, dated 24 February 1689/90 was written when the testator was 'weake in body but of sound and perfect mind.' Sometime within the next month he died, as the will was proved on 24 March 1689/90. Morgan was living at that time in the parish of St. Martin's, Ludgate, and asked to be buried in the rites of the Church of England.[44] There is no mention of children, and his wife Elizabeth was his chief heir and executrix, although 'overseers' were associated with her in the administration of the will. There is a distinct flavour of family animosity in the early provisions, wherein William left a small sum in trust for his brother Roger 'so long as he shall behave himselfe civily and with due respects to my Wife and Overseers and noe longer.' The same provisions and wording were used for a bequest to his sister Anne, wife of Mountford Balliedon. The bequests were to be increased 'when my Prints, copper plates, bookes and mapps shall be disposed of.' A number of friends were left £5 apiece (in some cases less) to buy mourning, and £5 was set aside for distribution to the poor.

Concerning the office of Master of the Revels in Ireland, Morgan bequeathed 'the said office and my estate and interest therein with the perquisites, benefits and advantages and appurtenances . . . unto my deare and loveing wife Elizabeth' for her arranging of its disposition. Whether the patent should be sold, leased or disposed of in some other fashion was to be left to the executors. The money thus raised was to be divided as follows: two-fifths 'to my said dear wife'; two-fifths to Joseph Ashbury and his heirs; and the final fifth to the aforementioned brother and sister of the testator.

The most complex of the provisions dealt with 'the government of the Company of Actors or Comedians belonging to the Theatre at Dublin.'

This authority, Morgan attested, was granted to him and his heirs forever under the Great Seal of England. Whatever profits might be made from the governance of this company, together with Morgan's share in the theatre and in its stock, 'or any the shopps, Cellars or other parts thereof or thereto belonging' were to be divided into ten parts. Five of these went to his wife. Another part was assigned to Edward Corker, Esq., with whom Morgan had earlier left his power of attorney, and who is here described as 'my worthy friend.' To Corker's eldest daughter Jane was left the reversion of two other parts (not her father's). Joseph Ashbury inherited one part; another went to John and Anne Richards; and the last two were assigned to Morgan's brother and sister. Presumably from this multitude of heirs, Ashbury was able to buy enough shares to manage the theatre until the early eighteenth century.

With the death of Morgan, the publication and advertisement of Ogilby's work ended also. Books are not altogether dead things, as a contemporary of Ogilby averred. Such immortality as Ogilby obtained may most justly be ascribed first to his own industry in the preparation of his writings and then, no less important, to his publicizing of them, in a variety of ways. His contemporary fame and future reputation will be treated in Chapter VIII. It can fairly be said here, however, that it was because Ogilby acted as printer-publisher and not as writer only that he made his name one of consequence in his own lifetime and even after his death.

VI

The Great Atlases

Exclusive of the *Britannia*, John Ogilby published seven large folios on foreign lands (often called 'atlases') between 1669 and 1673. His turning from classical verse to descriptive prose was a deliberate move, inspired in part by the success of his first venture (on China), and in part because he sensed the growing interest among Englishmen in the vast and strange areas now becoming more accessible to trade and even to conquest. Of the 'God, gold and glory' trilogy, the first element — conversion of the natives to Christianity — seems still to have been undeveloped. But the possibilities for increasing England's trade and extension of her national prestige (themes on which Ogilby had touched in the *Entertainment*) were certainly evident in his collection of materials and produced a commensurate effect in the considerable market that the volumes commanded. In his dedication of *Africa* to the monarch, for instance, Ogilby devoted a paragraph to the praise of 'Your own Bright Star, . . . Your Metropolis, Your Royal City Tangier, which Seated on the Skirts of the Atlantick, keeps the Keys both of the Ocean and In-land Sea.'

Ogilby's 'atlases' have been, on the whole, neglected in any modern assessments of the man's work. Their chief value, it would be reasonable to assume, lies in their contemporary stimulation and educative value to their readers. Since they represent a significant portion of his publications, however, they merit examination both as to content and to influence.

Ogilby's plan, as announced in the Preface to Africa,[1] was to cover the entire world, not with 'atlases' in the modern sense, but rather with available and up-to-date translations of various accounts. These emphasized the travels of various figures (generally ambassadors or Catholic missionaries), strange customs and outlandish wonders, and even some haphazard geography of the relatively unknown regions of the world. Ogilby projected a five-volume series: Africa, America, Asia, Europe, Britain. The fourth of these volumes was never printed or even, so far as evidence points, begun. The last volume — *Britannia* —was treated far differently from the strange regions represented by the first three volumes (see Chapter VII for a fuller treatment of *Britannia*). But, although the original plan was not wholly fulfilled, Ogilby did produce four additional volumes, which belong in the 'atlas' category. These were three volumes on China (1669, 1671, 1673,) and one on Japan (1670). All these books profited from Ogilby's earlier publishing experience. They were folios printed on fine paper, with large clear print, heavily illustrated with figures in strange costumes and postures and even containing some maps, which have an original charm of their own. In general, the volumes were so produced as to constitute a handsome addition to any library. In the absence of international copyright, Ogilby needed only to search out the most up-to-date and available works on the area he wished to treat. Then he had these translated (usually from the Dutch, but sometimes from Spanish or Portuguese). And, finally, money having bought brains, he could announce proudly an elaborate subject on his title page, often adding 'English'd by John Ogilby.'

It seems likely that, in all these volumes, Ogilby commissioned translations of the works he had obtained and at various points added his own comments. He also set artists to copying illustrations from the books he was using. Sometimes an English title was added to a print; at other times the original legend was erased and English words inserted. Small changes were often made also in the illustrations and the maps. As with the 'author,' so with the artist. Wenceslaus Hollar and other artists signed plates that they had copied from Continental editions. Such procedure was standard for the time, of course. Furthermore, the translated atlases that Ogilby produced were intelligible to Englishmen as well as useful. Hence the translations sold in quantities as the originals would never have done. In addition to making a solid business profit, Ogilby was educating Englishmen about a variety of lands. The government was favourable to the venture: Arlington's name appears on the licence for the first (1669) atlas, dated 19 March 1666/7. Far more valuable was the copyright from the King appended to *Africa*. It covered, for a period of fifteen years, Ogilby's sole right to reproduce all his works so far printed and including the projected atlas.[2]

Although all these volumes are derivative in content, they vary considerably in the style and care with which they were produced. The first, *An Embassy from the East-India Company of the United Provinces to the Grand Tartar Cham Emperour of China* [hereafter called *Embassy to China*], was printed in 1669 and attained considerable success. The greater part of it was a translation of the account of the embassy (in Dutch) by Jan Nieuhoff, who had been 'Steward' of the ambassadors. Also printed with this, however, was a letter from Father John Adams, a Jesuit, who had been working in China to counter the aims of the Dutch embassy; and, thirdly, there was a small section of 'remarks' selected from a large volume, *China monumentis, qua sacris qua profanis, illustrata* (1667), written by another Jesuit, Father Athanasius Kircher. These materials, it was claimed on the title page, were 'Englished in 1669 and set forth with their several Sculptures by John Ogilby, Esq., Master of His Majesties Revels in the Kingdom of Ireland.' The claim of authorship was reiterated in the statement that this was 'Printed by John Macock for the Author.'

The contents of these works were not, of course, the choice of Ogilby. They reflect, rather, the special seventeenth-century interests in strange

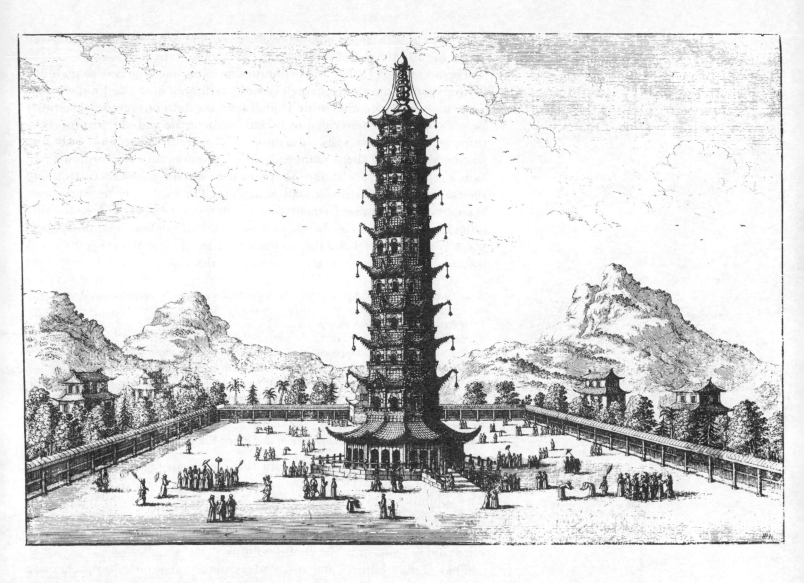

lands: concern about fantastic religious practices, sexual deviations, cruelty, marital customs, unusual costumes. Such subjects appear often, frequently with no apparent connection to adjacent portions of the text. On title pages and at times in headings, however, more dignified and comprehensive areas are indicated: for example, the description of cities, rivers and mountains, flora and fauna, government, language and manners.

This first of Ogilby's atlases was in many ways a typical one. After Nieuhoff's account of the embassy, there was his 'General Description of the Empire of China.' In it were included the drawing of some Chinese characters (p. 159), a discussion of Confucius and Chinese philosophy, the clothing worn by Chinese, including a depiction of the bound feet of women, various burial customs, and an illustrated tale of beggars who tormented themselves (pp. 170-71) in order to beg more successfully. The chapters on natural features included (pp. 264-65) a description and representation of that new fruit 'ananas' [pineapple], and a variety of animals. In the section on the history of the emperors of China, the Tar-

11) *The Pagoda at Paolinxi*, Embassy to China, *1673*
The Library, Lehigh University,
Bethlehem, Penna., USA

97

tars, shown with their characteristic drooping moustaches, were given credit for bringing peace to the land.

The account of Father Adams, quite hostile to the Dutch, was included in the volume, no doubt bringing some satisfaction to the English, who went to war three times with Holland in the latter seventeenth-century before consenting to be ruled by a Dutchman at the end of that time. The third portion of the work, drawn from Father Kircher and with new pagination, was really a compendium of remarks on the 'antiquities' of China, compiled from various sources, some of which stretched back into the early part of the century. This section included inscriptions, missionary accounts and random statements on various regions of China. Like the first (Nieuhoff) part, it was lavishly illustrated; throughout, emphasis was placed on the unusual and the magnificent (the Chinese Wall, pp. 97ff.). A pagoda, engraved by Hollar, was carefully described

This tower has nine rounds, and one hundred eighty four steps to the top; each round is adorned with a Gallery full of Images and Pictures, with very handsom lights (as is exprest in the annexed Print). The out-side is all Glazed over and Painted with several Colours, as Green, Red, and Yellow. The whole Fabrick consists of several Pieces, which are so Artificially Cemented, as if the work were all of one Piece. Round about all the corners of the Galleries, hang little Bells, which make a very pretty noise when the wind jangles them: The top of the Tower was Crowned with a Pine-Apple, which as they say, was made of Massy Gold. From the upper Gallery you may see not only over the whole City, but also over the adjacent Countries to the other side of the River Kiang.

There are some misplaced pages in this section of Ogilby's work. Stories and information (often of dubious validity) were provided in abundance. The volume was in no way, however, a systematic history or even a contemporary description on reasoned terms of the vast empire of China. Even such a helpful device as a full Table of Contents (which Kircher had supplied) did not appear in the Ogilby volume.

That Ogilby himself and his readers were under no misapprehension about the actual authorship of this work appears in a note to the reader at the end of the volume (p. 106 of the Kircher section): 'Those that are earnest to make further scrutiny in quest of all these Wonderful Relations, may resort to the Author [Father Kircher] himself, and to those in his Quotations.'

The *Embassy to China* was filled with illustrations, a number signed and one dated 1668 (by Hollar). Sometimes they are precise depictions (as in the pineapple plate). At other times, they were apparently drawn from verbal description and fall short of conviction. The double-page map of China (adapted from the one in the Nieuhoff volume, but showing certain differences) was signed by Wenceslaus Hollar. It shows in its orthography some of the pronunciation of Chinese as the West understood it at the time. 'A Wall 300 leagues long' appeared in the north, weaving in and out of the mountains. Blank spaces on the map served, as usual both then and later, for depiction of strange animals. Archibald Erskine, Esq., paid for the plate in Ogilby's volume, and was duly commemorated in an elaborate cartouche (see following illustration).

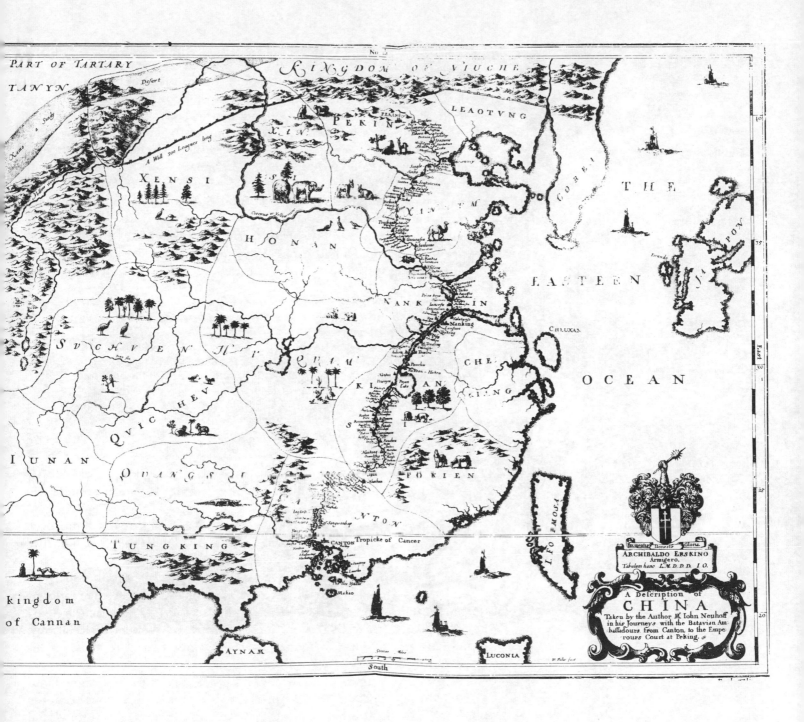

12) *Map of China*, Embassy to China, *1673*
By permission of the Folger Shakespeare Library, Washington, DC, USA

Aerdbeevinge tot JEDO . Earthquake at JEDO
Erdbeben zu Jedo .

13) *Earthquake at Jedo*, Atlas Japannensis, *1670*
By permission of the Folger Shakespeare Library, Washington DC, USA

The two volumes that appeared in 1670 (*Africa* and the *Atlas Japannensis*) seem very different in the effort involved and the effects achieved in their production. *Africa* was the first volume of Ogilby's announced 'Atlas,' and had received a high degree of advance publicity. The Japanese folio was a work extraneous to the major volumes: it was simply a translation and printing of a book that had apparently come to hand and might be presumed to find a market among the growing number of buyers of Ogilby's atlases.

To discuss the lesser Japanese volume first, it must be said that it was an impressive folio, as large as the *Africa,* and filled with illustrations. It was dedicated to the King, the tone of its contents being described in the dedication: 'These Strange and Novel Relations . . . being A Book of Wonders.' A variety of accounts were printed by Ogilby in this work, taken, as he says, from 'several Writings and Journals by Arnoldus Montanus.[13] These writings in turn, however, were originally derived from various people, some of them early sixteenth-century Jesuits. Although Montanus had supplied an index and a list of illustrations, Ogilby failed to adopt such useful devices. He did not even use chapter headings, and his marginal summaries, though useful, simply emphasize the lack of consistent treatment of material. Ogilby scarcely distinguishes between one writer and the other, as he prints descriptions of an earthquake in Jeddo, a singular method of abortion in Formosa (p. 51), varieties of tortures (pp. 269-71), and a picture of beheadings, with blood actually spurting from a neck from which the head has been severed (p. 198). Occasionally, the reader comes with relief upon a less exotic aspect of so-called Japanese life, such as the making of porcelain (p. 434) or the characters and derivation of the Japanese language (pp. 363, 366).

Ogilby's first remarks in the *Atlas Japannensis* reflected the interest in natural science so common at this time. The volume opened with a discussion of the earth and sea as a round globe and then a description of new ideas on space: 'Incircling this our Terrestrial Orb at an unmeasurable distance, sparkle the Innumerable Lights, in the immense expansions of the Firmament' (p. 1). He moved on from there to a description of the earth, the peoples on it, and finally the discoveries of new worlds. One of Ogilby's own quotations (from the third book of the *Aeneid*) on the venturing forth into the unknown was rather gratuitously included, and this led to an unusual comment. Despite his involvement with the classics, Ogilby apparently at times placed himself on the side of the Moderns as against the Ancients. Describing the various aids to navigation known to the seventeenth-century, he noted 'that now, by the help of the Needle [compass], our Modern Navigators often run safely that in ten days, which Aeneas, Ulisses and other Antients Navigators, still fearing Shipwrack, made a ten years pudder of' (p.5).

All in all, as Ogilby said in his final paragraph to the reader, this was a 'large account' of the wealth and wonders of Japan, the latest and fullest to be made of that island, 'reaching within three years of this our present Publication.' Though long, he hoped the volume would not be boring, the material being so strange that 'hitherto, we presume, [it] hath scarce reach'd any English Ear.' Japan, he acknowledged, was only a 'by-Volume,' inserted within 'our great Atlantick Work.' The volume on China had undoubtedly suggested the one on Japan; and Ogilby promised, that if Japan were well received, there would be another volume on China, even more lavishly illustrated. He made that promise good.

Africa, printed also in 1670, by Thomas Johnson for the Author, was the first volume of Ogilby's great Atlantic or English Atlas. Perhaps its most valuable aspect was the lengthy Preface, portions of which have already been quoted, and which is Ogilby's only autobiography (limited, unfortunately, to the years of his life between c. 1650 and 1670). In this Preface, dated 28 April 1670, were intermingled memories, ambitions, and political and literary criticism of a variety and perspicacity to whet the appetite for more of such data. Without what Ogilby wrote there, pitifully few details on his life and especially his thinking would exist.

It is from the Preface that we learn of Ogilby's attempt, after so many translations, at writing his own epic, the abortive 'Carolies.' The loss of this in the Fire, coupled with the destruction of his stock of books, brought him, says Ogilby, to 'a low condition, groaning under a double burthen of Sickness and Poverty, and almost quite despairing.' That unquenchable vigour of spirit reasserted itself, however. Ogilby was reminded that many of his friends and patrons rallied to him more 'when under a Cloud than after Shining in full Lustre.' Furthermore, he sensed that, since the Restoration, patrons and courtiers no longer pursued their interests in retirement, but were increasingly involved with the world about them. That world was expanding in size, in variety and opportunity. Ogilby moved consciously to acquaint Englishmen with this new world.

He left his pursuit of the classics with less regret, since he sensed that already the temper of his time had changed. Now there was increased interest in 'Rough Satyr, Rude Travestee, and Rhime Doggerel.' Satirical himself, he noted 'That we in this more Refin'd Age, speak better things *ex tempore,* than what hath been Recorded by the whole Rabble of Antiquity.' The old learning was now considered fitting only for schoolboy themes, which 'our Brisker Youth, and more Sublime Wits, should be asham'd to peruse, much more to follow.'

Then, in one of his most quoted sentences, Ogilby announced his future intent: 'Thus a new Gaggle drowning the old Quire of Melodious Swans, I resolv'd to desist, and shutting up the Fountain of the Muses, left Clambering steep Pernassus, and fell into the beaten way, and more frequented Paths of Prose.' The success of his first venture, the *Embassy to China,* confirmed him in this resolve and he determined thereafter to make prose 'the whole Business of my Pen.'

His endeavour, he resolved, should be of the greatest magnitude; and so there was advanced his project of the atlases of the four regions of the world. To return then, to *Africa,* Ogilby said that, while working on that volume, he came upon a full new work on Africa in the Dutch language, written (or organized) by Dr. Oliver Dapper. Dapper, a Dutch geographer and physician, may well have been the inspirer of Ogilby's style in atlas-making. Dapper used many sources, some obscure and ill-known, others recent, all of which he incorporated into his own writing. Ogilby followed this technique. Dapper's literary style was characterized by both profuseness and diffuseness, with the quality of organization notably lacking. Again, this describes Ogilby's own work. Also like Ogilby, Dapper appreciated and commissioned illustrations of high quality, and his books were valued and translated on the Continent.[4]

Ogilby used the same frontispiece as had Dapper, the same title page and the same map (a few unimportant lines were added). Ogilby made some interesting additions on his own, however. First, he used folio sheets approximately one-third larger than those of Dapper, a fact that added to the impressiveness of his volume. Then, presumably in an effort to guide his readers through the mass of material and as a testimony of various sources consulted, Ogilby included a two-page 'Catalogue of Names' of writers, ancient and modern, who had, he said, led him by the hand through the vast area of Africa. He cited first ten authors (chiefly Dutch) of general assistance, and then proceeded to note those who had been most helpful in each of his seven designated regions. Among these, besides Dutch writers, there were numbers of Portuguese, Spanish, Italian and French authors; and not omitted were some of the famous names of antiquity, such as Strabo, Pomponius Mela and Ptolemy. Ogilby attempted, in fact, an annotated, though incomplete, bibliography in these pages.

Since the 'English Atlas' was intended as an encyclopaedic history of the world, in the first volume, *Africa*, he included, as Dapper had done, the widest variety of natural features, animal, vegetable and mineral; social customs of all kinds; and specialities of various countries or regions. The author distinguished and subdivided the continent into seven great regions: Egypt, Barbary, Biledulgerid [Numidia], the Sahara, the Land of Negroes, Lower Ethiopia and Upper Ethiopia (the whole of these latter two stretching southwest to northeast, from below the Congo to the Red Sea). He included also a section, as had Dapper, on 'Islands' adjacent to the continent. Towns and mountains were grouped by region in yet another table. Dapper's map bearing the imprint of Jacob Meurs was included, with no changes in legend or content. A dedicatory cartouche in the lower left corner remained blank, presumably testimony to Ogilby's inability, in this instance, to find a patron for the unsigned plate. The map is reasonably accurate, with relatively few blank spaces, its chief failure lying in distortion and disproportion rather than in incompleteness. Age-old names of renewed modern interest appear, such as 'Biafara regnum' and 'Zaire lacus.'

As one of the most visually minded men of his century, Ogilby intended to illustrate lavishly his various works in this multi-volumed 'atlas,' as he had done with his translations. He included in *Africa* a double-page spread on the pyramids (between pp. 76 and 77). There were also drawings of pyramids to scale, a lurid print of the spoliation of an ancient tomb filled with mummies, and the depiction of some mummies and their cases (pp. 83-85). He used numbers of marginal references to the many authors cited in the front of the volume. Some of the marginalia seem without real

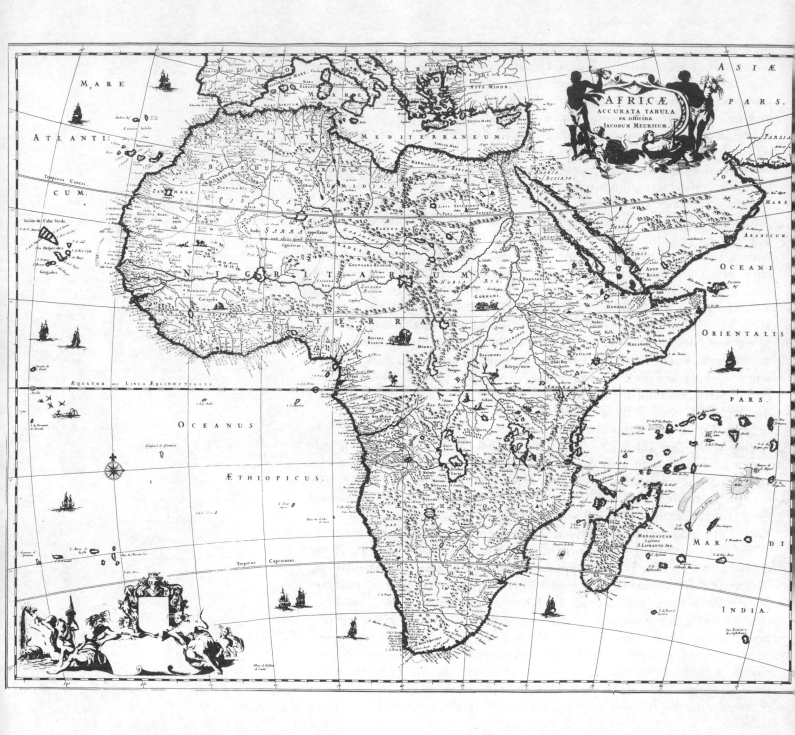

14) *Map of Africa, Africa, 1670*
By permission of the Folger Shakespeare Library, Washington DC, USA

justification, as in the comment on the city of Fez, opposite a description of its 250 bridges with shops on both sides: 'Like London-Bridge before the Fire' (p. 188). On the other hand, another of his marginalia (p. 53) shows some of Ogilby's frustration as he wrestled with various conflicting sources and attempted a reconciliation. This comment, dealing with the mouths of the Nile, was original with him:

What ever was, or is their number, antient or modern Maps vary among themselves; for whereas Ptolomy hath set forth nine, Hondius in his Map of Africa makes but eight, and in that of Europe, ten. Ortelius in the Map of the Turkish Empire setteth down eight, in that of Egypt, eleven: And Maginus in his map of that Countrey, hath observ'd the same number: And if we enquire farther, we shal find the same diversity and discord in divers others. Thus we may observe that this Account hath been always different concerning these Ostiaries [estuaries] of the Nile.

Although both Dapper and Ogilby cited classical geographers and writers of prose, only Ogilby inserted classical poets. Not only Homer, Virgil and Aesop did he use, as might be expected, but Horace as well, contributing a literary quality to his *Africa* that was lacking in the Dutch volume. There were additions of special interest to English readers also; for example, the story of the attack on the English vessel *Mary Rose* by pirates, illustrated by a plate (between pp. 218 and 219) done by the engraver Hollar, who had had the misfortune to be on board during the engagement. Ogilby also included Joseph Sprat's relation of some English merchants who climbed to the top of Teneriffe (pp. 736-41). And as further orientation to his English readers, Ogilby included in his marginalia of the 'Induction' (p. 1) an addition to some of Dapper's calculations: 'Concerning this, see Mr. Norwood's Experiment, or Sea-mans Practice. As likewise Mr. Oughtred's Treatise of Navigation, at the end of his Circles of Proportion.' It seems clear that Ogilby attempted, whenever possible, to introduce subjects of particular interest to Englishmen, and his acquaintance with various technical manuals is probably to be attributed to his current association with members of the Royal Society.

The strangeness of the essential Africa was stressed: in Negro-land, the inhabitants of the Gold Coast practised the deliberate debasing of gold in order to trick Europeans, were expert in dancing and drumming, and remained ineradicably pagan (various pages between pp. 419 and 463). Theories about the unknown interior were given at length, and, already in 1670, Ogilby was inciting Britons to think about the location of the sources of the Niger (pp. 316ff). There was a natural emphasis on Tangier, England's only foothold on the continent, and a part of the dowry of Charles II's queen. Two double-page maps of the city appeared (between pp. 196 and 197), showing, as completed, improvements to the harbour that were only in prospect and never actually finished. This was indeed an 'English Atlas,' in which Ogilby reported: 'The Garrison of English now there fear not at all what the power of the Moors can or dare do by Land,' and boasted, in the same fashion, that Tangier might now 'speak with any that pass the Straits of Gibraltar.' His national feelings showed again, in a later discussion (p. 376) of how the Dutch under 'De Rutter' in December 1664 took a small fort in the area of Sierra Leone from the English 'without reason' and stripped it of all valuables, such as elephants' teeth.

The description of Sierra Leone was an extensive one, taken from 'Jarrick.' Though not as yet noted for diamonds, the country supplied some gold and also slaves. The latter commodity was mentioned as being traded only by the Portuguese, and there was even a tale of some blacks selling a rival tribe to the Portuguese, an act described by Ogilby as a 'savage Tyranny' (p. 374).

Abyssinia, as an ancient Christian country on a pagan continent, received extended consideration, with several descriptions of Coptic practices and an attempt at a historical survey of the kingdom. Ogilby commented at some length on 'this supposed Prester John [who] . . . hath gotten many Names, to the great distraction both of Historians and Geographers' (p. 645).

In the light of later history, some of Ogilby's remarks and maps had perdurable interest. He included a particularly well-drawn map of the harbour of the Cape of Good Hope, with legends in Portuguese, Dutch and English, showing it had passed through a variety of printings (between pp. 584 and 585). He reported (p. 590) that

all the Kaffers [used interchangeably with Hottentots] are void of
Literature, stupidly dull and clownish, and in understanding are more like
Beasts than Men: but some by continual converse with European Mer-
chants, shew a few sparks or glimmerings of an inclination to more
humanity.

Malta's history and its exotic Knights were fully treated (pp. 745-63), and good maps of the island itself and of the city of Valetta were included. St. Helena (pp. 726-27) was described as a kind of earthly but uninhabited paradise.

Ogilby's treatment of the 'Islands' of Africa, which included all adjacent lands, ranging from Madagascar through the Canaries to tiny areas like St. Helena, added much to the comprehensiveness of his treatment of 'Africa.' On the other hand, the numerous engravings he printed of cities and ports (such, for example, as Luanda in Angola, between pp. 552 and 553) seem relatively undifferentiated, with ships and waves dominating the foreground, clouds the background, and the ostensible subject generally without much real character. Except for his occasional bias towards England, Ogilby kept his text free from personal comments, and did not draw moral lessons in the course of his descriptions. He had not done so with Aesop, though others had; and he left aphorisms alone in his 'Atlas,' although other gazetteers were to find sermonizing devices in accounts of strange lands and foreign peoples.

What is most disappointing about *Africa* to a modern reader is Ogilby's distinct lack of discrimination. He did indeed in this volume attempt to be systematic, consistent, comprehensive and honest in his attribution to previous writers. He even excised some of the less likely tales, as he explained in his Dedication to the King ('I . . . am busie exploding Old

Tales, Fictions, and Hear-says'). Certainly, in *Africa*, it is possible to locate an area on the map and find its description from the guide to regions printed at the beginning of the book. Furthermore, there is a List of Maps and Sculptures at the very end of the volume, which, while not complete, can be used to locate various specific places. The numerous authors, 'both Ancient and Modern,' upon whom he relied, however, included a wide variety of credulous story tellers, despite the author's avowal of not publishing 'anything, if possible, but undoubted Truth.' Perhaps, in consideration of the sizeable unknowns that Africa still conceals, too harsh a judgement on a seventeenth-century author's accuracy and credulity is unmerited.

That the appeal to his readers still emphasized the riches and the strangeness of these new lands appears in the author's customary final words to the reader (in *Africa,* p. 767):

Our next voyage (by God's conduct) we intend for America; hoping to receive that good Encouragement, that shall enable us to lead you through that New and Golden World, where you shall meet with the like, or more Variety of Wonders, than hitherto hath pierc'd any English ear.

So rapidly was Ogilby now moving on his project that, in the very year in which *Africa* appeared, he was advertising, on 22 November 1670, that *America* was 'now in good forwardness.'[5] In November 1671, he was able to advertise that *America* 'after much cost and pains' was in print and available at his own house or at a stationer's. In the next catalogue (February 1672), Ogilby noted that for the benefit of 'gentry that live far remote' he had appointed 'several noted Booksellers in many and chief Towns of England' and that a 'Specimen' of each volume so far published of his Atlas was available for inspection in their shops. No evidence exists of how many books of wonders such advertising sold. Frequent references to the coming volume on Britain were also made in these notices, however, and interest in *that* volume was to be evidenced throughout the country, as still extant letters show (see Chapter VII).

Ogilby's folio on *America* was probably the best of his foreign atlases, so far as content, style and organization were concerned. His strong sense of addressing himself to *English* readers was offered greater opportunity in this volume than before as he could tell of early English explorations and current English settlements. Again, Ogilby proclaimed on his title page the accuracy, the fullness and the recent nature of his sources. The conquests of Mexico and Peru were specifically noted, as well as the setting up of various European 'plantations' or settlements. And he included appendices on the Arctic, Tasman's discoveries (1642), and the Northwest Passage, among other things.[6] Some of this material, he claimed, was being printed for the first time, though he failed to identify just what that was. Ogilby signed himself 'Esq.' and used all his titles on this title page: 'His Majesty's Cosmographer, Geographic Printer and Master of the Revels in the Kingdom of Ireland.' He printed *America* himself and announced it for sale at his house in White Friars.

Over 150 authors, arranged in alphabetical order, were credited with having been used or mentioned, but many of these were simply familiars from antiquity: Virgil, Aristotle, Pliny, Strabo, even Moses and Tertullian. Among more recent commentators Nieuhoff, Las Casas and Scaliger were mentioned. It is noteworthy that although, both for content and illustrations, Ogilby was certainly most indebted to Montanus' work on the new world, he failed to mention this author.[7] As the books on America by Montanus and Ogilby both appeared in 1671, the latter must have arranged for swift purchase of the Montanus volume and its immediate translation. There are many obvious similarities in the two folios. Each has the same frontispiece illustration, but the Meurs imprint in Montanus' book has been erased from the plate in Ogilby's volume. A large map of north and south America by Gerard a Schagen, printed by Meurs, was also copied for Ogilby, but the latter made some changes of importance on it. The organization of the contents was generally the same, too. Ogilby's *America* in many respects is far more attractive to the eye than Montanus'. Instead of double columns on each page, Ogilby used his usual type, larger and clearer than Montanus'. Both books have marginal annotations, but Ogilby's are more legible because they are less crowded. For once, however, the illustrations in Ogilby's work are clearly of inferior quality, though they are numerous and keyed to the text.[8]

America was, of course, an easier territory to cover than Africa. Nevertheless, Ogilby clearly improved his organization in the second volume of the 'English Atlas' over that in the first. His volume of *America* was divided into three parts (called by him 'books'), the first containing the stories of various expeditions; the second treating North America, most of Central America and the Caribbean; and the third finishing the continent of South America. This was essentially Montanus' organization, but a reader of the Dutch volume would have had to page through it to discover the plan. Ogilby, on the other hand, provided an elaborate Table of Contents, divided into books, chapters and sections; his table was clearly keyed to the pages, with headings usually only a few folio leaves apart. A chapter number appeared at the top of each page as a further guide. And each chapter and section was clearly set forth in the text and given its own heading.

Though his 'sculptures' may have disappointed subscribers accustomed to his more finished engravings, Ogilby's prose in this volume was both smoother and more interesting than in any other atlas. Perhaps because he had more sources available to him in English, or perhaps because he had talked himself with eyewitnesses of the still new-found continents, he wrote with a freshness and vividness that Africa and Asia could not evoke.

His descriptions of the strange new animals (all from pp. 147-50) are among his most realistic; for example, the raccoon:

A deep Furr'd beast, not much unlike a badger, having a Tail like a Fox, as good Meat as a Lamb. . . . In a Moon-shine night they go to feed on Clams at a low Tide, by the Sea side, where the English hunt them with their Dogs.

The 'musquash' [muskrat] which provided small stones 'sweet as Musk' interested Ogilby, too:

15) *Map of America, Ogilby,* America, *1671*
The Library, Lehigh University, Bethlehem, Penna., USA

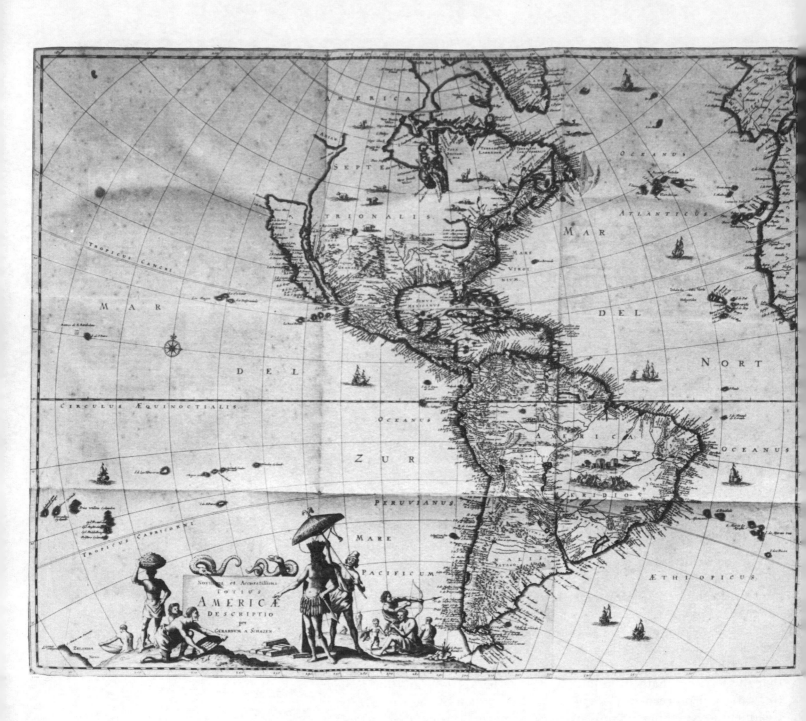

16) *Map of America, Montanus, America, 1671*
- *By permission of the Folger Shakespeare Library, Washington DC, USA*

These Skins are no bigger than a Coney-skin, yet are sold for five Shillings apiece, being sent for Tokens into England; one good Skin will perfume a whole house full of Clothes, if it be right and good.

The 'humbird' was 'one of the wonders of the Countrey, being no bigger than a Hornet, yet hath all the Dimensions of a Bird . . . For Colour, she is as glorious as the Rain-bow.' Sharks, however, though often caught, were 'good for nothing but manuring the land.' Ogilby told his readers also about the many kinds of troublesome flies in New England, especially the 'Musketor': 'Many that are bitten will fall a scratching, whereupon their Faces and Hands swell.'

Ogilby's early pages were concerned, as in *Africa*, with setting the general background of the continents he was describing. He disagreed firmly with those who held that the ancients had known the New World, and held that it was 'an empty Countrey' (p. 16) when the first settlers arrived. He showed a wide acquaintance in his second chapter with the many writers of antiquity who speculated on unknown lands, as well as with the difficulties of Christians in reconciling the existence of a world unknown in Christ's time and thereafter, and so ignored by most theological writers. Ogilby criticized received opinions freely, but then added: 'We must needs confess, that contradiction is not difficult; but it is something of Work, when we have beaten down a well-fortifi'd Opinion, to set up somewhat, in stead thereof' (p. 35). His own view was that a series of 'planters' and 'plantations' had populated America, shortly after Noah's flood, even as the Saxons had invaded the Britons, and the Normans came after both. Throughout the argument, Ogilby followed Montanus closely, as he did through the long story of many early explorers. Even Montanus' section on four English expeditions, on which Ogilby might have been expected to elaborate, followed the Dutch account. He did make one attempt to introduce a contemporary English note, by quoting some lines from 'Our Modern Poet, Mr. Dryden, in his *Indian Emperor*' (p. 15). The passage involved the reporting to Moctezuma (the Aztec Emperor) of the arrival of ships from over the sea, bearing men speaking strange tongues and firing guns. Unfortunately, Ogilby introduced this as occurring in Peru, a slip of which many of his readers were probably happily unaware.[9]

With the beginning of the second major part, the description of North America, however, Ogilby abandoned Montanus for his own better — and more national — sources. In the section on 'New France,' he mentioned that the territory 'hath been long in dispute between Us and the French' (p. 133), and proceeded to give the English version of the case. Ogilby's treatment of New England took twenty-nine pages, as compared with Montanus' one and one-half, and the English accounts, as mentioned above, are rich with realistic detail. Government and religion were discussed at length, with many curious American customs delineated. The 'Laws and Methods of Government' of New England, Ogilby observed, 'are wholly of their own framing' (p. 163). As an Anglican, he enjoyed the differences of religious opinion that had developed among the dissenting churches in that area. He was amused at the spectacle of Dr. Bastwick, 'who spoil'd so much Paper in railing at the Church Government of England, and crying up Liberty of

Conscience,' now sharply criticizing some of the leaders in the new world. In a number of places, Ogilby printed his (or his informants') appreciation of the North American Indian (p. 151: the marginal comment calls these 'Aberginians'):

In a word, take them when the Blood skips in their Veins, when the Flesh is on their Backs, and Marrow in their Bones, when they frolick in their antique Deportments and Indian Postures, they are more amiable to behold (though onely in Adam's Livery) than many a trim Gallant in the newest Mode.

The style in which masculine hair was worn in the new world was of interest to Englishmen moving to the era of great wigs (pp. 151-52):

Their black Hair is natural, yet is brought to a more Jetty colour by Oyling, Dying, and daily dressing; sometimes they wear it very long, hanging down in a loose dishevel'd Womanish manner, otherwise ty'd up hard and short like a Horse Tail, bound close with a Fillet . . . They are not a little Phantastical in this particular; their Boys being not permitted to wear their Hair long till sixteen years of Age . . . The young Men and Soldiers wear their Hair long on the one side, the other being cut short like a Screw; other cuts they have as their Fancy leads them, which would torture the Wits of the most exact Barber to imitate. But though they are thus proud of the Hair of their Head, you cannot wooe them to wear it on their Chins, where it no sooner grows, but it is stubb'd up by the roots . . .

Montanus, of course, had much to say of 'New Netherland,' its discovery, natives, colonization and resources. Only at the end of his account did he acknowledge that it was now 'Nieuw-Jork.' Ogilby, on the other hand, captioned a section (pp. 168-83): 'New Netherland, now call'd New York' [it became English in 1664]. Much of his account followed Montanus, but Ogilby gave the story of the transfer of sovereignty with pride, and went on to discuss the area around Delaware Bay, control of which the English likewise had assumed.

Moving on south, he treated Maryland in 'a new Description,' not found in Montanus, including the names of the incumbent governor and council in 1671. He proceeded thence to Virginia. More space was given in the section to history and documents (including the story of Powhatan, Captain Smith and Pocahantas) than to detail of the countryside and products of England's first settlement in the new world (pp. 192-205). Ogilby did give the estimated number of English inhabitants in Virginia in 1671 as between 30,000 and 40,000; the colonists were well supplied with grain, livestock and fruit, of the last 'whereof they make great quantities of Cyder and Perry' (p. 197). No mercantilist, apparently, Ogilby noted that the Virginians now had enough land, and more, planted in tobacco, and suggested that they would soon 'provide themselves of all Necessaries of Livelyhood' by producing their own commodities instead of importing them. Although black slaves had been in Virginia since 1619, their impact on the colony was still slight, and nowhere does Ogilby mention them in his treatment of English colonies in North America.

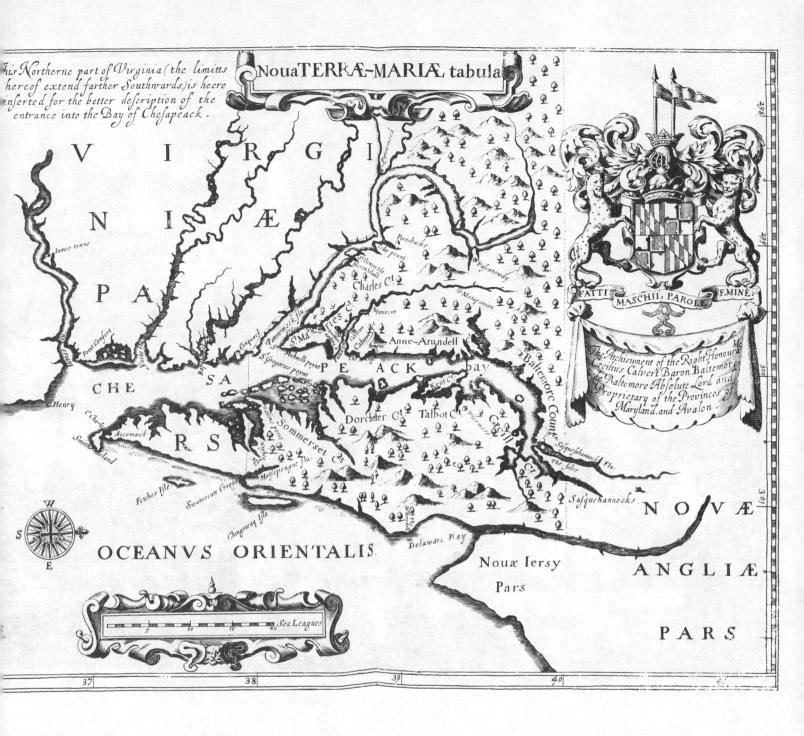

This Northerne part of Virginia (the limitts hereof extend farther Southwards,) is heere inserted for the better description of the entrance into the Bay of Chesapeack.

NouaTERRÆ-MARIÆ tabula

VIRGINIÆ PARS

CHESAPEACK bay

FATTI MASCHII, PAROLE FEMINE

The Atchievment of the Right Honourable Cæcilius Calvert Baron Baltemore de Baltemore Absolute Lord and Proprietary of the Provinces of Maryland, and Avalon

James towne

Point Comfort

C: Henry

C: Charles

Accomack

Smiths Island

Powtomack

Portobacke

Cedar Poynt

Stickienill Isle

Heron Island

Charles Ct.

Passatoway

Matapanian

Patuxent

Anne-Arundell

Potomeck flu.

S.t Ma

S.t Gregories poynt

Michaell poynt

Calvert Ct.

Kent Ct.

Baltemore County

Cecill Ct.

Susquahannock flu.

The Sales

Sasquehannocks

NOVÆ ANGLIÆ PARS

Dorchester Ct.

Talbot Ct.

Wicomeco

Sommerset Ct.

Watkins poynt

Matapongue flu.

Fetches Isle

Swansecutt Creeke

Chingoteag Isle

OCEANVS ORIENTALIS

Delaware Bay

Nouæ Iersy Pars

5   10   15   20   Sea Leagues

W   N   S   E

37   38   39   40

17) *Map of Maryland, Ogilby, America, 1671*
By permission of the Folger Shakespeare Library, Washington DC, USA

18) *Arx Carolina, Ogilby,* America, *1671*
The Library, Lehigh University, Bethlehem, Penna., USA

Again adding more than Montanus, Ogilby included (pp. 205-12) a section on 'Carolina' (of which Lord Ashley, donor of the large map of the Americas, was a Proprietor). So recently had the area been named that Ogilby, to identify it, began with: 'Carolina is that part of Florida which lies between twenty-nine and thirty-six Degrees and thirty Minutes of Northern Latitude.' The section on Carolina is filled with specific detail as to climate, products and inhabitants. The very favourable description of this region may well be attributed to Lord Ashley's consistent propagandizing for colonization and his particular current interest in the Carolinas. The songs of the Indians 'are not harsh or unpleasing, but are something like the Tunes of the Irish,' Ogilby wrote. And again, he praised (though seeing all this through someone else's eyes) the nobility of the 'savage,' while almost denying that that was an appropriate name (p. 209). He asserted that the problems of the French and Spaniards in Carolina were occasioned by their own evil acts, as the good relations prevailing between Indians and truthful Englishmen proved. Never had the Indians in the Carolina region taken advantage of the settlers' needs: 'a sort of fair Dealing we could scarce have promised them amongst civiliz'd, well bred, and religious Inhabitants of any part of Europe.' And he noted further the Indian aversion to salt and to liquor, 'to the latter whereof, their large Growth and constant Health, is perhaps not a little owing' (p. 210).

The names and titles of the Lords Proprietors were given, and their generosity to settlers recorded. Finally, a model plan for a colony, drawn up by 'My Lord Ashley,' was printed at the end of this section. There was even a plate not to be found in Montanus: a double-page view of a fort, headed 'Arx Carolina,' showing considerable shipping, some land transport, and the garrison's guns, pointing out in all directions toward the unknown wilderness that totally surrounded it.

With the treatment of Spanish Florida, Ogilby reverted to following Montanus, using the same prints (though not so many) and often the same marginalia, although occasionally inserting segments of material not in Montanus or changing the order in which the latter treated his areas. There were large sections on Peru and Brazil in South America, and the last page listed the holdings of various European powers in the new world. 'The Spaniards possess the greatest and best part of America,' Ogilby noted; but he began with English holdings, and they made a respectable showing. Of the Northwest Passage, he wrote that 'nothing considerable hath been done in this grand Enterprize, but by the English' (p. 674). As in *Africa*, his listing of double-page maps on the final (unnumbered) page served as an additional index.

A comparison between the map of the Americas (by Gerard a Schagen) as printed by Meurs for the Montanus volume and by Ogilby for his book reveals a number of differences, both substantive and aesthetic. At first glance, both seem the same, except for Ogilby's erasing of Schagen's name and placing his own with 'Cosmographum Regium' over it. Closer inspection reveals, however, a number of changes that show Ogilby had his English readership well in mind. 'Nova Albion' appears in much larger letters in Ogilby's version (at the north of the 'island' of California, which had lost the peninsula status it had had in the earlier seventeenth century). Sir Francis Drake's name is added to California, as well. 'Jamaica,' instead of being hidden among the Caribbean islands, stands out clearly. New England is much better defined, and New York, New Jersey, Maryland, the Carolinas and Virginia are also distinctly shown.

In addition to substantive changes, Ogilby made many others that were pleasing to the eye. Essentially, he removed materials that were too crowded on the original. He lightened the shading of coastal waters, took away numerous (quite genuine) mountain ranges, and lessened the number of cities shown; altogether, he produced a much clearer and pleasanter map to view, while emphasizing English explorations and settlements.

On the other hand, the 'American' figures in the lower left corner were clearly copied by no master or even very competent hand. Change for the sake of change alone occurred in the various ships that were scattered about the map; they have been altered in position, but seemingly without any reason. The cost of this map Ogilby managed to raise from the donor commemorated in the cartouche: Anthony, Lord Ashley, Baron of Wimburn, Chancellor and Sub-Treasurer, later to become the first Earl of Shaftesbury. The then Lord Ashley, an influential minister, was deeply concerned with the success of English 'plantations.' His name as donor of this map may strengthen the assumption that someone put Ogilby in the way of talking with men familiar with the English part of the New World.

A comment on the quality of one portion of Ogilby's *America* occurred in its reprinting in the mid-nineteenth-century. W. Wemyss Anderson, Esq., a highly enthusiastic proponent of Jamaica, reprinted Ogilby's description of Jamaica, adding an introductory chapter and notes. Presumably, he found, almost two centuries later, that Ogilby's account had sufficient authenticity and appeal to be usefully reprinted.[10]

Another folio was produced by Ogilby in 1671, his *Atlas Chinensis* (or *China*), a second volume on China, which was promised in his book on Japan. The title page credited Montanus with collecting the materials, but also stated that the work was 'English'd and Adorn'd with above a hundred several Sculptures, By John Ogilby, Esq.' Thomas Johnson printed this for Ogilby, whose own press was presumably engaged in this year with the production of *America*. As with the earlier volumes on China and Japan, the *Atlas Chinensis,* while handsomely printed, filled with illustrations and embellished with marginalia (chiefly paragraph or subject heads), was neither an easy nor a very meaningful book to read. There was a dedication, again to Charles II; and on the reverse of the dedication were placed directions to the printer for positioning the 'whole-sheet' [double-spread] prints, a fact which gave some guidance to the reader as to location of contents. Missing, however, were such aids as a table of contents or the keying of chapter heads to page numbers. Much of the contents must have been of minimal interest to Englishmen, consisting as they did of the attempts of the Dutch government in Batavia and the Dutch merchants to open trade channels with the xenophobic empire of China. Such items as reprinted letters, suggested treaties and lists of gifts exchanged between the two parties could hardly have been significant to many English readers and might have been placed in an appendix, if they were included simply to swell the size of the volume. As printed in English, the *Atlas Chinensis* was much too unedited to stand with *America*, or even *Africa*, regarding the interest of its contents for Englishmen.

From the frontispiece reprinted by Ogilby, it is clear that *China* was produced in the same year (1671) in which the original volume appeared, and must again have involved a hasty translation and the copying of selected prints — all this while the more original work was being done on *America*. No doubt Morgan by now was experienced enough to handle one volume, presumably the less important *China*, while Ogilby took charge of the other. That may help to explain the absence of personal remarks, of touches of individuality and of quotations from the classics, all of which characterize *China*. The usual irregularity prevailed in the illustrations, with some legends in Dutch, some in English, some in both languages.

After the conclusion of the story of the embassies (p. 364), matters of somewhat more general interest appeared in the volume, although again without obvious organization. The ancient history of the 'Chineses' [a consistent usage] was given, beginning in 2952 B.C. (p. 395), and lists of emperors followed. A number of subjects were treated, set off by headings, such as 'Feasts,' 'Marriages,' 'Funerals' (twenty folio pages on this subject) and 'Government.'[11] Pages and pictures of instruments and acts of torture (pp. 434-37) were included, credit given to the Chinese for gunpowder and printing, and their art critically examined.[12]

Father Nicholas Trigaut and Martin Martinius were cited regularly in another subsection on the description of China, (pp. 459ff.) Long lists of provinces followed, which suffered from difficulties of transliteration as well as of translation, and from the absence of any map or organization of the dozens of names listed. A section on 'Roads and Distances of the Great Cities of China, one from Another' (pp. 543ff.) may have stimulated Ogilby in his planning of *Britannia* to some extent, although the material is relatively simple and not pictorially displayed.

A group of four double-page prints brought authentic art before the readers of the *Atlas Chinensis*. The first print of the group was the most elaborately copied, with a Buddha on a lotus pad, crowned with two circles and bearing the original Sanskrit swastika on his breast. The figure immediately before him was identified in the text as Confucius ('Confut'); more tentatively, Mencius was said to be the square-hatted figure in the centre of the print. The second illustration showed a more static representation of a ceremonial act of worship, with the figures in this, as in the previous illustration, making the Indian [not Chinese] gesture of *namasti*. The chief note of interest in this print lay in the identification of the figure at centre right as the third great Chinese philosopher, Lao-tse. Foliage, costume, the placing of figures, the lack of perspective, the attempt to show delicate brushstrokes in these illustrations: all witnessed to fidelity in the copier of the original, and must have given many Englishmen their first experience of genuine Oriental art, as contrasted with the usual Europeanized faces and costumes, and the customary European stylistic treatment.[13] The text described the figure being reverenced as the goddess

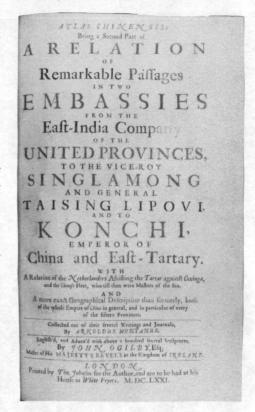

19) *Title page*, Atlas Chinensis, *1671*
The Library, Lehigh University,
Bethlehem, Penna., USA

117

20) *Worship of the Buddha,* Atlas
Chinensis, *1671*
The Beinecke Rare Book and
Manuscript Library
Yale University

'Pussa,' to be identified with the Greek Cybele and the Egyptian Isis.

The *Atlas Chinensis,* over 700 pages long, included writings on ships, roads, rivers, agriculture, plants, animals, birds and a host of other items. Organized by table, by relationship or even alphabetically, the information would have been quickly available (even if its accuracy were questioned). As it stood, however, Ogilby's *China* was a sprawling seventeenth-century volume, much in need of the neat organizational table often to be found helpfully inserted in such volumes by eighteenth-century readers. It is probably chiefly this lack of organization that has kept Ogilby's atlases from being known in later centuries.

Two years later (1673), Ogilby reissued the 1669 *Embassy to China* of Nieuhoff-Adams-Kircher. The title page calls it a second edition, and it was printed by John Macock for the 'Author,' Ogilby. The 1673 volume is on larger folio leaves than that in 1669; there are changes in the placing of illustrations, in punctuation and spelling and in the use of endpieces. On the whole, however, so far as content is concerned the 1673 'edition' is a reprinting of 1669. Often one or the other issue of the *Embassy of China* is to be found bound with the *Atlas Chinensis.*

The *Atlas Chinensis,* like that on Japan, was a 'By' volume. The original

plan for the regions of the world continued, however. In November 1673, Ogilby gave notice that 'Asia, the First Part' was available at his house for 30 shillings (in quires) and at 20 shillings for subscribers.[14] There was destined never to be a second part of Asia, but Ogilby had already in his 'By' volumes covered the eastern part of that continent.

The folio on *Asia* consisted primarily of materials on Persia and on the Indian (Mogul) Empire, with lesser materials on smaller areas in and around those two larger groupings. The title page proclaimed the material as taken from the 'most Authentick Authors' and the work contained maps and illustrations in considerable numbers. Ogilby printed this book himself, with his now customary full title on the title page. The dedication to the King spoke of this as 'This Fifth Volume of His English Atlas,' although it was only the third of the originally announced volumes. It may be that by now Ogilby was considering *China* and *Japan* as additional volumes to *Africa* and *America*. A 'new Map of Asia' (by F. Lamb) appeared in *Asia*, dedicated to the ruling body of the East India Company.

In organization and content, *Asia* was similar to the poorest of Ogilby's atlases. Under 'A General Description' almost any material could be included, sometimes contradictory to what had appeared elsewhere; and the

21) *Worship of the Buddha,* Atlas Chinensis, *1671*
The Beinecke Rare Book and Manuscript Library, Yale University

119

22) *Flying Fish*, Embassy to China, *1673*
The Library, Lehigh University, Bethlehem, Penna., USA

23) *The herb Cha (tea)*, Description of China, *1673*
The Library, Lehigh University, Bethlehem, Penna., USA

unusual, the unbelievable and the unpleasant were inevitably emphasized. Language was examined (e.g., pp. 59, 86, 129-33), the chewing of betel nuts discussed (p. 106), and the fearful practice of *suttee* described (pp. 121-22). The annotations were generally paragraph guides or summaries rather than genuine additions. Sir Thomas Herbert's *Travels*, first published in 1634, were cited (p. 5) for the benefit of English readers, and the nascent power of the East India Company made India of greater English concern, even in 1673, than were China and Japan. In general, however, *Asia* was another 'book of wonders,' although a fifteen-page 'Table' at the end of the volume helped impose some order on the massed tidbits of information in the work. A page of directions on the illustrations gave further assistance in locating materials, providing one had already read the book or knew the material fairly well. On the whole, however, Ogilby's last volume on foreign lands was less orderly than *America* or even *Africa*. He may never have taken pains with his Asian materials or perhaps the subject matter defeated him. Whatever the cause, that continent, despite three volumes and hundreds of pages devoted to it never benefited from a clear or systematic survey of extant materials in print or from first-hand conversation between Ogilby and Far East travellers.

Ogilby used his City contacts to good effect in publicizing his work during these years. By 1670, when he was permanently settled again in London, he began a series of presentations to the Court of Aldermen, after the fashion of his earlier presentations to the Merchant Taylors Company and to the Commons. On 28 July 1670, the Court ordered a payment of £20 'for the present he hath made of the tome of his English Atlas (printed upon imperiall paper) [perhaps the volume of *Africa* which appeared that year] unto this Court.' Another £20 was granted on 18 October 1670 'for the good encouragement of his studies,' when Ogilby presented his *Atlas Japannensis*, and yet another £20 for *Atlas Chinensis* on 2 May 1671.[15] A few months later (14 September 1671), the Chamberlain was ordered to pay John Ogilby, Esquire, £40 'for the rest of his works, namely his Royall Bible [the Bible is already 'his'] in two volumes, Homers *Iliads* and *Odysses*, Virgil, *Aesop* the first and second part and the *Kings Entertainment* now brought into this Court for the Cittyes use.' And by 12 December of that year, when John Ogilby was granted £20 for his *America*, 'a Large Volume in Imperiall paper now presented unto this Court,' he had received from the City Treasury £120 within a year and a half for the presentation of some eleven volumes.[16]

In producing these folio atlases, Ogilby was joining a large number of travel writers in his century, as his practice of using their materials makes clear. He shamelessly pirated authors — Montanus, Nieuhoff, Dapper, Kircher — and their publishers, but then so did most other writers. He knew and quoted some English authors, such as Purchas and Herbert, but he preferred material that was up to date. In seeking consistently to print the latest reports, he found the Dutch incomparably the most prolific producers, and so made the greatest use of them. When nothing more recent was offered, however, he moved to Spanish, Portuguese and other sources, not omitting, in his earlier travel folios, to cite numerous classical writers.

Ogilby's 'Atlas' was essentially a series of travel-description books, despite the presence of maps. His compilations were no more heterogeneous than those from whom he took material. Indeed, in the case of Montanus' *America*, Ogilby followed, in parts of his own *America*, the organization, examples and language of the Dutch volume. He did not, as stated before, use his volumes as the means of political or religious exhortation or even of generalization.[17] Ogilby seems to have sought for recent material, in large (sometimes overwhelming) amounts, and for excellence in its technical presentation. It was in this last area that his most outstanding contribution in printing travel books was made. Imperial-sized folios, fine paper, clear type, large margins, handsome and numerous illustrations, drawn and engraved by the best illustrators he could find: these were characteristic of Ogilby's travel books, as well as of most of his other productions. Although the maps he showed were generally copies from another volume, he could and did improve at times (as in the map of the Americas) on what he found. There was, however, nothing in these maps to indicate the cartographical contribution that he was to make in the publishing of *Britannia*.

Not all in Ogilby's time wanted size and grandeur in their travel books. George Meriton, another successful writer, put the opposite position vividly:[18]

As some stomachs, at the sight of a large Table plentifully furnished, instantly lose the Edge of Hunger, so may thine at the sight of several large Folio's [sic] on this Subject.

His work, he said, was *magnum in parvo* and *Veritas in Omnibus*. He cheerfully noted that he had copied it all, and actually much of his writing on the New World is almost a century old. Nevertheless, his octavo had successes where Ogilby's folios never penetrated. *Magnus in parvo*, whether up-to-date or not, has its own appeal.

Richard Blome was another writer of travel books whose titles and publication dates make him appear a close competitor to Ogilby for the attention of the English public. The differences in size and opulence between his works and Ogilby's, however, were great, and the prospective buyer, looking at the quires of Blome and Ogilby at his bookseller's, could easily see how unlike the bound volumes would be. The rival whose work came closest to that of Ogilby was Moses Pitt, who produced four folios of an *English Atlas* between 1680 and 1683. He followed many of Ogilby's practices, such as setting forth proposals[19] and obtaining patrons. Less successful than Ogilby in dealing with the financial part of his ambitious project, Pitt ended by being imprisoned for debt.

Ogilby's project of covering 'the four regions of the world' he did not entirely complete. Europe was untouched, and the 'British Monarchy' became transformed into a true atlas, the *Britannia*. That atlas, however, covered only England and Wales. It is curious that Ogilby never undertook to write about or illustrate his native land, Scotland. It is more unfortunate still that he wholly ignored Ireland, parts of which (unlike Scotland) he must have known very well indeed, from residences there in the 1630's, the 1640's and the 1660's. Since, however, it was the strange and the wonderful that attracted him and that he gave to his readers in his travel books, it is perhaps not surprising that Ogilby postponed treating more familiar areas until there was no time left for him to do so. His final achievement, *Britannia*, stands in its own category within his work.

VII

Last Ventures: THE BRITANNIA

When he wished to catch a market or pay tribute to a royal patron, Ogilby could have a volume ready for the press in a few months. For the production of one book, however, he spent years of planning and much money. The work changed its form and title under his hands more than once, and he only just finished it before his death. That volume was the *Britannia;* the story of its conception and making is also the story of John Ogilby's last years.

In the late 1660's, after his final return from Ireland, Ogilby resumed the close contacts with the City that he had enjoyed during and just after the Restoration. The double catastrophes of the Plague in 1665 and the Great Fire in 1666 had left London devastated but resilient. In his Dedication of *Africa* to the monarch, Ogilby reflected on the phenomenon of London's rebirth:

*No Work appears more Perspicuous than that Stupendious Miracle! the
Raising from a Confused Heap of Ruines (sooner than some believ'd they
could remove the Rubbish) Your Imperial City, already looking down,
though Private Houses, upon former Publick Structures, hereafter to be
the Business of Foreign Nations to See and Wonder at.*

Ogilby was himself an active part of this 'Stupendious Miracle,' working, along with William Morgan and others, as one of the sworn viewers of the City, under the general direction of Robert Hooke, who became the City Surveyor.[1] This work, commissioned by the Common Council and involving the personal interest of the sovereign, brought Ogilby into direct contact with yet another group of men, many of them Fellows of the Royal Society. In addition to Hooke, such men as Wren, Boyle, Aubrey and Evelyn were active in plans for the rebuilding of London. Former and present boundaries were surveyed, the settlement of property issues was undertaken and, most important of all, there evolved the transformation of burnt-out medieval London into a more spacious and far more healthful metropolis. Certainly, the streets were enlarged, and the Plague failed to reappear significantly after 1666. A lecturer at Gresham College wrote to Wren in 1707:

*I and every Body must observe with great Satisfaction, by means of the
Inlargements of the Streets; of the great Plenty of good Water, convey'd to
all Parts; of the common Sewers, and other like contrivances . . . it is not
only the finest, but the most healthy City in the World.* [2]

Ogilby worked hard at the assignment as 'sworn viewer' — not a light task
for a man in his late sixties and early seventies. Characteristically, he
profited as well from this work and its associations. For instance, a new and
handsome Royal Exchange was erected, with space for shops under the
north and south porticos. It was at a meeting of a subcommittee mulling over
this plan (on 26 March 1670) that Ogilby made a special plea: [3]

*Upon Mr. Ogilby's further request to have a shop at the Royal Exchange
belowe, and shewing how much it concerns him, after his greate pains and
charge in writing and printing a description of 'Affrica,' to have a publiq
place to put the bookes off, the Committee promised that he shall be
accommodated with one of the shops at the east or west end of the
Exchange, upon like terms as others shall take and pay for other shops there.*

At some time during this period, Ogilby moved south across Fleet Street,
from his former dwelling in King's Head Alley off Shoe Lane, and into a
house in Whitefriars. As a 'sworn viewer,' he would have been travelling
constantly about devastated London, watching its rebuilding. Possibly with
the memory of the Fire still clear, he decided to live nearer the river. He is
not listed as living in Whitefriars in 1667, but by 21 April 1669 he had paid
6s.8d. to have a foundation laid out for a new house in Whitefriars Lane. [4]
Three days later, the description of his property was set forth:

*containing upon the front North and South 30 foot whereof the passage is
to be 10 feet and the said Oglebee to have liberty to build over the
passage 20 feet Eastward and the other 20 feet to be 50 feet East and West
in depth.* [5]

Partial records exist for his residence in this location, which was in
Farringdon Ward Without, Whitefriars precinct. Among the assessments
for an eighteen months' tax (Act 25 Chas. II c. 1), Ogilby is listed for five
quarters from May 1673 to June 1674. The next extant assessment for this
precinct is dated 1677, after his death. The records, in which Ogilby is
variously listed as 'Mr.' and 'Esq.', show him to have been one of the heavy
taxpayers in his ward, assessed at 6s.8d. as 'landlord,' presumably a property tax. They show further that he drew his water supply from the New River
Company, to which he paid a 2½d. tax, rather than from the Thames. [6]
Neither in King's Head Court nor in the parish of the Ward of Farringdon
Without is Mrs. Ogilby listed. Nor is William Morgan's name to be found.
In 1677, however, Morgan did live in the same ward as the Ogilbys had
done, and paid a tax ('landlord') assessment there. It was much lower —
2s.6d. — than his grandfather's (6s.8d.) had been, and Morgan's water bill
stood at only 1/3d. [7] So apparently he did not occupy Ogilby's former
home, but a humbler dwelling not too far removed.

A book of assessments for the watch exists for the year after Ogibly's death and gives an idea of those who lived nearby, some of whom he surely, some he probably knew.[8] Lady Davenant, widow of his old friend Sir William, was listed, together with 'Mr Betterton' and others of the Duke's Playhouse in Lincoln's Inn Fields. James Shirley, perhaps a son of Ogilby's now deceased colleague in Ireland, lived in Shoe Lane. Thomas Shadwell, with whose name and writings Ogilby was later to be infelicitously linked, lived in Salisbury Court, adjacent to Whitefriars. And John Dryden was near there, on Fleet Street.

It is from Robert Hooke's *Diary* (which does not begin until March 1672) that most of the evidence comes of Ogilby's involvement with City planning.[9] Hooke knew Wren and Boyle even before becoming Curator of Experiments for the Royal Society, and for a time its Secretary. His rare combination of the scholar's learning and the artisan's craftsmanship made him one of the most valuable members of that society.[10] Throughout 1673, 1674 and 1675, Hooke's association with Ogilby was very close, the two men sometimes meeting weekly or more often, according to the *Diary's* record, while at other times drifting apart for several months.

Hooke, like most of the intelligentsia of Restoration London, was a collector of Ogilby volumes. He bought 'China' [apparently the *Embassy to China*] on 20 March 1673. Seven months later (11 October), he 'received from Ogilby the second part of China [*Atlas Chinensis*] unbound', probably as a gift for his services. On 12 December Ogilby promised to send in Africa and America to Hooke, who was helping regularly with the production of the *Britannia* by now. And on New Year's Day, no doubt as a gift, Hooke noted that *Asia* [not *Africa*] and *America* had arrived. On 22 May of that year 'Ogylby sent 2 voll. of Aesops fables . . . Folded Aesops.' And on 6 January 1676, Hooke purchased for 2s.6d. 'Mr. Ogylbys Roads,' the pocket volume for travellers rather than the library folio.

The strength of the association between Hooke and Ogilby lay in their work on restoring London, however, and not on Ogibly's travel books. Surveyor and sworn viewer gradually found a joint interest in Ogilby's ambitious plans for mapping England, and many of Hooke's recorded notes deal with his help to Ogilby, help in matters of surveying, in new ideas on engraving and in introductions to useful people. In the laborious work of surveying English counties (never completed) and of compiling an atlas of English and Welsh roads (the *Britannia*), Hooke was assuredly a sustaining and innovative force upon the now aging Ogilby.

It is possible from the closely packed pages of Hooke's *Diary* to recreate more details of Ogilby's life in these years (though little of his temperament) than at any other time. The men met most often at Garaway's, a coffee (and tea) house in Exchange or Change Alley in Cornhill. It had become well known also as a location for lotteries, and a lottery of Ogilby's was held there in February 1673.[11] Ogilby may have had a permanent table there, where he was regularly or frequently to be found. At any rate, Hooke certainly met him there constantly in the 1670's, and often Wren and Aubrey were present as well. Sometimes, Ogilby's younger assistants, William Morgan and Gregory King, whom Hooke apparently liked, were in the company. And often there was also Richard Shortgrave, a surveyor and a man clever with his hands, who served as 'Operator' of the Royal Society. Shortgrave became involved in preparing Ogilby's road maps, signing three of them, as King did for two.[12] Another figure employed by Ogilby during these years was William Leybourne, who worked on the large map of London. These men met regularly, sometimes daily, in various combinations, doing much of their work apparently in the congenial and stimulating atmosphere of London coffee houses. Although Garaway's seemed to be Ogilby's special location, he often met Hooke at the Spanish Coffee House, at Joe's, at the Rainbow or one of the many other such harbours of refreshment that London then provided. Once (9 August 1673) Hooke and Ogilby together visited Hollar, who was still working for Ogilby in these years. In the next month (27 September), Hooke and Ogilby met at Gresham College, a place they must often have visited. They went together also to wait upon the Lord Mayor and to the Sessions House (19 January 1673/4). Now and again, a small detail emerges from the dry record of events: 'To Ogylby, Shortgrave and he squabbled' (12 December 1673); 'Met Ogylby at Garways, he slipt away' (11 November 1673). More than once Hooke 'missed Mr. Ogylby,' who presumably sometimes had business to attend to at his printing shop as well as at Garaway's. Once (this was at Joe's in Mitre Court, Fleet Street) Hooke served as 'witness to a bond of his [Ogilby's] and Morgans to Brook, plaisterer, for £50 as he told me' (20 January 1674/5). Although the diarist visited and dined with many others, such as Aubrey and Wren, he did not mention social contacts beyond the coffee-house and business kind with Ogilby. The latter never attained membership in the Royal Society.[13]

If Hooke's acquaintance with Ogilby began, as seems likely, during their work concerning the restoration of London, it reached its strength — even a kind of intensity — over Ogilby's plans for his atlas, *Britannia*. Although Hooke owned many of Ogilby's foreign atlases, it seems improbable that those 'books of wonders' stirred his scientific and technical mind very deeply. But the project and prospect of actually mapping Britain's roads, of getting together maps and accurate descriptive accounts of the counties of England and of some of the large cities — such prospects as these, all of which Ogilby announced at different times, were of great concern to Hooke. He gave his support to a variety of projectors of atlases, now one and now the other, as some projects failed and others rose. None wholly fulfilled Hooke's hopes. For a few years, however, he gave strong support to Ogilby's plans, and he cannot have been wholly dissatisfied with the results.

R. A. Skelton[14] has described the milieu and some of the specifics in map-making when Ogilby entered that phase of his career. It seems reasonable to assume that the elderly publisher might have produced his first vision of a 'Britannia' through his usual methods of subscription and lottery. Had he used outdated but available plates and somewhat updated descriptions — practices common at that time — he might have published the work early in the 1670's and reaped sizeable profits, as he did with the great atlases. He vastly increased his later stature, however, by rejecting that route, probably because of his new contacts with Fellows of the Royal Society, and especially because of Hooke's interest. The costs of the new scientific procedure were very high indeed. Instead of entertaining his readers and occasionally instructing them as he did in the great atlases, Ogilby in the *Britannia* was to set new and long-lived standards of accuracy and utility. He created a different, and far more significant, aspect to the existent taste for maps, which currently showed itself, for example, in the use of such devices on playing cards.[15] Customarily, maps had been regarded for their beauty, their exoticism or, conversely, for their familiarity; antiquity of production regularly took place over accuracy.

It must be counted as a misfortune that Ogilby was in his seventies when he undertook the mapping of Britain. Had he begun ten or even five years earlier, he might have achieved what he hoped for and what he promised. It is possible to glimpse at intervals what he was planning, then what obstacles he faced, and finally the compromises for which he settled. In 1670, Ogilby apparently had in mind a travel book on England, similar, though more detailed, to the volumes he would publish on Africa, America and Asia. He planned at that time to make 'The Description of the British Monarchy,' as he then designated it, the third volume in his 'English Atlas,' to be published after *Africa* and *America*. In an advertisement in the *Mercurius Librarius*, he urged all who had useful information on the subject to supply him with it.[16] Presumably, at this point Ogilby envisaged a historical, geographical, genealogical volume on England and Wales, no doubt lavishly illustrated. (A treatment of Scotland and Ireland was apparently never in his plans.)

A year and a half later, in another advertisement (20 November 1671), Ogilby referred again to this volume. It was now called 'Britannia'; it was still to be the third volume of the Atlas; and it was announced as 'now ready for the Press.' In fact, it was nowhere near that state, as the remainder of the notice made very clear. Ogilby, by royal command, was 'to make a particular Survey of every County,' and this was still to be done. Admittedly, this was to be 'his greatest undertaking,' and he called again for gentlemen in all counties to submit to him pertinent information. Those nobility and gentry who wished special notice of their families and estates were requested to forward such items to the author. Various plans of a similar nature were under way in other quarters, and probably stimulated this unfounded claim of 'Britannia's' readiness. In fact, the notice just prior to Ogilby's dealt with a new map of England, showing highways and roads. In the catalogue for 24 June 1672, Ogilby stated that 'very speedily' he would have ready a sample of one county, available for inspection in various towns; and early the next year, his standing lottery for both the 'Description of Britain' and the 'general Survey of England and Wales' was announced as open at Mr. Garaway's Coffee House. In the Term Catalogue for Michaelmas 1673, Richard Blome was advertising his *Britannia,* which, though much less ambitious than Ogilby's, was nevertheless a threat to it. The same catalogue carried a notice from Ogilby that *his Britannia* was 'now prosecuted with extraordinary vigour; which by reason of the Actual Survey and largeness of the design being a Work of infinite Charge,' subscribers were urged to apply.

Some evidence remains of Ogilby's success in attracting the participation of the nobility and gentry in his projects. As early as 3 March 1671, Ogilby sent receipts to Sir George Fletcher and Sir Daniel Fleming, the latter of Rydal Hall, Westmorland, for their purchase of *America*. The publisher continued his contacts with Fleming, who was to prove a useful, though presumably unpaid, agent, for Ogilby's design of mapping the large cities of England.[17] About a year after the first letter, Ogilby wrote to Fleming again, stating that he had received the material on the residences and coats of arms of Fleming and his friend Fletcher, presumably for insertion into the proposed county history of Westmorland. Perhaps in answer to a query from Fleming, Ogilby added that he was interested only in obtaining information not as yet in print or such as would correct what had been printed in error. Ogilby mentioned also that he was looking for donors of plates (royal whole sheets) of the cities of Carlisle, Berwick and Newcastle, each to cost £20 or possibly 20 marks. 'But whatever it costs, I shall returne them by dedication and inscription with the armes of the donor.'[18]

In other letters, dated from November 1673 to May 1675,[19] Ogilby continued his correspondence with Fleming, discussing the progress of his work and his need for further support. Apparently, Fleming exerted himself on Ogilby's behalf, for he enlisted a neighbour, Sir Richard Graham, who promised to pay for the plan of the city of Carlisle [never executed].[29] It is possible that Fleming interested other patrons also, and it seems certain that in many parts of England there were gentlemen who were involved in Ogilby's plans and ready to contribute to their accomplishment. One of these, was the Earl of Denbigh, who supplied Ogilby with funds as well as with information on his own ancestry and some description of Denbighshire, presumably for another projected county history.[21] Irregular though such sources of income must have been, they were surely valuable as a stimulus for sales and for publicity, particularly in such outlying regions of the kingdom as Westmorland and Denbigh.

Royal patronage was more extensive than such intermittent assistance as described above; Charles II, however, showed his favours in a variety of ways that managed to avoid the outright contribution of cash. One of the most important grants obtained by Ogilby was a royal warrant of 1670, permitting him to import 20,000 reams of royal 'or other sort of paper' without paying customs duty, over a period of five years.[22] Inasmuch as Ogilby was interested in producing only fine and expensive volumes, this royal favour was a decided financial assistance. In the following year, in a notice addressed to J.P.'s and other local officials, 'our Trusty and Wellbeloved John Ogilby, our Cosmographer' was given access to all church books and other public records, and any queries he might make received royal approbation.[23]

Financial difficulties had accumulated by 1672, and Ogilby appealed for futher assistance. The King appointed, on 6 February 1671/2, a committee consisting of the Earls of Bridgewater, Sandwich, Essex and Anglesey and the Lord Holles. They examined the work already completed and the contemplated project in its entirety. They then reported 'after full consideration and debate at severall meetings' on 9 April 1672. Their verdict on the work was favourable, and they urged its support. Charles himself subscribed £500 toward its completion, and later another £500 was subscribed in the name of his Queen. The King suggested that others should aid the project insofar as they could, and a subcommittee of the Earls of Bridgewater and Anglesey and Lord Holles were to view the process from time to time and report to the King on the matter.[24] As a further aid, Ogilby received, on 18 December 1672, a licence for setting up lotteries, to further the sale of his books and increase his income, in England and Wales for a period of six years.[25]

Mingled hope and despair affected Ogilby as he became more deeply involved with the 'Britannia' and found the mapping of roads, counties and cities as well as the general description of England and Wales becoming a monumental task: one worthy of pursuing but requiring more money and energy than he, now in his early seventies, could well supply. His contacts with the men of the Royal Society had been helpful, no doubt; but they had brought (especially Hooke) new standards to his work — standards of measurement, precision and verification that were to absorb unexpected amounts of time and money. The 'Britannia,' whatever its ultimate form, would not be a slapdash reprinting of Gamden or Leland; it would not even follow the techniques of those informed and earnest but pre-scientific recorders. In his last years, Ogilby was dealing with new men making different demands upon him from any he had known before. He dimly perceived that he was engaged in a wholly new endeavour for him; he was proud of his last and greatest work. But he must often have wished for the easier, earlier times when a quickly translated text, beautifully printed and brightened by exotic illustrations, would satisfy his subscribers.

As a sample of his mingled pride and frustration, it is worth quoting at some length an advertisement of about this time.[26] After announcing the completion of a new map of Middlesex, 'Actually Survey'd' and promising that the whole of Great Britain would receive the same treatment, the notice continued, expressing gratitude for

. . . *Special Encouragement from the King's Most Excellent Majesty, and several of the Nobility: And we should be in much greater forwardness, if such Persons as seem willing to be Concern'd, would so seriously consider the Nature of the Work, as to agree in a chearful Unanimity, and not distract and discourage us with their different, if not contradictory Sentiments about it: Some crying, with an unreasonable Impatience, When will it be done? . . . Others, on the contrary, making a Pretense of their Wonder, and that indeed with somewhat more of Reason, that so Ample a Work should have so short a Time, as Two Years prefix'd for the finishing thereof: Which, nevertheless, we should not despair of performing, could we, in stead of Objections and Demurs, meet with that seasonable Support and Encouragement which is absolutely necessary for the Promoting and Expediting of so Useful and Grand a Design.*

As an inducement for additional subscribers, Ogilby invited those interested to visit his house in Whitefriars to see what had already been done (spread about, no doubt, in the front room), and to view also the work in progress, with Gregory King and Richard Shortgrave, among others, probably to be found engraving in some of the rooms to the rear. It need not be doubted that inducements for lotteries would also be at hand, and that all of Ogilby's books would be available, with a variety of bindings, special illustrations and the opportunity for a personal dedicatory page open to a patron willing so to immortalize himself.

Although it is unclear at just what point Ogilby became H.M. Cosmographer, he was so referred to in a licence for a lottery granted in January 1673, and probably obtained that honorific and useful title sometime in 1671.[27] The licence, procured by Coventry, was good for the period of six years. In the Bodleian, MS. Aubrey 4, fol. 220, there is a royal warrant of 24 August 1671 referring to John Ogilby as Royal Cosmographer.[28] The *Proposals* for this lottery were elaborately set forth. Ogilby represented his volumes at high prices in this prospectus.[29]

Money — in increasingly large sums — was to become the great obsession of Ogilby's last years. It was natural that Ogilby should look to the Common Council of London and to the Court of Aldermen for support of his venture. The Aldermen's interest, of course, centred on the full treatment of London that Ogilby proposed. On 20 February 1672, the publisher asked and the Court ordered that no one should interrupt or harm his proposed work by attempting to publish the same project.[30] It seems probable that two drafts of a petition (on two sides of the same sheet) date from about this time (1671 or 1672).[31] The petition is headed 'The humble Address of John Ogilby Esq., Citizen and Merchant Taylor of London, his M^aties Cosmographer.' It is addressed to the Aldermen and mentions the encouragement they have already offered the petitioner, as well as the support of the king and many of the nobility. Some progress has been made, and specimens of work already done were apparently to be submitted with the petition. 'But a work of this nature far exceeding his Private Ability,' Ogilby requested from the Court a subscription that would be a 'a Royal Example to the Rest of the Cities of England,' in the hope that *Britannia* would prove 'a lasting Monument to succeeding ages.'

In the summer of 1673, Ogilby presented this or another of his petitions calculated, as usual, to capture the attention and aid of those to whom it was submitted. He told the Court that 'he intends to be very perticular and accurate in the description and illustration of the severall parts and government of this Citty and therein hath already made some good progresse.' On 3 June 1673, he was granted £100, with the promise of more when he should have completed his work. Then, faced perhaps with a steady flow of such petitions, the Court decided to appoint a committee to examine Ogilby's work, to report its progress, and to advise on the continuance of support. On 19 June 1673, in a long entry concerned with the proposed *Britannia,* the Court of Aldermen granted a licence to proceed, subscribed £200 for support of the work, and encouraged companies and corporations to do the same. It also set up the aforesaid committee to examine Ogilby's progress, consisting, among others, of Sir Robert Vyner, Sir Thomas Player and Robert Hooke.[32]

On 10 February 1674, the Committee reported to the Court that *Britannia* 'will be a worke of great paines & Art and of very great benefitt & use to this Citty, & that the said Mr. Ogilby hath made very good progress therein.' They recommended, and the Court advanced, another £100 to the publisher. Six months later (19 July 1674), the Chamberlain was instructed to authorize City officials and employees to draw up memorials concerning the history of the City for Ogilby's work.[33] During these years, the Court of Aldermen continued to show interest in other of Ogilby's volumes, by paying him substantial sums for the presentation of various of his works. [34] Throughout 1673, 1674 and early 1675, Robert Hooke helped steadily to raise funds for this last great work of Ogilby's. When Ogilby showed Hooke some of the early 'sheets' for the volume, Hooke 'wrote him a report to the court of Aldermen' (9 January 1674). The scientist accompanied Ogilby to the Lord Mayor's residence and to the Sessions House ten days later. Still another ten days after that, they went together to the Guildhall, 'about map of London.' In the next month Hooke recorded that he 'wrote his [Ogilby's] address to Justices at Hickes Hall' (13 February 1674). In the following month, 4 March, at the Spanish Coffee House, Hooke 'Writ addresse to Merchant Taylors.' On 19 March, Hooke 'Drew the uses of London map,' presumably for submission to various patrons. He was, as stated above, at Ogilby's house/shop about the 'suit' on several occasions, once specifically on 28 March. On 23 May 1674, again at the Spanish Coffee House with Ogilby, Hooke 'corrected two addresses.' On 30 June, Hooke 'Wrot his [Ogilby's] addresse for records of City.' Presumably, Hooke was lending his knowledge and authority to Ogilby's varied presentations for which funds had been requested from various City bodies. Hooke added technical advice, too, on how to make letters for headings of the strip maps and on how to show ascending and descending ground. Ogilby rejected, however, the use of the more advanced 'waywiser' that Hooke recommended (adapted perhaps from a study of French map-making); he used instead the two men walking with the measuring wheel and the surveyor directing them on horseback, as shown on the title page of *Britannia*. By early 1675, however, Hooke's interest in Ogilby's project was cooling. One of his last references came on 9 February 1675: 'Ogylby and [Gregory] King shewd designe of Epitomising the sheets to serve for universal and particular mapps which I directed him how to doe in plates and to fold.'

Thereafter, few references to Ogilby occur, as Hooke shifted his interest in map- and road-making to other projectors, notably to Moses Pitt and Robert Plot. Both seemed for a time more likely to create the kind of scientific project that Hooke desired rather than Ogilby's slowly emerging *Britannia*. In the end, however, neither Plot nor Pitt contributed anything outstanding. Hooke's assistance to Ogilby meanwhile had been steady and informed — perhaps invaluable. Even though withdrawn at the end, it must be counted one of the substantial factors in the production of the *Britannia*.

Royal help had been promised as well. Ogilby, in the *Proposals* mentioned previously, had noted the King's encouragement to subscribers, 'His Majesty leading the Way by a Royal and Munificent Subscription' (£500 for himself and another £500 for his consort, Queen Catherine of Braganza). Sums of such magnitude were precisely what Ogilby most

24) *Title page*, Britannia, *1675*
By permission of the Folger
Shakespeare Library,
Washington DC, USA

needed. Unfortunately for him, Charles's patronage, though graciously worded toward artists and scientists, was directed financially into quite other areas. On 20 April 1673, a request of Ogilby's to import special paper for his *Britannia* was granted.[35] Within the warrant, however, was included the statement that the customs duty on such paper would amount to £1,000. This duty was waived, as being a substitute for the contribution of the King and Queen to such a worthy project. And so no cash actually passed from King to subject.

If royal patronage could not be commanded in pounds and shillings, there was still royal good will, and it could be counted on in other ways. In February 1674, Ogilby was granted a new title, or rather an addition to his earlier one. He became 'His Majesty's Cosmographer and Geographick Printer,' with a salary of 20 marks [£13.6s.8d.] per annum. Included in the grant was the right to have his own printing house, for the printing of his own works, a privilege that he expanded, at least to some degree.[36]

The new title, proudly borne, was certainly a useful appendage to Ogilby, whose precise social status is never very clear in Restoration England. In the grant, Charles spoke of 'Reposing especiall Trust and confidence in the fidelity, circumspection and ability of my wellbeloved Subject and deponant John Ogilby Esq.' Ogilby remained 'Mr.' or 'Gent.' to a number of people, however. And even the elaborate title could not avail him against the continuing and unexpected costs of this last and new kind of endeavour. A licence of June 1674, authorizing importation of 10,000 reams of paper, notes that '*Britannia* . . . will require greater charge than he could foresee, being forced to new model the whole Design by reason of the Errors he hath found in several Maps and Charts he had occasion to peruse in relation to that Work.'[37] Four months later, in October, a warrant to import 12,000 reams of paper, custom free, was issued to Ogilby.[38] Though customs might be remitted, the cost of such amounts of paper was in itself a formidable expense.

Less expensive, but no doubt far more time consuming and trying for Ogilby was the selection and supervision of those doing the actual surveying for the *Britannia* and related projects. Ogilby himself was growing increasingly lame in his late years, and was still, as Hooke's 'Journal' attests, involved in the 1670's with the continuing reconstruction of London. It seems doubtful that he himself actually did any surveying for the *Britannia*, but he certainly supervised a number of people working throughout the country. Furthermore, he obviously checked the work sent or brought in. A record of the activities of two of his surveyors — John Aubrey and Gregory King — remains, written by the men themselves, although some years after the event.

Aubrey, of a higher station than Ogilby and with many friends, had lost his fortune in later life; he was persuaded, through both financial and personal considerations, therefore, to help in Ogilby's project. 'Dr. [later Sir Christopher] Wren, my deare Freinde,' Aubrey wrote to Anthony à Wood, had devised an occupation for him.[39]

*'Tis this — Mr. Ogilby is writing the history of all England: the map is
mending already. Now the Doctor told me that if that were all, it would
be no very great matter. He was pleased to tell him [presumably Ogilby]
that he would not meet with a fitter man for that turne then J.A. Now it's
true that it suits well enough with my Genius; but he is a cunning Scott,
and I must deale warily with him, with the advice of my friends. It will be
in February next before I begin, and then between that and November
followeing I must curry all over England and Wales . . . The King will
give me protection and letters to make any inquisition, or etc . . .*

Certain of Aubrey's facts were wrong; it was not a *history* of England that
Ogilby was planning. And Aubrey was not to be the sole worker on the
project, as his 'currying all over England and Wales' indicates that he
expected. Wren's actions as intermediary say something for his relations
with both men. And Ogilby's own reputation, at 72, as still 'a cunning Scot'
and one who must be negotiated with cautiously, is likewise revealed in the
letter.

In fact, it was only the county of Surrey with which Aubrey was delegated
to deal. His authorization, signed by Ogilby, was dated 2 May 1673, and he
actually perambulated the county from July to October of that year. At
that point Ogilby terminated his arrangements with Aubrey, saying he
would use 'what scraps he can get out of bookes or by hear say.' It was
probably lack of funds that brought about this decision, and, although
Aubrey left an unfinished manuscript on Surrey, it was not printed until
much later, long after Ogilby's death.[40]

Aubrey took with him on these journeys through Surrey a questionnaire
drawn up in 1672 by a number of people — Hooke, Aubrey, Wren, Ogilby
and Gregory King among them. These queries, two sets of which survive,
show the increasing interest in matters technological, scientific and
anthropological. Questions on the use of land, on antiquities, customs,
manners, tides and a variety of other items show that these queries were
designed to produce a 'natural history' of the sort to be found more
frequently in the following century.[41]

Gregory King also set down his recollections of working for and with
Ogilby in the 1670's (see Chapter V). He went out into the countryside,
measuring roads, and was also active in the printing shop, engraving maps
of the counties of Middlesex and Kent. He collaborated, he said, with
Robert Felgate in surveying Essex. Speaking in the third person, as was his
custom in the 'Autobiography,' King noted that 'in the middle of Winter
1672 in very severe cold weather they [he and Felgate] took the
Ichnography of Ipswich in Suffolk and Maldon in Essex, which were
afterwards very curiously finished and sent to those two places.'[42]

King claimed a considerable role in the whole range of map-making
activities under Ogilby's general supervision. He extended the scale of the
map of London, originally drawn by William Leybourne, drawing some of
the plates and supervising the rest. In the spring of 1674, he undertook the
survey of Westminster on the same scale as London, and, with Felgate's
assistance, did that job in twelve months. He made digests of historical
notes (presumably after perambulations on the spot, such as Aubrey's, had

25) *Aubrey's Authorization as Surveyor, MS, Aubrey 4, fol. 22lr Bodleian Library, Oxford*

To all and singular to whom these Presents shall come, I John Ogilby Esqr His Maties Cosmographer send Greeting. Know ye that by Virtue of his Maties Warrant under his Sign Manual dated the 24th of August ao Dni 1671 Authorizing Me to proceed in the Actual Survey of his Maties Kingdom of England and Dominion of Wales, I have constituted, ordaind and made, and by these presents do constitute ordain and make John Aubrey Esqr my lawful Deputy for the County of Surrey and Parts adjacent. Willing and Requiring in his Maties name, All Justices of the Peace, Mayors, Bayliffs, Shiriffs, Parsons, Vicars, Church-wardens, High Constables Constables, Headborows, and all other his Majesties Officers, Ministers and Subjects whatsoever to be aiding and assisting to my said Deputy or his Agents in the said Actual Survey; and upon his reasonable request to admit him free Access to all Publick Registers or other Books wherby the Geographical and Historical Description of His Maties said Kingdom of England & Dominion of Wales may be any ways promoted or Ascertaind. Given under my hand and Seal, the 2d day of May ao 1673. ~~~~~~

John Ogilby

proved too expensive), did some engraving of strip-map plates and oversaw the drawing of others. Furthermore, he set up 'a lesser Lottery' at Bristol in 1673 and managed it successfully. With all allowances for King's enthusiasm for his own abilities and achievements, he seems to have been an efficient and reliable worker. Certainly, Hooke preferred him to Morgan, Ogilby's long-time assistant.

The kind of field work that King, Felgate, Aubrey and others acutally did can perhaps be visualized more clearly from a rough draft of such a survey that is still extant in the British Library.[43] The drawings are in a variety of hands, some more competent or more artistic than others. There are signs of haste and omission, such as one would expect in on-the-spot work. There are comments in other hands on errors made ('This Survey is Extreamly Erronious,' fol. 141), and corrections appear. The trick that Hooke had specifically suggested, and that Ogilby used in the *Britannia*, appears in these drawings, that of showing hills or mountains sloping upward as the road ascends and down again as it descends. Ogibly's three forms of calculating distance are used also in this survey book: the horizontal distance (apparently calculated from already existing maps); the statutory (the newly calculated) and the customary mile (longer, invariably, though not in any precise fashion) than the new waywiser's more accurate compilation.

Pages of calculation appear on these sheets — the work of a surveyor in the field, apparently, together with lists of distances, the depiction of open and enclosed fields, manors, castles, churches, windmills, coal pits and a toll booth. There is also a reminder of how remote Yorkshire was in the seventeenth century and later, in the description of 'No man's moor.' Some of these sheets have drawings in a very rough state; others are quite polished. A number, as indicated above, show later changes and corrections. There are blank folios mixed in, as 'Mr. Brown' presumably did not finish his survey. For whatever volume this record was compiled, it seems to give a brief glimpse of the surveyor at work on the roads of England, with measurement and calculation his primary concern, but concentrating, as a close second, on his task of describing the terrain surrounding the roads, including both natural and man-made features.

In the years before the great volume of *Britannia* finally appeared, 1675, some of the by-products of the road-mapping were printed. In 1672-73, there were county maps of Kent, engraved by Francis Lamb, at one-third inch to a mile, and of Middlesex, engraved by Walter Binneman, at two-thirds inch to a mile.[44] The map of Kent, suitably dedicated to the Archbishop of Canterbury, stated that it was a 'new Map . . . actually Survey'd and the Roads Deliniated.' Very detailed, it showed the hundreds of Kent and various towns, houses and other features, all keyed to an explanatory table. The scale in English miles was given at the bottom.[45] The map of Essex by King and Felgate was not engraved until 1678, after Ogilby's death.[46] Aubrey's survey of Surrey was apparently never completed, and mapping of the other counties of England was presumably not even begun. Although a map of Ipswich was made in 1674, it was not printed until 1698, when a local man, Thomas Steward, undertook it.[47]

The plan to map the city of Carlisle apparently never advanced very far.

Several months before *Britannia* appeared, Ogilby wrote his last will, dated 27 February 1675. He designated himself as esquire and stated his residence as being within the parish of St. Dunstan in the West. His entire estate was left to 'my deare wife Christian Ogilby and to William Morgan, her grandchild,' both of whom were also named executors.[48] The most-quoted portion of the will deals with his commission to Morgan to 'carry on my undertaking of the King's Brittania [sic].' Mistress Ogilby was to be maintained according to her proper condition, and Morgan was especially charged with looking after her. Four men, presumably the closest of Ogilby's friends, were named as 'overseers,' the first being 'my very Good Freind Sir Samuel Clarke' (presumably one of Ogilby's City acquaintances). The others named were Thomas Stanley the elder, with whose son Ogilby was associated in the patent for the theatre in Ireland; Edward Sherburn (later knighted), who had been in the household of Ralph, Lord Hopton in the 1640's, and whose associations with Ogilby probably went back through the decades; and William Ford.

Six months after making his will, Ogilby saw his last great dream take realistic shape with the publication of the *Britannia*. The large folio, with strip maps of all the major and some of the secondary roads in England, together with brief descriptions of the chief cities, was printed in September 1675 and perhaps presented in person to the King and Queen, as a later representation indicated. In its comprehensiveness, its incorporation of new devices of computation and delineation, and in its opulence of paper, design and decoration, it immediately set a new standard for map-making in England. Far different from Ogilby's atlases of foreign continents with their fanciful stories and often bizarre pictures, this volume was an attempt at a scientific study not only of the roads but also of the terrain and habitations on either side of the roads. As such, it had genuine appeal to the growing body of men who appreciated exact and verifiable factual information. Furthermore, in a country whose gentry still had strong attachments to the county of their birth, the detail with which various localities were shown was appealing, and reinforced the growing antiquarianism and appreciation of local history. Finally, for the traveller, an often unlucky but far from unfamiliar figure of the seventeenth century, Ogilby's *Britannia* had much utility: it gave him precise distances, locations of towns, and the best prospect of comprehending what his journey involved. Handsome though the volume was in its entirety, many owners did not hesitate to cut out strip maps of their local areas or of the places to which they were journeying, and presumably carried these strips with them. A number of such loose strips came to rest in various collections. Others no doubt were lost or destroyed after their immediate use was fulfilled.

A work of such precision and utility constituted, of course, an irresistible object of piracy to the map-makers of later Stuart London. Ogilby included an 'Advertisement' in at least one copy of *Britannia* that complained of this and took steps to counter it.[49]

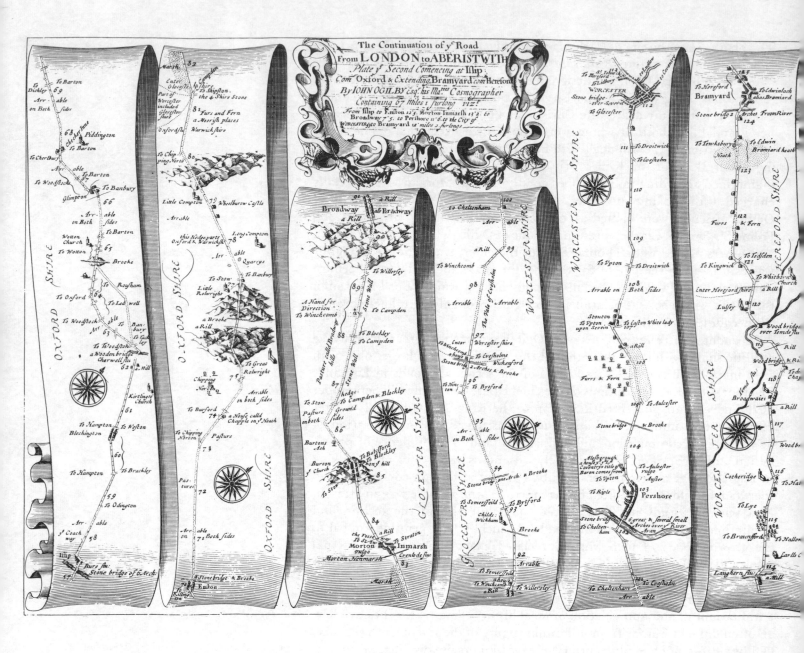

26) *Strip Map*, Britannia, 1675
By permission of the Folger Shakespeare Library, Washington DC, USA

Mr. Ogilby finding certain Tables Taken out of his Britannia, Publish'd with Mr. Speed's Maps, under the Title of The Principal Roads and their Branches, &c. Hath Publish'd his own Tables of all the Roads, with the Computed and Measur'd Distance betwixt every Town, and the Distinction of Market and Post-Towns, the Price 1s.

For the same sum there was available a new large-scale sheet of all the roads of England. And a Book of Roads, called *Itinerarium Angliae*, which showed the roads without the commentary, was issued at the cost of 40s. Included in these volumes were careful instructions on how to use the newly computed and delineated maps, and often tables of distances between cities were added as well.

Although in his will, Ogilby had claimed to be in sound health, his charge in that document to Morgan to complete the *Britannia* showed an awareness of failing health. Because of 'his age and growing infirmitys,' he petitioned his monarch for a reissue of his patent as Royal Cosmographer and Geographic Printer, this time the title to be held jointly with William Morgan. Ogilby surrendered the original patent, and a new and lengthy document, rehearsing the privileges of the earlier patent, was duly issued, granting the same annual fee, a renewed licence for a printing press and the copyright of all Ogilby's own works. Morgan's qualifications were set forth in this patent, as Ogilby's 'kinsman, Who is actually concerned with him in the sayd Worke and by his long experience in performance of that kind is (as Wee are credibly informed) fitly qualified for the management in the said offices and premisses.'[50]

The new patent assured Ogilby of continuity of his policies in the continued production of *Britannia* and the printing of various by-products. He remained distressed by the plagiarism of his efforts, however. An undated copy, without superscription or signature, stated that Ogilby was 'not to be hindered or molested in his work' and charged that no one else was to attempt 'the same design.' In fact, this document prohibited all others from making a survey or description of the City of London, a proscription certainly not followed.[51] On 6 January 1675/6, Ogilby signed in a firm hand a letter written for him, mentioning that he had been 'Long Lame,' and complaining of the pirating of some of his tables by the printers Bassett and Chiswell 'who Have Rob'd my Book.' He asked, and presumably received, leave to print a warning advertisement to that effect.[52] Six months later, Ogilby petitioned his old patron, the Duke of Ormonde, now Chancellor of the University of Oxford, for permission to run a lottery of his books at Oxford, a petition that was, as might be expected, granted, on 21 June 1676.[53] The summer of 1676, however, was the last in Ogilby's stressful life. He died ('gave way to fate,' in Anthony à Wood's often-quoted phrase) on 4 September 1676 and was buried next day in the vault at St. Bride's, one of Wren's new churches, which was not yet wholly completed.[54] Although St. Bride's was near Ogilby's last house in Whitefriars, he was, according to his will, of the parish of St. Dunstan's in the West. Nevertheless, St. Bride's, the Printers Church, was eminently suitable as a place of interment for one who had made his reputation and

139

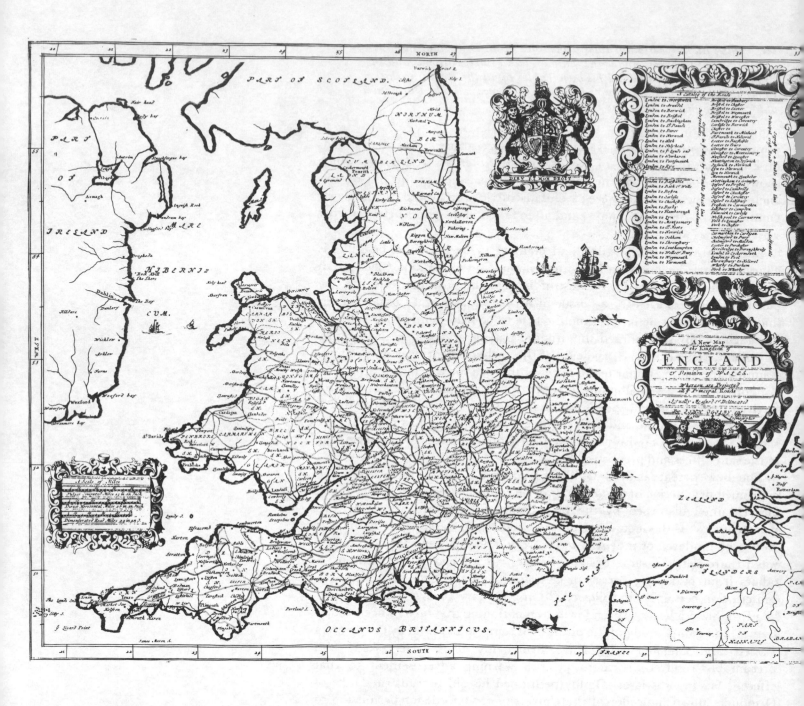

27) *Map of England*, Britannia, 1675
By permission of the Folger Shakespeare Library, Washington DC, USA

much of his livelihood from printing. The bombing of 1940 has eradicated all remains of his tomb.

The death of Ogilby's wife occurred in the year after his own, although no record of her will appears. It is from Aubrey that most of the information on Mrs. Ogilby is drawn, the same Aubrey whose notes on the Ogilbys contain an enticing combination of the probably correct, the provably wrong and the uncertain or unprovable. Aubrey's comments on Mrs. Ogilby place her as a native of Wiltshire (which is possible), never mention her marriage to Hunsdon, and identify William Morgan as an Ogilby grandson (incorrect), descended from an only daughter of the Ogilbys (any such daughter was almost certainly impossible). Mrs. Ogilby stirred Aubrey's interest for a particular reason. He recorded that she died in London three or four days before Christmas in 1677,[55] aged about 112. That number was later crossed out and in another place her age at death was given as near 90.[56] If Mrs. Ogilby indeed died at or near 90, it would mean that she was a decade or so older than her husband. It seems certain that she bore him no child.

One more important offshoot of the work on *Britannia* appeared, under Ogilby's name but after his death, as the legend composed by Morgan made clear. This was the great map of the newly reconstructed City of London. It was greatly admired and often cited; a copy dated 1676 survives, mounted and hung at the Guildhall.[57]

Almost of its own momentum Ogilby's work continued after his death, chiefly through the agency of his heir William Morgan, and through Morgan's use of familiar and previously proved methods of money-raising. In May of 1678, Morgan obtained a licence to import royal-sized folios for the continued printing of the *Britannia*.[58] He kept alive Ogilby's contacts with the Court of Aldermen, and in an order of 26 October 1676 was granted £100, on condition that each member of the Court receive a map of the City, and that individual ward maps be completed as well. The grant noted that Ogilby had 'by Encouragement from this Court in the Yeare 1673' undertaken the survey and description of the City.[59] Shortly thereafter, in April 1677, Morgan petitioned the Aldermen for further funds, and a committee was set up to investigate his request.[60] In September 1680 the committee reported favourably, and granted Morgan another £50, together with the profits from the grants to three new freemen of the City.[61] This was to encourage production of the 1681/2 map of London, Westminster and Southwark, the last ambitious venture to grow from the Ogilby-Morgan cooperation.

No doubt as a result of pressure from his new Cosmographer Royal and Master of the Revels in Ireland (to both of which positions Morgan had succeeded), Charles II, on 15 February 1681/2, recommended to the Vice Chancellors of the universities of Oxford and Cambridge that they procure copies of the new great map of London and place them in public rooms 'as usefull Ornaments.' The King himself intended to do this in his palaces and great offices and had, to that end, taken (whether by purchase or gift is left unsaid) 'a good Quantity of the said Maps.'[62]

28) *Advertisements*, Pocket Book of
Roads, *1679*
*By permission of the Folger
Shakespeare Library, Washington DC,
USA*

The decorative aspects of the map, in which Ogilby was likely to have had considerable influence, were striking indeed. At the upper left stood the Holbein Gate ('The King's Gate at Whitehall'). Next to it was the aforementioned picture of a kneeling Ogilby presenting a book of subscribers (to *Britannia*) to Charles II, standing with his consort, before the throne bearing the royal arms. Various figures in the background presumably represented courtiers, including James and Mary, Duke and Duchess of York, who were mentioned with the king and queen in the dedication. Morgan signed his name and gave his title as 'His Majesties Cosmographer,' while paying tribute to Ogilby who began 'the Actual Survey of England.' Below the gate appeared a kind of pear tree, with numberous noble and gentle names inscribed on individual pears (three of which remained blank). Other important names, often accompanied by the offices they bore, also appeared in the left portion of the map. A cartouche at the top, signed by Morgan, gave a second dedication to the monarch, again in Morgan's name.

Expenses already incurred and those continuing in the production of *Britannia*, however, were considerable, and Morgan pressed on with all the resources his relative had devised. In Hilary Term of 1676/7, Morgan advertised a lottery of all of Ogilby's works, with the lots to go at 20s. apiece. He noted in a broadsheet that the books would advance in price 'as hath done the Price of the Bible, which being sold by Mr. Ogilby for Thirty Shillings, is now rais'd to Five Pounds Ten Shillings; for that none of these Books will ever be Printed again.' Details of the values of prizes, the conditions, and the hours of the drawings were set forth at length, and William Morgan signed as 'Undertaker, at his House near the George Tavern in White Fryers.'[63]

Morgan received a bounty of £200 from the King, presumably in June or July of 1682.[64] In the same year (15 February 1681/2) Morgan obtained a copyright for the printing of his new maps for fourteen years. This copyright repeats the encouragement to officials to buy and hang these maps as mentioned above.[65]

Advertisements continued to appear in the term catalogues through the 1670's and 1680's, chiefly, but not exclusively, concerning *Britannia* and its offshoots. Around the time of Morgan's death (1690), the copyright of many of Ogilby's works passed from Morgan to other publishers and a variety of volumes using Ogilby's road calculations appeared. Ogilby's *Virgil* was still being advertised in 1711,[66] and the *Pocket Book of Roads* (of Ogilby and Morgan) was advertised as late as 1738, in an edition of the *Intelligencer or Merchants Assistant*.[67]

The publication and republication of Ogilby's work therefore continued for a number of years after his death, with the *Britannia* and its various connected elements receiving the chief attention, but with other volumes of his writings, chiefly classical translations, reappearing at intervals as well. In addition, of course, as various listings attest, the works already in existence remained in libraries, often read and generally cherished, for their opulence and cost, if for nothing else. At his death and for the next ten to twenty years, Ogilby's fame was considerable. Thereafter it rapidly faded. The reasons why remain to be considered.

THE
Traveller's Guide: D. *godfrey.*
OR, A MOST
EXACT DESCRIPTION
OF THE
ROADS
OF
ENGLAND.
BEING
Mr. *OGILBY's*
ACTUAL SURVEY,
And Mensuration by the Wheel,
OF THE
Great ROADS from LONDON
To all the Considerable
Cities and Towns in *England* and *Wales,*
TOGETHER
With the Cross-Roads from one City or
Eminent Town to another.

Wherein is shewn the Distance from Place to Place, and
plain Directions given to find the Way, by setting down every Town, Village, River, Brook, Bridge, Common, Forest, Wood, Copse, Heath, Moor, &c. that
occur in Passing the Roads.

And for the better Illustration thereof, there are added
TABLES, wherein the Names of the Places with their Distances
are set down in a Column, in so plain a manner, that a meer Stranger
may Travel all over *England* without any other Guide.

LONDON, Printed by *T. Ilive* for *Abel Swall,* and Sold by *Tim. Child* at the *White-
Hart,* and *R. Knaplock* at the *Angel* and *Crown* in St. *Paul's* Church-Yard, 1699.

BRITANNIA DEPICTA
OR
OGILBY Improv'd,
Being a Correct Coppy of Mr. OGILBY's
ACTUAL SURVEY of all ye Direct & Principal Cross
ROADS in *ENGLAND* and *WALES:*
Wherein are exactly Delineated & Engraven, All ye
CITIES, TOWNS, VILLAGES, CHURCHES, SEATS &
scituate on or near the ROADS, with their respecive
Distances in MEASURED and COMPUTED MILES.
And to render this WORK universally Usefull & agreeable, [beyond
any of it's kind] are added in a clear & most Compendious Method
1. A full & particular Description & Account of all the CITIES
BOROUGH-TOWNS, TOWNS-CORPORATE &c. their ARMS,
Antiquity, Charters, Privileges, Trade, Rarities, & with
suitable Remarks on all places of Note drawn from the
best HISTORIANS and ANTIQUARIES ——
By INo. OWEN of the MIDD. TEMPLE Gent.
2. The ARMS of the PEERS of this REALM who derive
their Titles from places lying on, or near the ROADS
3. The ARMS of all ye BISHOPRICKS & DEANARIES, their foun
-dation, Extent, Yearly-Value, Number of Parishes &
4. The ARMS, & a succinct Account of both UNIVERSITIES
& their respecive COLLEGES, their foundations Fellowships &
Lastly Particular & Correct MAPS of all ye Counties of SOUTH BRITAIN; with a
Summary description of each County, its Circumference, Number of Acres, Boro & Market
Towns & Parishes, Air, Soil, Comodities, Manufactures, & what each Pays in ye 4th Aide
The Whole for its Compendious Variety & Exactness, preferable to all other Books of
Roads hitherto Published or Proposed; And calculated not only for the direction of
the Traveller [as they are] but the general use of the Gentleman and Tradesman
By EMAN: BOWEN Engraver
LONDON Printed for & sold by Tho: Bowles Print & Map seller next ye ChapterHouse
in St Pauls Church Yard & Em Bowen next ye King of Spain in St Katherines 1720

---

29) *Title page,* Traveller's Guide,
1699
*By permission of the Folger
Shakespeare Library,
Washington DC, USA*

30) *Title page* Britannia Depicta, *1720*
*By permission of the Folger Shakespeare
Library, Washington DC, USA*

VIII

Contemporary Admiration & Posterity's Scorn

Public esteem was slow in coming to Ogilby, but, from the early 1660's onwards his name and work became increasingly prominent. The continuing success of his translations and of the *Entertainment,* as well as the consistent widespread support of his lengthy endeavours regarding the *Britannia,* constitutes the most reliable testimony to the esteem in which Ogilby was held in the 1660's and 1670's. This testimony comprised not only the view of the man but also some critical estimate of his works. Toward the end of his life, then, and for a number of years after his death, praise of Ogilby as a contributor to seventeenth-century taste was widespread.

If indeed Ogilby suited the taste of his times and in some ways influenced it, a brief discussion of what that 'taste' constituted is in order. It seems valid to suggest that, for a seventeenth-century Englishman, taste means a combination of Christian and classical virtues. In a literary sense, Ben Jonson had contributed much to the educated Englishman's idea of what constituted style. In the broader sense, the nation felt the shift in 'taste' from the bawdiness in life and language under James I to the refined and cultivated atmosphere under Charles I. The confused years of the Civil Wars drove 'taste' from men's thinking; but the rule of the saints in the 1650's consolidated most of the upper and lower classes into a concentrated dislike of repression of the old ways of living. By the time of the Restoration, 'taste,' again in the general sense, turned into almost unrestrained licence in word, dress and deeds, in reaction to the proscriptions of Puritanism.

It is against this broad background that the word 'taste' may be applied in examining Ogilby's life. It is true that the French were studying, analyzing and defining taste in the literary sense during his most productive years, and that he knew some French theatre of his time. It was not until a generation after Ogilby's death in 1676, however, that such judgements and discussions became common in England. For Ogilby himself and for his contemporaries, 'taste' would seem to have consisted of appreciation of writing that touched, with respect and knowledge, the bases of religion, the classics, veneration for the monarchy, and a kind of diffused national feeling that adumbrated future glories. There are, of course, numerous expressions in his time of the inevitable individual like or dislike of a particular work. But this is generally stated as a personal feeling, and not exalted into an aesthetic or philosophical argument.

Anthony à Wood offered a contemporary commendation in his usual backhanded fashion, remarking on 'John Ogilby, who was a prodigy in that part of learning which he professed, considering his education.' Later, he praised Ogilby's 'excellent invention and prudential wit,' noting that, despite various misfortunes, Ogilby always rose again and 'never failed in what he undertook.' Wood's often-cited conclusion on the matter was that at Ogilby's death 'many persons of great knowledge usually said, that had he been carefully educated when a young man, in a university, he might have proved the ornament and glory of the Scotch nation.'[1]

A more considered judgement was printed in 1675, in Edward Phillips' *Theatrum Poetarum*, or a Compleat Collection of the Poets. Phillips, a nephew and student of John Milton, dedicated his volume to two men well known to Ogilby, Thomas Stanley and Edward Sherburn. His praise of Ogilby and of his work was generous:[2]

One of the prodigies of our Age, for producing from so late an initiation into Literature, so many large & learned Vol. as well in verse as Prose: in Prose his Volumes of the Atlas, *and other Geographical Works, which have gain'd him the Style and Office of his Majestie's Cosmographer; in Verse his Translat. of* Homer & Virgil, & *which is the chief of all, as Compos'd* propria Minerva: *his Paraphrase upon* Aesop's Fables, *which for Ingenuity & Fancy, besides the Invention of new Fables, is generally confess't to have exceeded what ever hath been done before in that kind.*

Phillips gave more space to Ogilby's achievements than to those of his uncle Milton. His criticism of Dryden (the writer from whom flowed the greatest obloquy to Ogilby later) was centred on the Poet Laureate's 'French way of continual Rime' and to Dryden's adapting his gifts too much to the temper of his time. Others known to Ogilby were treated by Phillips: Davenant and Hobbes, the latter of whom, it will be remembered, praised Ogilby's edition of Homer even while publishing his own translation. James Shirley and Katherine Philips, both of whom shared Irish associations Ogilby, were given a meed of praise, as were Thomas Stanley, Elkanah Settle and Thomas Shadwell. Settle and especially Shadwell, by evoking Dryden's wrath, were fated to join Ogilby in the doom of derisive laughter.

It may be that as a Scotsman Ogilby was not considered qualified to appear in Fuller's *English Worthies* (1662) or in William Winstanley's *England's Worthies* (1660). A quarter of a century later, however, the latter published *Lives of the Most Famous English Poets* (1687). In it, after dismissing Milton's fame and memory because of his 'treason,' Winstanley printed an encomium (pp. 195-96) on Ogilby, taking many of the phrases from Phillips, and adding an admiring comment of his own on the *Entertainment* and on the quality of paper, printing and design characteristic of all of Ogilby's works.

In the following century, Theophilus Cibber collected a number of facts about Ogilby, citing Wood in particular. In successive paragraphs, Cibber mingled conflicting critical opinions on Ogilby's work, quoting first Phillips' praise and then some denigration by Pope. Cibber took ultimate refuge in praising Ogilby's industry and filial piety, and failed entirely to use the word 'dull' — the most characteristic comment applied to Ogilby in the eighteenth century.[3]

The change from acceptance and even praise of the man Ogilby and his works began with one writer, Dryden, and with a specific piece of literature, 'MacFlecknoe.' The offhand opinion concerning Ogilby's literary talent therein expressed has remained essentially unchallenged in the past three centuries. It was almost by inadvertence that Ogilby appeared in 'MacFlecknoe.' Vast piles of commentary choke the way to an understanding of the origins and significance of that clever, brief satire. Without entering into them, it is perhaps sufficient to say that it was Thomas Shadwell who was Dryden's chief target in 'MacFlecknoe' (written c. 1678 and published pseudonymously in 1684). Ogilby made only two appearances in the satire, linked in one line with his friend James Shirley and with Heywood, and a second time, more significantly, referred to as 'uncle' to 'MacFlecknoe,' the epitome of dullness. The theme of Ireland was recurrent in the poem (the almost unknown Flecknoe was an Irishman), and that may have suggested Ogilby's name to Dryden. Clever as it was, 'MacFlecknoe,' which Dryden acknowledged only in 1692, would hardly have reversed critical opinion on Ogilby; in fact, it had relatively little impact on the fame of Heywood and Shirley.

The importance of Ogilby's inclusion in 'MacFlecknoe,' then, did not consist of the two slighting references to him in that poem. It was rather the portent of a marked change in taste — a word indefinable in English because it is so variously definable — that was developing toward the end of the seventeenth century. Dryden himself with his writings on style taught English writers and readers alike an entirely new set of values from the ones they had cherished earlier. And Dryden very much disliked Ogilby. It was essentially through his early attempts at translating Virgil that Dryden became convinced of Ogilby's disservices to literature.

As early as 1685, Dryden had made up his mind about the classical translations of Ogilby and the iniquities they represented. He was working on some translating of his own at the time, and had some hard words to say about the abuse suffered by Virgil, Homer and others 'by a botching interpreter,' very probably Ogilby. He continued: 'What English readers unacquainted with Greek or Latin will believe me or any other man, when we commend those authors, and confess we derive all that is pardonable in us from their fountains, if they take those to be the same poets, whom our Ogilbies have translated?'[4] Somewhat later, in discussing portions of Virgilian translation that he had undertaken, Dryden mentioned how difficult he found that poet. 'All that I can promise for myself,' he said, 'is only that I have done . . . better than Ogilby, and perhaps as well as Caro.' He admitted to using poetic licence at times, in opposition to the sense of the commentators and added, with assurance: 'It may be I understand him [Virgil] better.'[5] Certainly, then, Dryden had read at least some of Ogilby's

Virgil — and with distaste. Clearly, he determined to try a different approach to Virgilian scholarship from that used by Ogilby. He would abandon the pentameters and hexameters with their weighted syllables based on the classical languages, and turn to the heroic rhymed couplet, with ten-foot iambic lines. Ogilby had rhymed his couplets (considering always the resistance of English to absolute rhyming); but he had varied his stresses in a fashion more Latinate than Dryden was willing to consider.

In a lengthy 'Introduction' to his translation (1694), Dryden never mentioned Ogilby's name, although he lavished praise upon a manuscript translation of Virgil by the Earl of Lauderdale, and thanked Congreve for his assistance. Dryden noted also that he had 'all the arguments in prose to the whole translation' — probably a custom followed by all translators of the time. He defended himself also against the charge that he 'Latinize[d] too much,' a charge that might be more appropriately applied to Ogilby. To look at a page of the Ogilby folio of the *Aeneid* is to see a work engaged with all the trappings of contemporary scholarship. To pick up Dryden's *Aeneid* is to be forced to concentrate on the verse — no marginalia, no cognate readings from the Greek, no learned or amusing speculations on various topics. Dryden's *Aeneid* was to be read as a work of art, not to be admired as a compendium of learning. In this new style, new words became modish; old ones were often declared rough and unpoetic. For the modern reader, accustomed to a formidable series of literary experimentations in later times, the variations between Ogilby's and Dryden's styles, while apparent, may not seem to represent the intolerably crude as against the elegantly smooth, which is the reaction that Dryden taught his readers to feel. Compare, for example, the following lines from the eighth book of the *Aeneid*, first from Ogilby, then from Dryden:

Whilst, in Aeolian Caverns Lemnius sweats,
Hastning the work, blest Morn from humble seats
Evander Rais'd, and chirping Birds did call
Up, with sweet notes, under his Palace wall.

———————

While, at the Lemnian god's command, they urge
Their labors thus, and ply th' Aeolian forge,
The cheerful morn salutes Evander's eyes,
And songs of chirping birds invite to rise.

The second selection is easier to follow, and avoids some of the inversions and Latinate sentence structures so dear to Ogilby. But to read, not four, but forty, lines of Dryden can bring a sense of sameness in words and realization of the use of 'poetic' elaboration to round out the meter that may lead some to prefer the tougher and cruder ('sweats,' for example) language of the older writer. It might be remarked, parenthetically, that the *reading* of an epic, particularly in translation, would seem to be one of the acquired tastes, and not a natural one, for most people in the twentieth century.

Another contrast, this from the second book of the *Aeneid*, tells the story of Laocöon's warning against the Greek horse. Thus, Ogilby:

Laocöon first, follow'd with many Friends,
Chafing, in haste the lofty Tower descends,
And calls from far: What Frenzy can besot,
Mad men to think Greek Presents veil no Plot?
Or to suppose the Enemy is gone?
What! is Ulysses yet no better known?
Either the Foe within this Monster lurks;
Or the huge Machin's rais'd against our Works,
The Fort being view'd, the City to surprize;
Trojans beware, within some Mischief lyes;
Be what it will, Greeks bringing Gifts I fear.

Then, Dryden:

Laocöon, follow'd by a num'rous crowd,
Ran from the fort, and cried, from far, aloud:
'O wretched countrymen! what fury reigns?
What more than madness has possess'd your brains?
Think you the Grecians from your coasts are gone?
And are Ulysses' arts no better known?
This hollow fabric either must inclose,
Within its blind recess, our secret foes;
Or 't is an engine rais'd above the town,
T' o'erlook the walls, and then to batter down.
Somewhat is sure design'd, by fraud or force:
Trust not their presents, nor admit the horse . . . '

The latter version, longer by one line, is more relaxed, less urgent than Ogilby's. On the whole, however, there are fewer absolute differences between the two translators than might be expected, considering the usual critical judgements. Nevertheless, Dryden's reputation (based, of course, on more than translations) wholly eclipsed Ogilby's. He swung future criticism to condemnation of much of the earlier seventeenth-century writing, including writers other than Ogilby, as rude and barbarous. In later centuries, that judgement has come under closer scrutiny than when it was made, with some recent efforts at revisions.[6] The criticism of Ogilby's work did not extend, however, even with Dryden, beyond the verse; in 1694, Jacob Tonson published Dryden's *Virgil,* using 100 plates from Ogilby's 1654 *Virgil.*[7] And, of course, not everyone was immediately convinced by Dryden; Addison gave first place in Leonore's library to Ogilby's *Virgil* rather than to Dryden's, although it must be considered that looks rather than poetic content may have influenced that decision.

Again, in 1700, when Tonson produced Dryden's *Fables Ancient and Modern,* it was apparent that there had been a prototype of Ogilby's for Dryden to look at — but not to acknowledge. There is clear evidence that Dryden knew Ogilby's *Aesop* and *Aesopics,*[8] but no recognition of this was given. Instead, in a lengthy, unpaged Preface to the *Fables,* Dryden took occasion to counter some criticisms of his translation of Virgil. His detractor, a Rev. Luke Milbourne, had publicly declared his preference for Ogilby's version. Dryden responded that the world had paid Milbourne 'the same Compliment: For 'tis agreed on all hands, that he writes even below Ogilby: That, you will say, is not easily to be done; but what cannot M[ilbourne] bring about?'

That Ogilby's *Virgil* needed additional attack to satisfy Dryden and his friends may be inferred from two bits of verse, attached in the usual prefatory fashion, to the 1697 edition of Dryden's *Works of Virgil*. One of these, by a Henry Grahme, bemoaned the fate of Virgil, groaning long

. . . beneath the weight
Of mangling Ogleby's presumptuous Quill.

The other, a considerably longer 'poem,' and unsigned, likewise mourned that

. . . Ogleby, mature in dulness rose, [a line from 'MacFlecknoe']
And Holbourn Dogrel, and low chiming Prose,
His Strength and Beauty did at once depose.

The second writer urged upon Dryden one more labour: that of rescuing Homer from his previous translator:

To right his [Homer's] injur'd Works, and set them free
From the lewd Rhymes of groveling Ogelby.

The fashion was clearly set, that Ogilby was a writer to be scorned, and in some curious places it is possible to find Ogilby singled out for criticism. Samuel Garth wrote, in 1699, a satire on the Royal College of Physicians, and in an offhand couplet said:[9]

Had [Samuel] Wesley never aim'd in Verse to please,
We had not rank'd him with our Ogilbys.

Although Ogilby made two appearances in Pope's *Dunciad* (written and revised several times in the first half of the eighteenth century), there is no feeling of personal animosity apparent on Pope's part. Indeed, the references to Ogilby may be more a conventional tribute to a by-then accepted verdict than a reflection of Pope's own feelings toward an earlier translator of Homer. Joseph Spence collected a number of references to Pope and Ogilby.[10]

Ogilby's translation of Homer was one of the first large poems that ever
Mr. Pope read, and he still spoke of the pleasure it then gave him, with a
sort of rapture only on reflection on it.

'It was that great edition with pictures. I was then about eight years old.
This led me to Sandys's Ovid.'

On 16 June 1715, Pope had written to Broome, 'Homer . . . was the first author that made me catch the itch of poetry, when I read him in my childhood.' And at the age of twelve, Pope wrote a play based on the Iliad and acted by his schoolfellows. He had all the actors 'dressed after the pictures in his favourite Ogilby.'[11] Again, in discussing subscriptions, Pope stated (incorrectly) that Dryden's *Virgil* was the only work that had succeeded through subscription, 'and even that was [chiefly] on account of the prints, which were from Ogilby's plates touched up.'[12]

The two references in the *Dunciad* show little or none of the pejorative judgement that sprang from Dryden. One was a reference to Ogilby's *Aesop*, which quoted a line from that author:

So when Jove's block descended from on high
(As sings thy great fore-father Ogilby,)
Hoarse thunder to its bottom shook the bog,
And the loud nation croak'd, God save King Log.

The other presumably referred to the large folios produced by Ogilby:

Here swells the shelf with Ogilby the great

although the reference may also, of course, be considered as satirical. In any event, these were brief and minor inclusions in a lengthy and elaborate satire. From Pope himself there does not come the breath of withering scorn so characteristic of Dryden, although some Pope's editors are explicit about Ogilby's evils.[13]

Through the work of eighteenth-century arbiters, therefore, and of succeeding ones, Ogibly's fame became that of one of the worst poets in the English language, a man certainly not read but one of whom a variety of criticisms could be quoted. In a couplet whose rhyme scheme might have served as an example for Ogilby's strongest detractors, the greatest arbiter of all, Dr. Johnson, admonished in 'The Young Author':

Warn'd by another's fate, vain youth, be wise,
These dreams were Settle's once and Ogilby's.

To enter the many spacious chambers of Johnsonian criticism is, of course, well outside the scope of this discussion. And yet there is in Johnson's 'Life of Pope' a section that has pertinence for Ogilby as well, and may bear quotation here. While defending Pope's introduction of elegance and subordination of sublimity in his translation of Homer (especially in the Iliad), Johnson wrote:

I suppose many readers of the English Iliad, *when they have been touched*
with some unexpected beauty of the lighter kind, have tried to enjoy it in
the original, where, alas! it was not to be found . . .

To a thousand cavils one answer is sufficient; the purpose of a writer is to
be read, and the criticism which would destroy the power of pleasing must
be blown aside. Pope wrote for his own age and his own nation . . .

If this holds true for Pope, it should hold as well for Ogilby, who wrote also for his own age and nation, and who, in his own time and for several decades thereafter, was widely read by his countrymen.

* * *

To move to a conclusion on Ogilby and his career, it seems appropriate to indicate four or five major areas in which he gained both personal and professional acclaim during his lifetime and for some years afterward. There was first his devotion to the classics: Virgil, Homer, Aesop, and his 'edition' of the Bible. Next, Ogilby's undoubted loyalty to the Stuart line influenced his entire life, beginning with his service under Buckingham and Strafford, continuing under Hereford and Ormonde, and culminating in direct grants of honour and money from Charles II. This loyalty, signified in print through the handsome editions of the *Entertainment,* no doubt further enhanced Ogilby's reputation. The series of atlases on foreign areas, exploiting the rising expectations of trade and power among Stuart Englishmen, brought additional lustre to the name of Ogilby. Furthermore, his final work, the *Britannia* and its various by-products, evoked praise for its recording of national and local memorabilia; likewise, the introduction of some elements of new scientific ideas added to the publisher's fame. Lastly, the insistence of Ogilby on fine paper, excellent type and illustrations, and admirable design had an overall impact on his name and reputation that lasted well into the eighteenth century. An Ogilby folio was a work to be read with interest, as the Earl of Denbigh testified to Ashmole in 1672: '[I received] Mr. Ogilby's America last night, which [the night] I emploi'd for the most part, in the reading of it with much delight.' Such volumes would be remembered in later years with pleasure, as Pope's recollections of Ogilby's Homer proved. And sometimes Ogilby folios were held simply as an investment, and often paid off handsomely.

These very qualities, however, brought their own tribulations. As the vitality of the classics waned, the complex apparatus of scholarly commentary became less meaningful to readers, and Dryden's or Pope's versions of the great epics easily superseded Ogilby's massive folios. As for loyalty to the Stuarts, it was severely tried in 1688-89, and flowed in complex streams, Catholic and Protestant, after the accession of William and Mary. Dryden, who early produced a paean on Oliver Cromwell and ended life as a Roman Catholic, must have looked at times with envy on the simple but sustained loyalty to his monarchs that John Ogilby exhibited. So far as the foreign atlases were concerned, they were impressive show pieces, but in general were poorly arranged for information. They were succeeded, on the one hand, by more accurate and readable materials on foreign lands, and on the other by a whole literature of moral-satirical writings based on foreign or fantastic lands, such as Montesquieu's *Lettres Persanes* or the travels of Gulliver.

The *Britannia* and the road atlases best sustained the fame of John Ogilby; not until the early nineteenth century were their comprehensiveness and innovations wholly superseded. As for the look and feel of fine book-making, an art in which Ogilby excelled, it became a luxury reserved for bibliophiles, and not likely to perpetuate a popular reputation. Even so, had Ogilby's verse not been so severely criticized, he might — especially through his fables — have remained within the canons of minor but enjoyable writers. The judgement of the Augustan Age, however, went against him; the taste of his times changed shortly after his own time ended.

151

It is now worth reopening the question of Ogilby's merits and influence. In the light of much that has been forgotten, or never recognized as part of his contribution to society and thought, he might again be reread. Assuredly, this complex, wide-ranging and intriguing figure left a significant imprint on a variety of seventeenth-century activities and ideas.

Notes & References

CHAPTER I

1 MS. Aubrey 8, fol. 46, cited in A. Clark, ed., John Aubrey, *Brief Lives* (2 vols.; Oxford, 1898), II, 99-105.

2 Bodleian; Ashmolean 332, f. 35*v*. The second of these horoscopes is dated '20 Dec. 1653' (*Ibid.*, 243, f. 196). Both were probably cast at about the same time.

3 James, 6th Lord Ogilvy, and his namesake son, the 7th Lord, frequently appear in records of this time (the latter was created Earl of Airlie in 1639). The Factor of the Airlie Estates, Mr. D.L. Laird, very kindly searched the family records for a John Ogilby born in 1600, but with no success.

4 Merchant Taylors Guild Records, IV, 1595-1607, f. 246*r*. This volume gives the date of the Court Meeting at which Ogilby was admitted as 16 June 1606. In the Repertory records in the City of London Record Office, the same information is given as of 3 June 1606. Indices to these records are imperfect; for example, no mention of the name 'Hunsdon' could be found.

5 Merchant Taylors Company, Freemen, 1530-1928.

6 Merchant Taylors Company Records, IX, 1636-1654, f. 435. See also C.M. Clode, *Memorials of the Guild of Merchant Taylors* (London, 1875), p. 187. City records exist of those men made free by virtue of membership in Livery Companies, but the Merchant Taylors' records of such freemen do not reach back to Ogilby's time. I am indebted to Mr. Cedric Holland, who checked Guildhall records for me on this point in November 1971.

7 There are numerous references to Ogilby in the Aubrey MSS. in the Bodleian. They are concentrated in two printed sources, the *Brief Lives,* noted in footnote 1, on pp. 99-105 and in John Aubrey, *Letters by Eminent Men and Lives of Eminent Men* (3 vols.; 1813), III, 466-470. These accounts, although full of detail, are sometimes confusing and sometimes incorrect. For want of any other sources, the material that cannot be disproved is generally accepted. I have offered reasons where I demur to an Aubrey statement.

8 Clark, ed., *Brief Lives,* II, 99, and Aubrey, *Letters . . . and Lives,* III, 466.

9 K.B.9.

10 S.M. Kingsbury, ed., *Records of the Virginia Company of London* (4 vols.; Library of Congress, 1906), III, 51-53, cited from a Bill of Complaint and its answer of November 15 and 30, 1613, in Chancery Proceedings, Jas. I, Bundle U, Nos. 2/55.

11 John Samuel Ezell, *Fortune's Merry Wheel: The Lottery in America* (Harvard University Press, 1960), pp. 4-7.

12 A book called 'The Lottery for Virginea,' which contained the names of the winners, was entered at the Stationers' Company on 2 July 1612. A search for the volume, apparently made before 1890, produced no copy. Alexander Brown, *Genesis of the United States* (2 vols.; first published, 1890; reprinted, New York, Russell and Russell, 1964), II, 571.

13 Aubrey quotes the motto printed on his father's lot: 'I am a poor prisoner, Got wott, God send me a good lott, I'le come out of prison and pay all my debt.' *Letters,* 1813, II, 466.

14 Ezell notes, pp. 14ff., the sale of books as part of various estates in eighteenth-century America; but Ogilby's example as a bookseller using lotteries to aid sales apparently did not cross the Atlantic. For a chronological survey of English lotteries, see C.L. Ewen, *Lotteries and Sweepstakes* (London, 1932; reissued by B. Blom, 1972).

15 This is printed as 'The Third Universitie of England,' bound with Stow's *Annales* [London], 1631, but dated 24 August 1612. In Beinecke Rare Book Room, Yale University.

16 Clark, ed., *Brief Lives,* II, 28.

17 Bacon published an essay (XXXVII), 'Of Masques and Triumphs,' in his third and last edition (1625). 'These things are but toys,' he observed. 'But yet, since princes will have such things it is better they should be graced with elegancy, than daubed with cost. Dancing to song is a thing of great state and pleasure.' It may be inferred from the latter statement that the high leaping and buffoonery so congenial to James did not equally enchant his Lord Chancellor.

18 Hugh Ross Williamson, *George Villiers, First Duke of Buckingham* (London, 1940), p. 72.

19 Clark, ed., *Brief Lives,* II, 28.

20 Herford and Simpson, eds., *Ben Jonson* (11 vols.; Oxford, 1950), X, 437, 612.

21 *Ibid.,* pp. 92-94.

22 Fifty years later, Wycherley, in 'The Gentleman Dancing-Master,' performed in 1672, made it clear that a dancing master must be able to sing and to play the violin. Without these accomplishments, he simply could not qualify. Ogilby certainly had some skill at music. He wrote a number of songs for *The Entertainment* and supplied songs for at least one of Katherine Philips' plays in the 1660's, in Dublin.

23 A reference to apes occurs in Jonson's *The Gypsies Metamorphosed:*
   A Gipsie in his shape
   More calls the behoulder,
   Then the fellowe wth the Ape,
   Or the Ape on his shoulder. (11. 715-718)

24 P.R.O., S.P. 16, Vol. 66, No. 63; Vol. 67, No. 78; and Vol. 68, No. 62. Hopton served in the Mansfeld expedition as a Lieutenant-Colonel. For a recent biography, see F.T.R. Edgar, *Sir Ralph Hopton: The King's Man in the West (1642-1652),* Oxford, 1968.

25 P.R.O., S.P. 16, Vol. 91, No. 87, fols. 174v and 175.

26 P.R.O., Warrant Office 55, 1682-1684. I have paged through the volumes mentioned. Further records exist concerning these ships, their provisioning, and the auditing or survey of their stores. There are several references in other places to the *Report*, but none mentions the name of her captain.

27 P.C. 2/42, fol. 596.

28 S.P. 16, Vol. 239, No. 69.

29 *Ibid.*, 69I.

30 *Ibid.*, 69II.

31 The manuscript Privy Council Registers are not indexed by individuals, but I have paged through the meetings of the period under consideration without finding any reference to Ogilby.

32 Appended to one of the horoscopes cast by Ashmole for Ogilby (see note 2, the first citation, above) is a list of events, chiefly in cipher, which Ogilby must have related. I have already mentioned the importance of accuracy in the casting of horoscopes; any errors in fact that may have been listed herein should be attributed to Ogilby's faulty recollection. Ashmole and Ogilby first met in October 1653 (C.H. Josten, ed., *Elias Ashmole, 1617-1692*, 5 vols.; Oxford, 1966, II, 655). Of the six items listed, one stated that in August 1633, Ogilby entered Strafford's service. It is curious that the date of his injury in the masque does not occur. The only events noted that were prior to 1633 were a broken leg at eight years of age and a 'double quotidian ague for eighteen weeks' in 1625. *Ashmole*, II, 655, n. 4.

33 The story of Ogilby's life in Ireland has already been told, by William Smith Clark, *The Early Irish Stage* (Oxford, 1955), chapters II, III and IV. Clark's emphasis is on Ireland and the theatre rather than on Ogilby. He acknowledges the importance of Ogilby in Irish theatrical history, however, and his work supersedes the earlier histories of the beginnings of Irish theatre, namely, W.R. Chetwood's *General History of the Stage* (London, 1749), La Tourette Stockwell's *Dublin Theatres and Theatre Customs* (Kingsport, Tenn., 1938), the work closest to Clark in scholarly terms, and Peter Kavanagh, *The Irish Theatre* (Tralee, 1946).

34 S.P. 63, State Papers Ireland, Vol. 345, No. 50.

35 Stockwell, p.4, and Clark, p. 27, point out this likelihood. Clark notes (pp. 26-27) that in January of both 1634 and 1636 there were theatrical performances at the Castle. As at least the first of these was by 'gentleman performers,' Ogilby may not have been in charge of it.

36 See Clark, Appendix D, 'Actors and Actresses at the Dublin Theatres, 1637-1720.' According to an eighteenth-century account, there were about 8,000 Dubliners in 1644, roughly two-thirds Protestant, and somewhat over half of the total female (a preponderance that may be attributable to the number of female servants). Walter Harris, *The History and Antiquities of the City of Dublin* (Dublin, 1766), p. 336.

37 A play by Thomas Randolph, 'Aristippus or the Jovial Philosopher,' is listed as having been published in Dublin in the 1630's, but no evidence exists that it was presented there. *Catalogue of Early Dublin-Printed Books, 1601 to 1700,* compiled by E.R. McC. Dix. Introduction and Notes by C. Winston Dugan (3 vols.; Dublin, 1898-1912), Vol. I, Pt. II, 1626-1650. Randolph's is the only play listed in this early period.

38 See Clark, Appendix C, 'Plays Acted at the Dublin Theatres, 1637-1720,' and pp. 32-37.

39 Copies of both these printings are in the Folger Shakespeare Library.

40 G.E. Bentley, *The Jacobean and Caroline Stage* (7 vols.; Oxford, 1941-68), II, 517-518. Bentley suggests that some day a connection between Ogilby and the Phoenix will be uncovered.

41 Aubrey adds other details about this first stay in Ireland that seem less credible: he states that Ogilby's task was 'to teach,' and remarks that he wrote a fine hand. Later, he amplifies the 'teaching' as meaning the instruction of Lady Wentworth and her children in dancing. This may have been an incidental task for Ogilby; but the organization and management of the theatre would seem to have been a fairly

155

full occupation. Aubrey also states that Ogilby began to paraphrase Aesop's Fables at this time, a statement in flat contradiction to Ogilby's own autobiographical comments in the Preface to *Africa,* to be discussed later.

42 Patent Roll C. 66/2995, 13 Chas. II, pt. 40, no. 37; Clark corrects Stockwell on the dating of this, p. 31.

43 John 5th Marquess of Ely, *Rathfarnham Castle. Adam Loftus and the Ely Family.* Printed for private circulation, no date. 'A Biographical Sketch of Rathfarnham,' dated 1905, concludes the book. See especially pp. 87-88.

44 Mr. John Bebbington, F.L.A., City Librarian and Information Officer of the Central Library in Sheffield, kindly informed me (in 1971) of this fact.

CHAPTER II

1 Hooke notes his doing it; presumably to communicate with foreigners, in 1673. *Diary of Robert Hooke, 1672-1680,* ed. H. Robinson and W. Adams (London, 1935), p. 58.

2 Cf. Pope's story of his admiration for Homer, created by his first encounter with that poet in Ogilby's translation of the *Iliad.* This occurred in 1696, when Pope was eight. Joseph Spence, *Observations, Anecdotes, and Characters of Books and Men, Collected from Conversation* (ed., James M. Osborn; 2 vols., Clarendon Press, 1966), I, 276.

3 *The History of the Worthies of England,* ed. P. Austin Nuttall (3 vols.; London, 1840), III, 287. The *Utopia* of Thomas More (1516), considered a clever but dangerous book, was not translated into English until 1551.

4 Proby of Emanuel was an original Fellow of the Royal Society whose name disappears from Society records after 1664. See Thomas Birch, *History of the Royal Society of London* (4 vols.; Johnson Reprint, N.Y. and London, 1968), I, xlii. The poem is copied in a commonplace book in the Bodleian: MS. Rawl. poet., 246, fol. 2. Proby appears, *passim,* in Hooke's *Diary.*

5 Register General in Guildhall, London. There is no pagination of the folio. This entry occurs about two-fifths of the way through. Ogilby had the husband's customary difficulty with the date of this event. He apparently told Ashmole that it was in February 1650. Josten, ed., *Ashmole,* II, 655, n. 4.

6 PROB. 11/211, now in Public Record Office.

7 Aubrey states categorically that Ogilby married the daughter of a certain Fox, servant to the Earl of Pembroke, who lived at Netherhampton, near Wilton in Wiltshire. But since Aubrey also states that Elizabeth Morgan was Ogilby's daughter and William his grandson, some reservations must be held about the entire entry. Aubrey and Ashmole agree that Mrs. Ogilby died in 1677, one year after Ogilby. Aubrey, in different manuscript leaves, gives her age as 'neer 90,' with the '90' substituted for '100' and 'circiter 112,' with the '112' scored out. She seems clearly not to have been a youthful widow at her second marriage in 1650.

John Bunyan used the name 'Christian' for his male protagonist in *Pilgrim's Progress* (1678); when the second part was published, in 1684, Christian's wife was called 'Christiana.'

8 See Chapter I, n. 40.

9 Clark's notation about two children of Ogilby dying in Dublin in the 1660's may involve a reference to some other Ogilby. *Early Irish Stage,* pp. 66, n. 5. For further discussion of this point, see Chapter III, note 48.

There was a John Ogilby, collector of customs in Dublin in the 1660's who seems *not* to have been the printer-publisher. There may have been other Ogilbys in Ireland as well. The records for that country are imperfect.

10 See Henry R. Plomer, *Dictionary of Booksellers and Printers,* 1641-67 (London, 1907) for information on the Crooks and other publishers mentioned.

11 Stationers Register Book for Entry of Copies, Liber E, fol. 136.

12 C.M. Clode, compiler, *Memorials of the . . . Merchant Taylors,* p. 187.

13 It is interesting that of the seven dedicatory poems in this volume of Shirley, one is by Thomas Stanley, who was to be associated with John Ogilby two decades later in the second patent creating Ogilby Master of Revels in the Kingdom of Ireland.

14 For a full discussion of Ogilby's *Aesops* and comments on the man himself, see the excellent article by Marian Eames, 'John Ogilby and his Aesop' in *Bulletin of the New York Public Library,* LXV (1961), 73-88.

15 See Ben Edwin Perry, *Aesopica* (Urbana, Ill., 1952). The lack of an authentic or closed Aesopic canon encouraged experimentation in verse and content. Other useful treatments of the Aesopic tradition can be found in Earl Miner's 'Introduction' to a facsimile edition of Ogilby's *Fables of Aesop* (1668), published by the University of California, 1965, and in John J. McKendry, *Aesop: Five Centuries of Illustrated Fables* (Metropolitan Museum of Art, 1964). In the former is reprinted a copyright that Ogilby had obtained in 1665.

16 Anon. pamphlet, *The Swearers, or, Innocence Opprest and Sacrific'd* (London), rebound 1935. In British Library, 112.d. 15. The Thirteenth Fable of the Aesopics (1668 ed., p. 31) contains the notable phrase 'Praise-Jove Bare-bones.'

17 Aubrey says: 'His Odysses came out in 1665. People did then suspect, or would not believe that 'twas he was the author of the paraphrase upon Aesop, and to convince them he published a 2d volume, which he calles his Aesopiques, which he did during the sicknesse, in his retirement at Kingston upon Thames.' Pepys testifies to the anticipation that a new edition of Ogilby's *Aesop* could bring: 'I by Coach to Mr. Cades, the stationer. Here I understand that Ogleby is putting out some new fables of his owne, which will be very fine and very satyricall.' 27 June 1666. Mynors Bright, ed., *Diary* (London, 1889), VI, 92.

18 Some of Hollar's prints are dated as early as 1652. For material on Hollar's relations with Ogilby, see K.S. Van Eerde, *Wenceslaus Hollar: Delineator of His Time* (Folger Shakespeare Library, 1970), especially Chapters V and VI. For the dating of Hollar drawings, see Gustav Parthey, *Wenzel Hollar: Beschreibendes Verzeichniss seiner Kupferstiche* (1853; reprinted, Amsterdam, 1963). See also Edward Croft-Murray and Paul Hulton, *Catalogue of British Drawings,* Vol. I: *XVI and XVII Centuries* (London, 1960).

19 De la Cerda's first edition, that of the *Eclogues* and *Georgics,* appeared in Madrid in 1608. His first full and excellent edition appeared at Lyon in three parts, 1612-19. A second edition appeared in three volumes, printed at Cologne in 1628. I have used the third edition, also printed at Cologne in three volumes, 1642-47. The editions from 1619 to 1647 were folios. Another edition, in octavo, appeared in 1680, long after Ogilby's versions.

20 *Thesaurus graecae poeseos ex omnibus graecis poetis collectus,* 1612; *De symbolica Aegyptiorum,* 1623; and *Polyhistor Symbolicus,* 1631.

21 For more details, and a confirmation of Ogilby's pioneering in the area of subscriptions in the latter seventeenth-century, see Sarah L.C. Clapp, 'The Subscription Enterprises of John Ogilby and Richard Blome,' *Modern Philology,* XXX (1933), 365-379. Quite probably as an alert young man, Ogilby had noted and approved the enterprise of his only apparent predecessor in book subscriptions, the learned John Minsheu.

22 *Ibid.,* p. 367.

23 Aubrey, who knew him, was convinced of Ogilby's classical knowledge. 'He printed

Virgill, translated by himself, into English verse . . . After he had translated Virgil, he learned Greek of Mr. Whitfield [believed to be David Whitford, a teacher in Shirley's school] . . . and grew so great a proficient in it that he fell-to to translate Homer's Iliads.' *Brief Lives*, p. 102.

24 *Iliad*, pp. 469-470.

25 Maynard Mack, ed., *Works of Alexander Pope* (10 vols.; London and New Haven, 1967), Vol. VII: *The Iliad of Homer*, pp. cviii, cxii, cxviii, cxx-cxxi, *et passim*. A travesty on the first two books of the *Iliad* was published by James, Lord Scudamore, at Oxford in 1665. His doggerel is of a type that later commentators ascribe to Ogilby.

26 Luther A. Weigle, 'English Versions Since 1611' (Chap. X), in S.L. Greenslade, ed., *Cambridge History of the Bible* (Cambridge, 1963), pp. 362-363. Plomer's *Dictionary* speaks of Field's many editions of the Bible, 'all of which were noted for the number and variety of misprints, the general badness of printing, and their excessive price.' A contemporary complaint on the sad state of printed Bibles and various suggestions for improvement appear in William Kilburne's proposals in BM, MSS. Room, Harl. 5908 and 5909.

27 See David Bland, *A History of Book Illustration* (University of California, 1969), pp. 186-191 and illustrations. What is most curious about 'Ogilby's Bible' is not the differences within various volumes, which are in most instances attributable to the different owners' whims; it is rather the fact that a poor and sloppy printer turned out such excellent plates or sheets as appear in Ogilby's folio. In the very year, 1660, in which Ogilby's edition appeared, Hills and Field printed and sold an octavo Bible without illustrations, which falls entirely within the category of contemporary and later judgements on Field's work.

28 That there were limitations in the appeal of this Bible appears from Pepy's comment (27 May 1667): 'There came Richardson, the bookbinder, with one of Ogilby's Bibles in quires for me to see and buy, it being Mr. Cade's, my stationer's; but it is like to be so big that I shall not use it.' Mynors Bright, ed., *Diary*, VII, 150.

29 Richard Baxter, *Autobiography* (ed. N.H. Keeble): Dent, 1974, p. 144.

30 669. f.26/44, numbered '41' in a contemporary hand.

31 See S.L.C. Clapp, 'Subscription Enterprises,' cited in note 21 above.

32 See Clode, note 12 above. The Virgil must have been the 1654 edition, as it is described as illustrated.

33 S.P. 29, Vol. 40, No. 66, fol 120.

34 *Ibid.*, No. 66I, fol. 122. The *Commons Journal.* References are for 27 December 1660 and for 8 July 1661.

35 S.P. 44, Entry Books, Vol. 7, ff, 150-151. One of these documents is undated; the other is dated 8 July 1662.

36 A699 Bd. w. A700. See also Miner's 'Introduction' for a listing of editions of Ogilby's *Aesop*, which does not mention the 1673 edition.

37 Dugan, *Books Printed in Dublin*, II, 132. The second item appears from a Sale Catalogue of the library of William Elliot Hudson, in 1853.

CHAPTER III

1 See Coronation Chas. II, 1661, Bills, MS. 290/19 in the Corporation Record Office. The signature on the receipt does not appear to be Ogilby's own. He may at that stage have been too busy to go in person for the money. See also the petition in *Cal. S.P. Dom.*, 1660-61, p. 553.

2 Coronation Chas. II, 1661, Bills, MS. 290/34.

3 Folger Shakespeare Library, copy 0181, p(a*) Washington,D.C. The complex bibliographical history of Ogilby's editions of *The Relation of His Majestie's Entertainment* [generally called *The Entertainment*] has been explored in Fredson Bowers, 'Ogilby's Coronation *Entertainment* (1661-1689): Editions and Issues,' *Papers of the Bibliographical Society of America*, XLVII (1953), 339-355. Ogilby often made up volumes with special insertions as presentation items.

4 See Atkins and Overall, *Company of Clockmakers* (1881), pp. 91, 95 and numerous other references to various Morgans in the Court Meet Book for Clockmakers at the Guildhall.

5 *Register of Apprentices of the Worshipful Company of Clockmakers*, compiled by C.E. Atkins (1931). I have checked through the Court Meet Book and various lists of freemen and apprentices, all at the Guildhall, without finding there any certain record of this William Morgan's apprenticeship.

6 Coronation Chas. II, 1661, MS. 290/1, Corporation Records Office and Bills paid, MS. 289, Ex. GLMR, fol. 15r.

7 For the latest account of coronation pageantry from 1558 to 1642, see David Bergeron, *English Civic Pageantry, 1558-1642* (London, 1971). Other secondary works are Glynne Wickham, *Early English Stages* (London and N.Y., 1959) and Robert Withington, *English Pageantry: An Historical Outline* (Cambridge, Mass., 1918-20).

8 See John Nichols, *The Progresses . . . of King James the First* (reprint, 4 vols., by Burt Franklin, of edition of London, 1828), I, nos. 13 to 19 incl., for a variety of accounts, some with texts, of the 1604 procession and entertainment.

9 There was a parade in 1641 that constituted perhaps a miniature progress for Charles I, and was celebrated in two works, *Ovatio Carolina. The Triumph of King Charles* and John (?) Taylor, *Englands Comfort, and Londons Joy.*

10 'The King's Entertainment Through the City of London,' reprinted in Nichols, *The Progresses . . . of King James the First*, p. 388.

11 This will be treated below. For details, see Bowers, 'Ogilby's Coronation *Entertainment*.'

12 Folger Shakespeare Library, copy 0181, p. (a*).

13 'This entertainment was designed, and the Speeches made by a Person of Quality,' p. 9. It was presumably near this spot that there was represented the Royal Oak, transformed into a bearer of crowns rather than of acorns by Ogilby's fancy, and reminding viewers of the tree that sheltered Charles after the defeat at Worcester in 1651. Dryden refers to this in his 'Panegyric on His Coronation,' 11. 129-132, in *Works of John Dryden* (18 vols.; Walter Scott, ed., revised and corrected by George Saintsbury, N.Y., 1882), IX, 60 and note. On the title page the volume is described as 'Dramatic Works, Vol. VIII.'

14 Josten, ed., *Ashmole*, III, 822-825, including footnotes.

15 S.P. 29/33, no. 73, noted in *Cal. S.P. Dom.*, 1660-61, p. 553.

16 Copy 0181 at the Folger Shakespeare Library, top of p. 33; this appears as a notice set within lines drawn across the page.

17 There exist volumes with the 1662 text and Ashmole's name appended to his account in the Guildhall, London, and in Oxford and Cambridge. See Bowers, 'Ogilby's Coronation *Entertainment*,' pp. 350-354. Furthermore, in one of the Guildhall copies, as also in a copy in the Beinecke Library, Yale University, there are bound two issues of Ashmole's brief work, with differing title pages and slightly differing versions. Presumably, these issues were printed and made available at dif-

ferent times in 1661 and 1662 and eventually were bound together, without discrimination, as parts all of which pertained to the same event.

18 Josten, ed., *Ashmole*, III, 828-831.

19 *Ibid.*, III, 822-823.

20 S.P. 44/48, Entry Book 7, fol. 20. A pencilled notation in the margin dates this as of '1661 May.' The licence appears also in S.P. 44/7, Entry Book 48, fol. 24, dated from Whitehall, 25 April 1662.

21 Bowers, 'Ogilby's Coronation *Entertainment*,' p. 353.

22 *Ibid.*, p. 340.

23 *Ibid.*, p. 347.

24 It is ironical that Gregory King, probably a rival to Morgan as assistant to Ogilby in the 1670's, should have been in charge of the coronation ceremonial for James II, and may have used this redaction in his planning for that event. Further irony exists in King's belated production of his record of James's coronation — a record he finished only in 1688, by which time the interest in his account of that event was minimal. For still other issues based on the 1685 edition, see Bowers, 'Ogilby's Coronation *Entertainment*,' p. 355.

25 P.R.O., Patent Rolls, c. 66, 2932, No. 33, and Signet Books, Docquets, IND. 6813, folios unnumbered.

26 P.R.O., S.P. 63, Ireland, Vol. 304, No. 171. See Clark, *Early Irish Stage,* chapter III and Appendix A for the story and the documents of this episode and succeeding events regarding the Irish stage in the early Restoration days.

27 S.P. 63, Ireland, Vol. 345, No. 50. There is a brief reference to this episode, including some allusions to Ogilby, in Alfred Harbage, *William Davenant, Poet, Venturer, 1606-1668* (Octagon Books, 1971), pp. 143-144.

28 Sir Henry Herbert tried to re-assert his authority as Master of Revels in England after 1660 against Davenant and Killigrew. These three were apparently too involved in litigation among each other to become exercised over Ogilby's much smaller claim in Ireland. For further information on Herbert, see Arthur F. White, 'The Office of Revels and Dramatic Censorship During the Restoration Period,' Western Reserve University Bulletin, *Studies in English Literature,* New Series, Vol. XXXIV, Sept. 15, 1931, No. 13, pp. 5-45. Plomer, *Dictionary of Booksellers and Printers,* notes that John Crook was Printer General in Ireland in 1660.

29 P.R.O., IND. 6813, no pagination; this appears at the end of the March grants.

30 P.R.O., C. 66/2995, Patent Roll, 13 Charles II, Part 40, n. 37.

31 There had been booksellers and printers in Dublin in the 1630's, but probably very few. Some forty years after the Restoration, in May 1700, Dr. Narcissus Marsh, Archbishop of Dublin, wrote to Dr. Thomas Smith of Magdalen College concerning the library he proposed to build (still extant) in Dubin: 'Which will be of great use here, where is no public Library (that of the College being open only to the Provost and Fellows) and where the Bookseller's shops are furnished with nothing but new trifles. So that neither the Divines of the city, nor those that come to it about business, do know wither to go to spend an hour or two upon any occasion at study.' John Aubrey, *Letters . . . by Eminent Men . . .* (London, 1813; 3 vols.), 1, 105, Dublin in the 1660's could not have begun to compare as audience or market to the London to which Ogilby had been addressing himself for over a decade.

32 *Athenae Oxonienses* and *The Fasti* (Facsimile of London edition of 1820. 4 vols.; New York and London: Johnson Reprint, 1967), III, 742 [380].

33 S.P. 63, Ireland, Vol. 276, No. 62; Vol. 307, No. 201.

34 For details, see Clark, pp. 46-47, and especially p. 47, n. 3, as well as Appendix A.

35 See Clark, pp. 53-55, who discusses at length the arrangements of the Smock Alley Theatre and notes a ms. prompt book of John Wilson's *Belphegor* in the Folger Shakespeare Library.

36 Clark, pp. 57-58 and Appendix D.

37 S.P. Dom., Charles II, lviii, 15. S.P. 44/7. S.P. Domestic Entry Book, p. 181. Summarized in *Cal. S.P. Dom.* 1661-2, p. 455. See Clark, p. 57, notes 5 and 6.

38 Clark, p. 56.

39 *Ibid.*, Appendix C.

40 See William S. Clark, *Dramatic Works of Roger Boyle, Earl of Orrery* (Cambridge, Mass., 1937), 2 vols., and Kathleen Lynch.

41 Clark states that Orrery apparently sent a second play to the Duke of Ormonde (NOT *The Generall*), but that it was lost. *The Generall* is not polished in style, and no use was made of scene flats. *The Dramatic Works of Roger Boyle, Earl of Orrery*, I, 'Historical Preface.' See also Clark's Preface to *The Generall*, in which he suggests that it may have been staged in Smock Alley Theatre after its première at the Earl's house.

42 *Letters from Orinda to Poliarchus* (London, 1705), pp. 78-79 and p. 96. 'Poliarchus' was Sir Charles Cotterell.

43 *H.M.C. Report XI*, App., Pt. V, p. 11, cited in Clark, p. 61, notes 3 and 4.

44 See Philip Webster Souers, *The Matchless Orinda* (Harvard University Press, 1931, reprinted by Johnson Reprint Corp., 1968), p. 161. At the Folger, there is a 1663 edition of *Pompee*, which contains a page stating that the 'Prologue for the Theatre at Dublin [was] written by the Earl of Roscomon.' The third dance composed by Ogilby, in addition to the Gypsies and the Grand Masque, was a 'Military Dance.' Lord Orrery contributed £100 toward the costumes. *Letters from Orinda to Poliarchus,* p. 119.

45 See Clark, p. 65, and Souers, pp. 184-88.

46 *Cal. S.P. Ire.*, 1663-65, p. 87. 9 May 1663.

47 *Letters from Orinda to Poliarchus,* pp. 158 and 164.

48 See attached map, as also Clark, p. 66, notes 1 and 2. In note 5 of that page, Clark states that Ogilby's family remained in Dublin through 1667, and cites James Mills, ed., *The Registers of St. John the Evangelist, Dublin* (Dublin, 1906), to that effect. It is true that on page 268 there are references to two burials, 'One of Mr. Oglebyes familye in the Church' and 'One from Mr. Oglebyes, in the Church.' If not another Ogilby entirely, it may be that the 'family' referred to the troupe of actors. The actor Yeoghny's wife was buried in Dublin, and so were members of the Ashbury family (see *passim*, especially pp. 144, 239, 243).

49 On 26 December 1671, 'at a stage play at the great theatre in Smockalley, the upper gallery fell down (being burthened by [the] multitude of people therein) into the pitt, by which three persons were killed and many wounded.' Harris, *Dublin*, p. 347. There is no evidence as to the effect this had upon Ogilby's further involvement with the Irish theatre.

CHAPTER IV

1 Clark, *Early Irish Stage*, pp. 43, 54, 59, 91-92.

2 Charles Gildon, *The Life of Mr. Thomas Betterton* (Reprints of Economic Classics; New York: Augustus M. Kelley, 1970), pp. 15ff. First printed, 1710. Some of these

complaints have the characteristic touch of grumpy age contemplating feckless youth.

3 See G.M. Crump, *Poems and Translations of Thomas Stanley* (Oxford, 1962), pp. 354-366. See also A.C. Partridge, ed., *The Tribe of Ben,* pp. 124-125.

4 *Poems by Thomas Stanley, Esq.* [ed., Sir Egerton Brydges], London, 1814, reprinted from the 1651 edition. Introduction, p. xv.

5 Montague Summers, ed., *The Complete Works of Thomas Shadwell* (5 vols.; London, 1927), Vol. V, 'Introduction,' especially p. xxvi.

6 *Theatrum Poetarum Anglicanorum* (1675), p. 114. Phillips was somewhat critical of Dryden's style.

7 Peter W. Thomas, *Sir John Berkenhead, 1617-1679* (Oxford, 1969), *passim.*

8 Van Eerde, *Wenceslaus Hollar,* pp. 58-59, 61, 63.

9 Dryden, 'MacFlecknoe,' *Works of John Dryden,* Scott and Saintsbury, eds., Vol. X.

> *From dusty shops neglected authors come,*
> *Martyrs of pies, and relics of the bum,*
> *Much Heywood, Shirley, Ogleby there lay,*
> *But loads of Shadwell almost chok'd the way. (11. 100-104)*

10 Merchant Taylors Company Records, IX, 1636-1654, fol. 435. It is likely that Ogilby presented all his works to the Company at various times. The only one remaining in the Company's library today is a copy (1662) of the *Entertainment,* not containing any special dedicatory page, as might have been expected. If Ogilby's presentations were handed on to the Merchant Taylors School, they have vanished in the intervening centuries. Bruce Ritchie, a master at that school, has kindly checked that fact for me.

11 *Brief Lives,* II, 103.

12 *Athenae Oxonienses,* pp. 740-744.

13 Josten, ed., *Elias Ashmole,* II, 655; III, 1237, 1238, 1249.

CHAPTER V

1 There are standard works such as Plomer's *Dictionary of Printers and Booksellers* on this subject, as well as more obscure but still helpful writings, *e.g.,* Charles R. Rivington, *Records of the Worshipful Company of Stationers* (Westminster: Nichols and Sons, 1883) and an anonymous publication, *The Worshipful Company of Stationers and Newspaper Makers,* List of Exhibits, August 1951, in London Room of I.H.R.

2 Guildhall, MS. 6537.

3 DNB, no reference cited. See note 34 in chapter II.

4 S.P. 29, Vol. 40, fol. 125.

5 S.P. 29, Vol. 122, item 26, fol. 57.

6 *Ibid.,* item 27, fol. 58.

7 The Earl of Arlington's name is very often found signed to these grants or patents assigned to Ogilby. It may be the merest chance. Perhaps, however, Ogilby regularly approached Arlington as a conduit for some of these favours from the King. Arlington was a skilled and long-term courtier, generally in favour with Charles, and related by marriage to the Earl of Ossory, who was at least fairly well known to Ogilby.

8 S.P. 44/23, Entry Book, ff. 416-417 P.R.O. This latter warrant has been reprinted in the Introduction by Earl Miner to his Ogilby, *Fables of Aesop,* 1668. The num-

ber of printers in London was greatly reduced by the 1662 Licensing Act. See Michael Foss, *The Age of Patronage* (Cornell University Press, 1972), p.83.

9 S.P. 29/173, fol. 226, item 109.

10 *Ibid.*, fol. 227, item 110.

11 It appears also in S.P. 44/25, fol. 131.

12 Signet Office, Docquets, IND. 6815, fol. 328, P.R.O.

13 Rawlinson C. 514, vol. 19, Bodleian.

14 *Ibid.*, fol. 20.

15 *Ibid.*, fol. 39.

16 John Minsheu, *Ductor in Linguas, The Guide Into Tongues* (London, 1617), published a prospectus of his work and a list of subscribers, including royalty, high clerics and myriads of the Buckingham connection. It seems likely that Ogilby had come upon this prospectus and list and saw possibilities for his own purposes in it. *John Johnson Collection* (Bodleian Library, 1971), pp. 25-26.

17 *Ibid.*, pp. 105-106.

18 These figures are taken from a catalogue presumably of this sale at the Huntingdon Library, cited in Pepys, *Diary* (eds. Latham and Matthews, University of California Press, 1970 —, p. 48, n. 1. 19 February 1665/6). There is a reproduction of the Prospectus in Eames, 'John Ogilby and his Aesop,' p. 82.

19 It might be noted, in passing, that the British Museum was financed by a national lottery in the following century.

20 For further details, see Eames, pp. 73-88.

21 *Gentleman's Magazine*, Vol. 84, Pt. 1, p. 646.

22 F. Madan, *Oxford Books* (3 vols., 1931), III, 1651-60. In the paragraph at the opening of 1668, Madan erroneously states that Ogilby instituted the first lottery of books in England in that year.

23 C. Ewen, *Lotteries and Sweepstakes* (London, 1932; reissued by B. Blom, 1972), p.112.

24 *Gentleman's Magazine*, Vol. 84, Pt. 1, p. 646. Ogilby noted satirically 'that a money dearth, a silver famine, slackens and cools the courage of Adventurers: through which hazy humors magnifying medium Shillings loome like Crowns, and each Forty Shillings a Ten Pound heap.' Since the total value of prizes offered came to £13,700 and the sale of the 21,050 tickets amounted only to £4,210, Ogilby must have been relying heavily on the profit made in his printing house, or perhaps in his bindery, to justify the existence of such a lottery. It did have, of course, considerable publicity value, and Ogilby continued throughout his life to use it as a sales device.

25 Ewen, *Lotteries*, p. 112.

26 Bodleian; Wood, 658, fol. 792.

27 This portion of the document must have been written not long before Ogilby's Preface to *Africa* (1670); there are several similar turns of phrase.

28 Ogilby gives at some length his reasons for the change from classical verse to geographical prose in the aforementioned Preface to *Africa*, dated 28 April 1670. His arguments will be discussed at greater length in Chapters VI and VII.

29 Rawlinson MS. C. 514, f. 22. I have found no corroboration of the Bristol lottery. There may, of course, have been lotteries in several provincial cities.

30 Killigrew made the same claim in England, with only limited success. See Ewen, *Lotteries*, p. 117.

31 P.R.O., S.P. 63, Ireland, Vol. 331, p. 25. Ewen, *Lotteries*, p. 330, states that 'Robert Leigh' reported on this document on 7 February 1671/2.

32 For specific references, see Arber's *Term Catalogues*, Volume I. As the first of Ogilby's notices occurs in June 1670 and deals with his atlas project, this subject will be discussed at greater length in Chapter VI.

33 Miss Clapp has given a detailed account of the subscription operations of both Ogilby and Richard Blome in her article cited in Chapter II, n. 21.

34 Bodleian; Wood, 658, fol. 790. Miss Clapp prints this material, pp. 367-368. Ogilby estimated that he would make a profit of at most £2 on each plate. The estimate seems remarkably low. It would bring the actual cost of the plate to about £10. Inasmuch as Dugdale (see William Hamper, ed., *The Life, Diary and Correspondence of Sir William Dugdale* [London, 1827], *passim*) was paying Hollar only between £3 and £5 in the next two decades for his meticulous and highly regarded plates, it appears likely that Ogilby, not a man to lose in a business deal, was deliberately underestimating his profit.

35 For a description of the process, after the Great Fire, whereby 'the printer shrank and the bookseller grew in importance,' see Foss, *The Age of Patronage*, pp. 83ff. 'The caterpillar bookseller,' says Foss, 'was transforming himself into the full glory of the publisher, that radiant butterfly.' Foss, who does not mention Ogilby, fails thereby to note the latter's transformation from author to entrepreneur into bookseller and then on to publisher.

36 Translation of the *Visions of Don Francisco de Quevedo Villegas*, 5th ed., 1673, cited in Peter Ure, ed., *Seventeenth-Century Prose, 1620-1700* (Pelican, 1956), p. 56.

37 Stationers Register, Liber F, fol. 482, 2 May 1675. 'Mr. Guy' bought the copyright for this first Ogilby volume for 6d. from 'Mr. Rev. Took,' whom the widow Crook had married. Numerous copyrights were being bought up presumably as speculations, during these years, by Thomas Guy and Peter Parker, among others.

38 See, for example, the sale to a Thomas Lowndes on 10 September 1777, of one-sixteenth of the copyright of 'Ogilby's Roads' at £17.17.6., in B.M. MSS., Add. MSS. 38730, one half-sheet pasted on fol. 169, new numbering.

39 Guildhall MS. 2710/1, ff. 375, 397, 398, 421, 423.

40 There is a record of one of his trips in S.P. 44/51, fol. 132.

41 S.P. 63, Ireland, Vol. 343, no. 77B. This and the following document are printed in full in Clark, *Early Irish Stage*, Appendix A, pp. 189-193.

42 Signet Office, Irish Letter Books, 1/11, pp. 234-236.

43 A copy of the power of attorney is given in Clark, *Early Irish Stage*, p. 193. The original, he says, was destroyed in the Dublin P.R.O. fire in 1922. Clark gives the name as 'Corkey,' but judging from its use in Morgan's will several times, it must be 'Corker.'

44 P.R.O., PROB 11, 399, C/1/9.

CHAPTER VI

1 'Feeling (he said, in his dedication) a Spring of Youthful Vigour, warming my Veins with fresh Hopes of better Times,' he proposed 'A New Model of the Universe, an *English Atlas*, or the setting forth, in our Native Dress, and Modern Language, an Accurate Description of all the Kingdoms and Dominions in the Four Regions thereof.'

2 This grant was dated 1 November 1669. The licence for *Africa*, again by command of Arlington, was dated 20 April 1669. S.P. 44/30, fol. 127.

3 *Gedenkwaerdige Gesantschappen der Oost-Indische Maetschappy in 't Vereenigde Nederland aen de Kaisaren van Japan,* Amsterdam, 1669. There are numerous illustrations in this volume and copious marginalia. The double columns, however, crowd the appearance of the page; it is distinctly less handsome a volume than Ogilby's *Japan.*

4 The work of which Ogilby spoke in his Preface, *Naukeurige Beschryving der Afrikaenschen . . .* appeared in folio, in Amsterdam, in 1668. (I have used the second edition, 1671, *Naukeurige Beschrijvinge der Afrikaensche Gewesten.*) Ogilby must have obtained a copy almost at once and had it translated into English. He used many of the same regional divisions as had Dapper (including the curious and obscure 'Biledulgerid' for 'Numidia'). Dapper's later works on China, Asia and America undoubtedly also influenced Ogilby, although not to the same extent as for Africa.

5 Arber, *Term Catalogues,* 1668-1709. In the same notice, Ogilby called attention to his 'By, or Supernumerary, Volume, Entitled Atlas Japannensis . . . being a Book of Wonders.'

6 One unusual portion of the sizable appendix was a five-page (folio pages) vocabulary of Indian words used in Chile and their English equivalents, taken from a work by Elias Herkman and appearing on pp. 635-639.

7 *De Nieuwe en Onbekende Weereld: Beschryving van America en 't Zuidland,* printed by Jacob Meurs at Amsterdam, 1671.

8 Wenceslaus Hollar, one of Ogilby's favourite, though exploited, illustrators, was on special assignment in Tangier at this time, and apparently not available. Both Montanus and Ogilby, it will be remembered, produced their *Americas* in the same year; Ogilby was apparently in such haste to get out his work that he could not follow his usual practice of commissioning plates several years in advance.

9 Another error, this one of the eye, occurred on p. 166, where Ogilby twice printed 'Troquois' for 'Iroquois.'

10 Anderson credited Ogilby with the authorship, and gave the date, 1671, of *America.* His book, however, was entitled *Description and History of the Island of Jamaica,* Kingston, Jamaica; London and New York, 1851. It is interesting to compare Ogilby's serious and informative account of Jamaica with that of Ned Ward's *Trip to Jamaica* in 1698. The latter, a short diatribe against Jamaica and Jamaicans, roused public interest and became exceedingly, though briefly, popular. See Howard William Troyer, *Ned Ward of Grub Street* (1st ed., Frank Cass, 1946; Barnes and Noble Reprint, 1968), pp. 13-15. Blome in 1672 also published a *Description of the Island of Jamaica.*

11 In this section, p. 104, the translator used a word recently coined in England: 'Every Councellor consults with his private *Cabal.*'

12 B.S. Allen, *Tides in English Taste* (2 vols., 1937), (I, 237) credits Ogilby with the judgements herein given. They are, however, statements from Father Nicholas Trigaut, who admired Chinese painting but thought little of their sculpture (*China,* pp. 456-457). Even the 'horrible shapes' that Allen speaks of in regard to Chinese sculpture take on fuller meaning from examination of the Ogilby text: 'They cast also prodigious and horrible Shapes, both in Copper, Marble and Clay.' These presumably are the dragons and fierce dogs of China, 'horrible' in the sense of evoking fear rather than aesthetic distaste.

13 Cf., for example, Hollar's print of the Emperor of China, with elaborate European complexity and assured use of perspective, in Ogilby's second edition of *Embassy to China* (1673), facing p. 299.

14 Arber, *Term Catalogues,* Michaelmas 1673, the first notice under 'History.'

15 Corporation Record Office, Repertory 75, ff. 284 and 329*v* and Repertory 76, fol. 142.

16 Repertory 76, fol. 243*v* and Repertory 77, fol. 36*v*.

17 Contrast this with the popular work of Giovanni Botero, whose *Historical Description of the most famous kingdomes . . . of the worlde* was published in English in 1601, 1608, 1611, 1616, 1630. The author stated clearly that he was not only or primarily interested in events or descriptions but in the analysis of what makes kingdoms great. Such a goal shaped the form and argument of his work very differently from that of Ogilby.

18 *Geographical Description of the World*, 3rd ed., 1679, in Epistle to the Reader, A3.

19 Bodleian; Wood, 658, fol. 791. See also ff. 787, 792. Further information on him is available in Cox's *Reference Guide to the Literature of Travel*.

CHAPTER VII

1 Much of this story is told, although with almost no references to sources, in E.G.R. Taylor, 'Robert Hooke and the Cartographical Projects of the Late Seventeenth-Century (1666-1696),' *Geographical Journal*, XC (1937), 529-40.

2 'Dr. Woodward' was the writer, quoted in T.F. Reddaway, *The Rebuilding of London after the Great Fire* (London, 1940), p. 300. Letter originally cited on p. 285, n. 1.

3 Charles Welch, *Illustrated Account of the Royal Exchange* (London, 1913), p. 43. The story is given in quotation marks, but without a reference. I am indebted to Mr. Ralph Hyde, Keeper, the Print Room of the Guildhall, for this reference.

4 Peter Mills and John Oliver, *Survey of Building Sites in the City of London after the Great Fire of 1666.* (facsimile reproduction by the London Topographical Society, 5 vols.; 1962-67), I, 82.

5 *Ibid.*, III, 87*v*. Ogilby's neighbours are mentioned on p. 138 in the same volume, and a drawing of one side of his house appears in Vol. V, p. 81*v*. William Morgan's foundations in Crane Court near Fleet Street were laid on 6 November 1669, according to the same record, p. 116.

6 Corporation Record Office, Assessments Boxes 15.1, 23.13, 31.2 and 27.15. There are references in some of these records to an 'Inhabitant' tax, which may refer to 'Personal,' as opposed to real property. Ogilby paid an 'inhabitant' tax of 1s.6d. and a personal one of 6d. in differing quarters.

    I am indebted for these references and a number of others to the skill and kindness of Mr. James Sewell, Assistant Deputy Keeper of the Records.

7 Corporation Record Office, Assessments Box 61.26.

8 St. Bride's Booke of Assessment for the watch 1677/78. Guildhall, MS. 6613/1-3.

9 Hooke's 'Journal' exists in manuscript form in the Guildhall Library. The printed *Diary, 1672-1680*, ed. by H. Robinson and W. Adams (1935), is more accessible, though the index is not to be relied on.

10 See Margaret 'Espinasse, *Robert Hooke* (1956) and F.D. and J.F.M. Hoeniger, *Growth of Natural History in Stuart England* (Folger Booklet, 1969).

11 'Mr. Ogilby's office for carrying on his Description of Great Britain and his General Survey of England and Wales by way of a standing lottery, is kept at Mr. Garaway's coffee-house . . . ' Arber, *Term Catalogues*.

12 See Taylor, p. 532.

13 By an ironic quirk, Hooke failed to keep his journal from 28 August until 9

September 1676, and so left no record of his reaction to Ogilby's death on 4 September of that year. Since Hooke noted Shortgrave's death and burial in entries the following month, it is reasonable to assume that he would have left a comment on Ogilby had he been scribbling in his accustomed fashion when that event occurred.

14 *County Atlases of the British Isles, 1579-1850* (London, 1970), Appendix C, 'The London Map-trade before 1700,' pp. 231-50.

15 See, for example, King's reference to 'geographical cards' on p. 91 of his Autobiography, Rawl. C. 514.

16 Arber, *Term Catalogues*, Vol. I, 21 June 1670. There is an undated advertisement that may be in Ogilby's hand describing the 'English Atlas' as the publisher first envisaged it, probably in 1670. The final, fifth volume, the notice says, was to be 'the Concerns Onely of Great Brittain or our English Monarchy, Collected and Translated from most Authentique Authors and Augmented with later observations.' S.P. 29, Vol. 442, No. 16, sheet No. 1.

17 *Hist. MSS. Comm.* 25, Le Fleming MSS., No. 1197, pp. 75-76.

18 *Ibid.*, No. 1297, 27 February 1671/2, p.89.

19 *Ibid.*, pp. 105, 112, 119.

20 *Ibid.*, No. 1487, December 1673, p. 106.

21 Josten, ed., *Ashmole,* III, 1237 and 1238, n. 2. The Earl expressed his pleasure in *America*, and apparently had commissioned a special dedicatory plate for himself, to be placed in his copy. He enclosed five guineas for Ashmole to forward to Ogilby on one occasion. *Ibid.*, III, 1246, 1247 and n. 1.

22 P.R.O., Signet Office, Docquets, IND. 6815, fol. 328, June 1670.

23 P.R.O., S.P. 44 (Entry Books), Vol. 36, ff. 31-32. 24 August 1671.

24 *Ibid.*, ff. 93-95. A lengthy statement, endorsed 'Mr. Ogilby's Letter of Recommendation' and dated 11 July 1672, details these steps.

25 *Ibid.*, fol. 147. This appears again, together with a plea to justices of the peace and other local authorities to aid the lotteries in P.R.O., C66, 3140, No. 20, dated 31 January [1673].

26 Bagford Collection, fol. 49. These folios are not in consecutive order, having been abstracted from various sources.

27 P.R.O., Signet Office, Docquets, IND. 6814, fol. 588.

28 It was printed by Fordham in 1925 and mentioned again by Skelton, *County Atlases . . .* , p. 185.

29 P.R.O., S.P. 30/G.

30 Repertory 77, fol. 89*v*.

31 Sloane MSS. 3958, fol. 16*r* and *v*.

32 Repertory 78, ff. 185*v* and 207*v*-208*v*.

33 Repertory 79, ff. 105 and 292.

34 Repertory 78, fol. 250*v*.

35 S.P. 44, Entry Book, Vol. 26, fol. 155*v* and 156*r*. This also appears in P.R.O., IND. 6815, fol. 689.

36 IND. 6816, fol. 29. This appears also in P.R.O., C66, 3157, No. 20.

37 *Ibid.*, fol. 63.

38 *Ibid.*, fol. 93.

39 *Brief Lives*, ed. by Anthony Powell (New York, 1949), p. 124. 12 August 1672.

40 *Ibid.*, pp. 149-51 and *passim*.

41 J.B. Harley, in his Introduction to the facsimile of *Britannia* (T.O.T., Vol. II, 1970) reprints one set of questions as Plate 3. The queries appear in Bodl., Aubrey 4, ff. 243-44. One of these, annotated by Aubrey, states that the contents were considered at several meetings. Others besides Ogilby were sending out such queries about this time, as Stuart Piggott remarks in 'Antiquarian Thought in the Sixteenth and Seventeenth Centuries' in Levi Fox, ed., *English Historical Scholarship in the Sixteenth and Seventeenth Centuries* (Oxford University Press, 1956). Piggott stresses that the surveys were tilted to the scientific rather than the historical angle by the time of the latter seventeenth-century, p. 109.

42 King, Bodl., Rawlinson C. 514, fol. 21.

43 B.M. MSS. Room, Lansdowne MS. 895, ff. 138-228. This document has a cover entitled 'Mr. Brown's Survey Book' and it deals primarily with Yorkshire. It is generally assumed that it was a preliminary study for Warburton's *Yorkshire,* although there are no maps similar to those in 'Mr. Brown's Survey Book' in the copy of Warburton in Lansdowne MS. 913 or in Lansdowne MS. 895, 'Warburton's Collections for Yorkshire, Vol. VII, Miscell.' It might have been done for Ogilby, whose title page shows cherubs displaying York in the very centre of a strip map. Whatever the book for which it was taken, the survey gives an idea of what the mapmaker on the spot was looking for and what he saw. To my knowledge, 'Mr. Brown's Survey Book' has never been reproduced in print.

44 Skelton, *County Atlases* . . . , p. 186.

45 B.M. Map Room, 3055 (37).

46 One cartouche stated that this was 'Actually Surveyed' at three miles to an inch by Ogilby and Morgan, His Majesty's Cosmographers. Another cartouche gave the dedication to the Earl of Essex and was signed by Morgan alone, using the titles of Cosmographer and of Master of the Revels in Ireland. This map was printed separately by the Essex Topographical Society.

47 See the copy in Map Room, K to P [XXXIX]. Ralph Hyde of the Guildhall has been helpful in elucidating the evidence associated with this map, and with that of the town of Malden in Essex.

48 P.R.O., PROB. 11/352, on seven folios between 124 and 125.

49 B.M. Map Room, Map C.7.e.8.

50 P.R.O., C66/3184. 7 February 1675/6. This appears, in brief, under the date of October 1675, in P.R.O., IND. 6816, fol. 205, procured by Coventry.

51 Bodleian, Rawl. D734, Fol. 41.

52 S.P. 29, Vol. 378, No. 28, fol. 41.

53 *Hist. MSS. Comm.* 36, Ormonde MSS., N.S. IV, pp. 610-11.

54 Register of Marriages, Burials &c. from 1673 to 1695. Guildhall, MS. 6540/2.

55 Ashmole gives the date as 19 December 1677 and the hour as 2:00 p.m. (MS. Ashmole 1136, fol. 57v, cited in Josten, ed., *Ashmole*, IV, 1507).

56 The remarks on the Ogilbys and Morgan occur both in MS. Aubrey 7, ff. 19v and 20v, and in MS, Aubrey 8, ff. 44-47v. They are reprinted in Aubrey's *Brief Lives*, 11, 99-105 and in Aubrey, *Letters by Eminent Men* III, 466-70. See also Anthony à Wood, who, under the heading of 'Shirley,' gives a biography of Ogilby in *Athenae Oxonienses*, pp. 740-44.

57 The map has usually been dated as 1677, but the Guildhall copy is dated as of 1676, presumably printed after the month of September in which Ogilby died. It is a superb source of information about specific locations, even of obscure areas, of the London after the Fire. When it is supplemented by the five volumes of Peter Mills and John Oliver, *Survey of Building Sites,* these items constitute an unparalleled resource for the study of a seventeenth-century city.

58 P.R.O., Signet Office, Docquets, IND. 6817, fol. 24v.

59 Guildhall Records Office, Minutes of the Records of the Court of Aldermen, Repertory 81, ff. 337v-338r.

60 *Ibid.,* Repertory 82, fol. 142v.

61 *Ibid.,* Repertory 85, fol. 219.

62 Bodleian, Wood 658, fol. 776.

63 *Ibid.,* fol. 786.

64 In Bodl., Rawl. D. 874, fol. 41, there is contained a 'schedule' of receipts of payments for secret service by one Henry Guy, Esq. Among these is the note of the above-mentioned payment to William Morgan, Cosmographer, for his Survey of the City of London and Westminster. It is undated, but lies between documents of June and July 1682.

65 S.P. 44, Entry Books, Vol. 66, fol. 65.

66 Arber, *Term Catalogue,* p. 677.

67 Guildhall Library. Safe 2.

CHAPTER VIII

1 *Athenae Oxonienses,* III, pp. 740, 743, 744.

2 To be found under the heading 'The Modern Poets,' p. 114.

3 *Lives of the Poets* (5 vols.; London, 1753), II, 265-68.

4 *John Dryden: Selected Criticism,* ed. by James Kinsley and George Parfitt (Oxford, Clarendon Press, 1970), 'Preface to *Sylvae,* 1685,' p. 195.

5 *Ibid.,* pp. 198-99.

6 Richard F. Hardin, in his 'Preface' to *Michael Drayton* (University Press of Kansas, 1973), p. v, indicates just such a switch in the case of Drayton. Even more à propos is a sentence from Alfred Harbage concerning the opprobrious use of the term 'dead trees' for a number of authors not appreciated by Gosse in his *Shakespeare to Pope.* Harbage says, 'This arborous appraisal illustrates nothing so well as that critics, in practising their 'art of praise,' secrete by natural laws of compensation a quantity of bile that must be vented at intervals upon minor authors.' *William Davenant,* p. 5. See also an older work, Albert S. Borgman, *Thomas Shadwell, His Life and Comedies* (New York University, 1928, reprinted by B. Blom, 1969), especially the 'Preface,' p. v.

7 Kathleen M. Lynch, *Jacob Tonson, Kit-Cat Publisher* (University of Tennessee Press, 1971), p. 30. See also pp. 119-20 for Lynch's appreciation of the value of these illustrations in increasing the popularity of Dryden's translation.

8 See Earl Miner, *Dryden's Poetry* (Indiana University Press, 1971), pp. 157-58, 167-68; cf. also the same author's Introduction to a facsimile of Ogilby's *Aesop* (1668), wherein he singles out Fables XX and XL of Ogilby's as being especially influential on Dryden, pp. xi-xiii.

9 Reprinted in *Poems on Affairs of State: Augustan Satirical Verse, 1660-1714*, Vol. VI, *1697-1704*, Frank H. Ellis, ed. (Yale University Press, 1970), p. 107. Note 68 on that page quotes from a 1709 manuscript at Yale, which declares that Ogilby's name 'will, as long as the *English* Tongue lives, signify a *Poetaster*.'

10 *Observations, Anecdotes, and Characters of Books and Men, Collected from Conversation*, ed. James M. Osborn (2 vols.; Oxford, Clarendon Press, 1966), pp. 2-3, has a number of references to Pope and Ogilby.

11 *Ibid*., cited from Pope's *Works* (1751), IV, 17.

12 *Ibid*., p. 3. Dated 6-10 April 1742.

13 See Maynard Mack, 'Introduction' to the *Iliad* (Twickenham Edition of the Poems of Alexander Pope, 2nd ed., revised), VII, especially pp. cxviii, cxx, cxxi. In the same edition, see also James Sutherland, ed., *The Dunciad*, Vol. V, p. xlv. And, lastly, Spence, *op. cit.*, p. 2.

Bibliography

WORKS OF JOHN OGILBY Listed in chronological order, during his lifetime

Virgil's *Works*, 1649
Aesop's *Fables*, 1651
Virgil's *Works*, 1654
Virgil's *Opera* (in Latin), 1658
Homer His Iliads, 1660
The Entertainment . . . of Charles II, 1661
The Entertainment . . . of Charles II, 1662
Aesop's *Fables, Androcleus or The Roman Slave, The Ephesian Matron*,
   1665
Homer His Odyssey, 1665
Works of Virgil, Dublin, 1666
Aesop's *Fables, Aesopics*, 1668
Embassy to China, 1669
Africa, 1670
Atlas Japannensis, 1670
America, 1671
Atlas Chinensis, 1671
Aesopics, 2nd ed., 1673
Asia, 1673
Embassy to China, 2nd ed., 1673
Aesopics, 3rd ed., 1675
Britannia, 1675, 1676
Itinerarium angliae, 1675, 1676, (?)
Virgil, *Works*, 1675

OTHER WORKS including unpublished material

Two volumes of Homer, *Works* published in Dublin, 1669, listed as by
   'O'Gilby'
'The Merchant of Dublin,' a play, performed, but not published (contemporary reference only) (cf. John Ford, 'The London Merchant,'
   written between 1621 and 1638)

'The Character of a Trooper,' a character study or essay (contemporary reference only)

Miscellaneous maps of London and Edinburgh, and of the counties of Middlesex, Essex, and Kent. The most comprehensive collection of these maps is in the Map Room of The British Library.

Bibliographical Essay

The variety of John Ogilby's activities involves a commensurate diversity of sources that must be consulted by anyone tracing his work. Perhaps first in order of importance are the works published and/or written by Ogilby himself, which appear here in a separate listing, by chronology. Variations abound in Ogilby volumes, some attributable to the vagaries of the purchaser at the bindery, some presumably the result of differing issues rather than editions. To collate Ogilby folios is to discover the extent of these variations, but they seem to have little significance in themselves.

Only the scantiest of records appear in the Merchant Taylors Company Guild Records Book and the Stationers Company Register. In the Guildhall, both the printed and the manuscript copies of Robert Hooke's Journal mention Ogilby briefly. His marriage is recorded in the Register General there, but other sources, such as the Watch Books, cover just a few patches of time and space. Ogilby does not appear. The Guildhall Record Office has a few entries relating to Ogilby's life in London in his latter days.

In the British Library there are no manuscript references, although the Lansdowne MSS. 895 includes 'Mr. Brown's Survey Book.' The J. Bagford Collection (in the North Library), an extensive and heterogeneous compilation, illuminates a number of the areas — printing, maps, religion — in which Ogilby was involved.

A few references appear in the Bodleian that are related to Ogilby, specifically in the Wood MSS., the Aubrey MSS., the Ashmolean MSS., and Gregory King's account of his life in the Rawlinson MS. On the other hand, in places where one might have expected some record, nothing appears, as, for example, in the Index of Strafford Papers in the Sheffield Library, in the National Register of Archives, the Merchant Taylors School Library and among the papers of the family of the Earls of Airlie, whose family name John Ogilby bore and from whose general region he certainly came.

Despite the disappointing absence of Ogilby's name in various manuscript sources wherein it might rightly be expected, he made an impact upon a number of contemporaries. Both in John Aubrey's *Brief Lives* (2 vols.; ed., A. Clark; Oxford, 1898) and his *Letters by Eminent Men and Lives of Eminent Men* (3 vols.; London, 1813), there are references to Ogilby. Anthony à Wood (*Athenae Oxonienses* and *The Fasti*, New York and London, Johnson Reprint, 1967) purveys a considerable amount of his usual mixture of fact and fancy, treating Ogilby in his account of James

Shirley. The five published volumes of Ashmole's jottings (C.H. Josten, ed., Oxford, 1966) contain numerous references to Ogilby, although not everything that appears in the manuscripts. There are, of course, numerous references to Ogilby's works and projects in Arber's *Term Catalogues* (those dealing with the years 1668 to 1709). It is sad not to find a small character sketch by Pepys, although there are a few references; on the other hand, Edward Phillips, in *Theatrum Poetarum Anglicanorum* (1675), gives Ogilby far more space than might have been expected. Dryden and Johnson note Ogilby only to deride him; Pope's interest as a young boy in Ogilby comes secondhand from Joseph Spence, *Observations, Anecdotes, and Characters of Books and Men, Collected from Conversation* (ed. James M. Osborn; 2 vols., Clarendon Press, 1966). Subsequent historians of English literature ignore Ogilby or use him as a figure for ridicule. There has been no full-length biography of Ogilby. The latest work dealing directly with him is a brief account in German, beautifully produced, by Margaret Schuchard (Hamburg, 1973).

Only slight references occur in the Historical Manuscripts Commission volumes (25, the Le Fleming MSS. and 36, the Ormonde, n.s. IV). On the other hand, valuable, though scanty, evidence appears in Peter Mills and John Oliver, *Survey of Building Sites in the City of London After the Great Fire of 1666* (5 vols.; 1962-67). The manuscript materials, from which these volumes were taken, are in the Guildhall and do not add anything. T.F. Reddaway, *The Rebuilding of London After the Great Fire* (London, 1940) does not mention Ogilby, but gives a convincing picture of the process of rebuilding, in which Ogilby certainly had a part. There is one reference to the printer-publisher in Charles Welch, *Illustrated Account of the Royal Exchange and the Picture Therein* (London, 1913).

There are more omissions than inclusions of Ogilby's name in records left by contemporaries, perhaps because of his Scottish birth, his lack of university connections and his failure to connect himself with an important family by marriage. It is probably not surprising that he is not included in the numerous Buckingham biographies; they are useful for descriptions of the court background that Ogilby must have known as a young man, and for suggesting the atmosphere of lavish flattery that he administered to patrons all his life. Ogilby does not appear in Fuller's *Worthies,* nor in Evelyn. S.M. Kingsbury's *Records of the Virginia Company of London* (4 vols.; Library of Congress, 1906) has no mention of the successful Ogilby lottery. There are a few brief references in C.M. Clode's *Memorials of the Guild of Merchant Taylors* (London, 1875). Thomas Birch is silent on Ogilby in his *History of the Royal Society of London* (4 vols.; New York and London, Johnson Reprint, 1968), although Ogilby certainly knew and consorted with a number of early Fellows. He appears only once in Margaret 'Espinasse's *Robert Hooke* (second printing; University of California Press, 1962). Nothing (except printed poems) remains of any exchange between Sir William Davenant and Ogilby, despite the ocasions on which those two worked together or against each other (see Alfred Harbage, *William Davenant,* first printed, 1935; Octagon Books, 1971). Shadwell, whose name is so often linked with that of Ogilby in adverse criticism, has biographers (Albert S. Borgman, first published in 1928, reissued by B. Blom in 1969 and Alfred Harbage, *Thomas Shadwell, Life and Comedies,* New York University, 1928); and his collected works are published (Montague Summers, ed., 5 vols.; London, 1927). No scrap of evidence showing direct contact between him and Ogilby remains. Although Ogilby worked with and under Hopton for some time, he is not mentioned in F.T.R. Edgar's *Sir Ralph Hopton: The King's Man in the West* (Oxford, 1968). Ogilby's life showed a number of parallels to that of Sir John Birkenhead, but there is no reference to him in Peter W. Thomas's book (Oxford, 1969) on that royalist. Thomas Stanley, with whom Ogilby had business and presumably some social relationships, attracted a nineteenth-century editor (Sir Egerton Brydges, *Poems by Thomas Stanley, Esq.,* London, 1814), and one in the twentieth (G.M. Crump, *Poems and Translations of Thomas Stanley,* Oxford, 1962). Again no reference to Ogilby remains, and it is doubtless significant that Ogilby was not included in the list of friends whom Stanley commemorated in a poem on friendship. The social status of the printer-publisher probably precluded his entry into Stanley's circle.

A number of decidedly varied works are important either because Ogilby knew and used them or because they explain the kind of projects he initiated and works he produced. Giovanni Botero, whose *Historical Description of the Most Famous Kingdomes . . . of the Worlde* (various editions, 1601 to 1630) was popular in Ogilby's youth, produced the kind of generalised travelogue that Ogilby disdained to follow. On the other hand, J.L. de la Cerda, *Opera Omnia Argumentis, Explicationibus et Notis Illustrata* (of Virgil; 3 vols.; Cologne, 1642-47, with both earlier and later editions) was openly used and cited by Ogilby in his classical endeavours, as were other classical translators and commentators. For his atlases of Japan and Africa, Ogilby, in that pre-copyright age, took at will, and sometimes with amazing rapidity, large chunks, including maps, from the works of Arnoldus Montanus, *Gedenkwaerdige Gesantschappen der Oost-Indische Maetschappy in't Vereenigde Nederland aen de Kaisaren van Japan* (Amsterdam, 1669) and from Dr. Oliver Dapper, *Naukeurige Beschrijvinge der Afrikaensche Gewesten,* 1671 (this is the second edition, the one that I have used; the first appeared in Amsterdam in 1668, with a similar title).

Other works that Ogilby used for his atlas series were Montanus' *De Nieuwe en Onbekende Weereld Beschryving van America en't Zuidland* (Amsterdam, 1671) for his *America* volume and Jan Nieuhof, *Het Gezantschap der Neerlandtsche Oost-Indische Compagnie aan den Grooten Tartarischen Cham . . .* (Amsterdam, 1665) for *China.* For the latter volume, Ogilby also used, and gave credit to, Father Athanasius Kircher's works, especially *China Monumentis, qua Sacris qua Profanis, Illustrata* (Amsterdam, 1667). Of some bibliographical interest also is the reprinting of Ogilby's remarks on Jamaica by W. Wemyss Anderson in his *Description and History of the Island of Jamaica* (Kingston, Jamaica, 1851). Ogilby knew and quoted Sir Thomas Herbert's *Travels* (first printed, 1634), and he was probably familiar with the very different travel works of

George Meriton in that century.

Certainly, Ogilby knew and used, in the production of his *Entertainment,* Stephen Harrison's *Archs of Triumph* (London, 1604) and probably also Dekker's *Magnificent Entertainment* and Jonson's *Part of the Entertainment.* . . . He may have seen the account of Charles I's progress through Edinburgh in 1633, entitled *The Entertainment of the High and Mighty Monarch Charles.* . . . And possibly he knew two small works commemorating a 1641 parade of that monarch, entitled *Ovatio Carolina. The Triumph of King Charles;* and *Englands Comfort, and Londons Joy.* A recent excellent book illuminating the background against which Ogilby worked in producing the *Entertainment* is David Bergeron, *English Civic Pageantry, 1558-1642* (London, 1971); earlier such works are Glynne Wickham, *Early English Stages* (London and New York, 1959) and Robert Withington, *English Pageantry: An Historical Outline* (Cambridge, Mass., 1918-20).

Luther A. Weigle's 'English Versions Since 1611,' *Cambridge History of the Bible,* ed. S.L. Greenslade (Cambridge, 1963), provides a partial unravelling of some complications surrounding the production of Bibles in Ogilby's time. A number of puzzling queries remain, however, about the production of 'Ogilby's Bible' in particular.

A number of works treat the Aesopian versions made in Ogilby's and others' times. Among these are Ben Edwin Perry, *Aesopica* (Urbana, Ill., 1952); John J. McKendry, *Aesop: Five Centuries of Illustrated Fables* (Metropolitan Museum of Art, 1964); Earl Miner's 'Introduction' to a facsimile reproduction of Ogilby's *Aesop,* the 1668 edition (University of California Press, 1965) and Marian Eames, 'John Ogilby and his Aesop,' *Bulletin of the New York Public Library,* LXV (1961), 73-88.

On the problem of translation and on the currents of ideas passing from the continent to England, a number of volumes are suggestive. Generally, these raise questions rather than provide answers as to how translators and copiers worked. Two of the volumes I found helpful were Justin Bellanger, *Histoire de la Traduction en France* (Paris, 1903) and Dorothea F. Canfield, *Corneille and Racine in England* (New York, 1904). On the subjectively infinite question of taste, a question raised throughout this book, the following works should be mentioned: B.S. Allen, *Tides in English Taste, 1619-1800* (2 vols.; Harvard University Press, 1937); Geoffrey Scott, *Architecture of Humanism: A Study in the History of Taste* (2nd ed., 1924; reprinted, Gloucester, Mass., 1965); Raymond Nave, *Le Goût de Voltaire* (Slatkine Reprints, Geneva, 1967, from Droz, 1938), which discusses the seventeenth-century background to Voltaire; Roger Zuber, *Les 'Belles Infideles' et la Formation du Goût Classique* (Colin, 1968); H.S. Bennett, *English Books and Readers* (Cambridge, 1970); and Stuart Piggott, 'Antiquarian Thought in the Sixteenth and Seventeenth Centuries,' *English Historical Scholarship in the Sixteenth and Seventeenth Centuries* (Oxford, 1956). Of interest in discussing travel books (though not mentioning Ogilby) is R.W. Frantz, *The English Traveller and the Movement of Ideas, 1660-1732* (University of Nebraska, 1967, first published in 1934).

Ogilby's work on the first and second theatres to be founded in Dublin, both by him, is best treated by the last book on the subject, William Smith Clark, *The Early Irish Stage* (Oxford, 1955). Professor Clark had access to certain records, now destroyed, that make his book a source as well as a thorough account of the subject he treats. His interest, of course, lies in the theatre and not particularly in Ogilby. Somewhat earlier LaTourette Stockwell in *Dublin Theatres and Theatre Customs, 1637-1820* (1938; reissued, B. Blom, 1968) had treated the same subject. Peter Kavanagh's *The Irish Theatre* (Tralee, 1946) is of slighter value than either of the first two mentioned. Among the works that give evidence of Dublin in Ogilby's time is a small but interesting monograph by John, fifth Marquess of Ely, *Rathfarnham Castle. Adam Loftus and the Ely Family* (printed for private circulation, no date), a copy of which is in the National Library at Dublin. G.E. Bentley's *Jacobean and Caroline Stage* (7 vols.; Oxford, 1941-68) is evocative of the atmosphere that prevailed when Ogilby, a dancer and dancing-master, first entered the theatrical world. A.H. Nason's *James Shirley, Dramatist* (first printed, 1915; reprinted by B. Blom, 1967) treats one who was for some years a close associate of Ogilby's in the world of the theatre. Mrs. Katherine Philips, some of whose work Ogilby produced, is the subject of a biography by Philip W. Souers, *The Matchless Orinda* (Harvard University Press, 1931; reprinted by Johnson Reprint Corporation, 1968). Further information on the theatrical world at this time appears in Arthur F. White, 'The Office of Revels and Dramatic Censorship During the Restoration Period,' *Studies in English Literature,* XXXIV (September 15, 1931), 5-45.

The idea of using subscribers to support his work and the printing of their names probably originated with Ogilby's familiarity with John Minsheu's *Ductor in Linguas: The Guide into Tongues* (London, 1617), although he makes no such acknowledgement. The fullest treatment of Ogilby's involvement in this activity appears in Sarah L. C. Clapp, 'The Subscription Enterprises of John Ogilby and Richard Blome,' *Modern Philology,* XXX (1933), 365-379. The use of lotteries, which, in many instances, Ogilby combined with his subscription proposals, is explored in C.L. Ewen, *Lotteries and Sweepstakes* (London, 1932); John S. Ezell, *Fortune's Merry Wheel: The Lottery in America* (Harvard University Press, 1960); and the account in *Gentleman's Magazine,* Vol. 84, Pt. 1.

The very considerable subject of book-making in later seventeenth-century England is a necessary background for John Ogilby's most significant activity. Plomer's two dictionaries, of *Printing* and of *Booksellers and Printers, 1641-67,* are useful. So, of course, are the already mentioned Arber's *Catalogues,* as well as F. Madan's *Oxford Books* (3 vols.; 1931), and the curious three volumes of C.W. Dugan's *Books Printed in Dublin* (compiled by E.R. McC. Dix; Dublin, 1892-1912). Somewhat later in coverage but of interest are H.W. Troyer, *Ned Ward of Grub Street* (1st ed., 1946; Barnes and Noble Reprint, 1968) and Kathleen M. Lynch, *Jacob Tonson, Kit-Cat Publisher* (University of Tennessee Press, 1971). On the problem of censorship there is Joseph G. Muddiman, *King's Journalist: Sir Roger L'Estrange* (originally published, 1923; reissued by A.M. Kelley,

1971); treating one of Ogilby's specialities is David Bland, *A History of Book Illustration* (University of California Press, 1969).

Map-making is the achievement of Ogilby most admired by Englishmen of his own time and later. It is not surprising, therefore, that there is a considerable literature, some of it technical, on that aspect of his work. Sir Herbert G. Fordham's monograph, *John Ogilby, 1600-1676* (reprinted by Oxford from *Transactions of the Bibliographical Society,* 1925) is devoted primarily to an examination and assessment of Ogilby's contribution to the mapping of roads in England and Wales. Miss E.G.R. Taylor's article on 'Robert Hooke and the Cartographical Projects of the Late Seventeenth Century (1666-1696)' in the *Geographical Journal,* XC, 1937, 529-540, added considerable information on Ogilby's activities, although a lack of references has made it impossible to trace some of her statements. A handsome facsimile edition of the *Britannia* was produced by Theatrum Orbis Terrarum (5th series, Vol. II; Amsterdam, 1970), edited and with an introduction by J.B. Harley. Other works in this field, dealing directly or indirectly with Ogilby's mapmaking, include Ida Darlington and James Howgego, *Printed Maps of London, c. 1553-1850* (London, 1964); R.A. Skelton, *County Atlases of the British Isles, 1579-1850* (London, 1970); Philippa Glanville, *London in Maps* (London, 1972); and Helen Wallis and Sarah Tyacke, eds., *My Head is a Map* (Francis Edwards and Carta Press, 1973).

The maps commissioned and created by Ogilby and Ogilby/Morgan appear in various repositories. Among those I have used are the British Library Map Room, the Map Room of the National Library of Scotland, the London Museum (which has a rare original of a Morgan map) and the Print Room of the Guildhall. The largest collection I have seen is in the Map Room of the British Library. It includes the maps of Kent (1670), of Essex (1678), of Middlesex (1677?); the depiction of the Borough of Ipswich (1674), of the island of Jamaica (1671), and of a part of the plan of the Hospital of St. Katherine (1686). And it contains also the map of the City of London (1677), which Morgan produced just after Ogilby's death, another finished in 1681-82, and the Hollar map of 'The Country about fifteen Miles any Way from London,' drawn in 1670 and published in 1683. Some of these are copies. There are also many of the later editions and revisions of the Ogilby road maps, one dated as late as 1770. Some separates have disappeared, probably forever. In this field, I have essentially followed the work of trained geographers. The only original suggestion I offer is to look at 'Mr. Brown's Survey Book' in the British Library Students Room (Lansdowne MSS. 895) as an example of the kind of on-the-spot map drawing that must have passed, in great quantities, into Ogilby's publishing office, to be redrawn and recalculated, then to be engraved by Hollar or others, and finally printed by Ogilby and, in later instances, by Morgan.

There are a number of portraits of Ogilby. The earliest of which I know is one engraved by William Marshall in 1649. Marshall, who engraved the cut for Milton's first collected works, was an inferior craftsman who stayed on in Commonwealth England when most of the artists had gone. His oval frame, showing the subject's head, upper body and ill-made hand (the latter holding a medal of Virgil) portray Ogilby looking like a sober divine of the period, though with more luxurious curling locks than would have been expected. A later, folio-sized engraving, painted (or drawn) by Peter Lely and engraved by Peter Lombart is set in an octagonal frame, showing a more youthful, much handsomer man than the first engraving. It portrays only head and bust; the arms of Scotland appear below. A slightly different pose and somewhat sterner mien, drawn again by Lely and engraved this time by William Faithorne, again bears the lion of Scotland on a shield. These two latter portraits date from the 1650's and 1660's, when Ogilby was producing so many volumes and commissioned a leading painter to record his features. His portrait appears in some issues and not in others, no doubt according to the wish of the buyer. The card catalogue of the Map Room of the British Library lists a portrait by Fuller engraved by Edwards, another portrait in the Bodleian and a bust in the *Aesop*. Miss Schuchard reproduces two other pictures of Ogilby, neither of which have I seen. One is the Bodleian portrait done by Lely. The other is included in a nine-teenth-century work, from a picture now at Strawberry Hill. There is also the engraving of Ogilby tendering the *Britannia* to Charles II, which appears on Morgan's London map. Lely customarily improved his sitters' appearance; but, even allowing for artistic licence, Ogilby seems to have had a strong and attractive face.

If the records on Ogilby seem relatively slight, those relating to Morgan are even more vestigial. There is nothing left of the numerous missives that must have passed between the two men, ephemera dealing with publishing, with the Dublin theatre, the Fire, the Plague, new houses and the like. The lack of a direct male heir of Ogilby and presumably of Morgan as well would have contributed to the disappearance of what must once have been a considerable amount of paper.

Morgan, of course, does appear in warrants and patents, in wills and in City records (as recipient of City money and as taxpayer). He is probably one of the William Morgans listed in Charles Edward Atkins, *Register of Apprentices of the Worshipful Company of Clockmakers of the City of London . . . 1631 . . . to . . . 1931* (privately printed, 1931). Background material on Morgan's company, in which he played a role as member if not as a watchmaker, appears in Atkins and Overall, *Company of Clockmakers* (1881), Baillie, Clutton and Ilbert, *Britten's Old Clocks and Watches and Their Makers* (London, 1956, 7th ed.), and G.H. Baillie, *Watchmakers and Clockmakers of the World* (3rd ed., reprinted; London, 1963). Morgan's advertisements continue for a time after Ogilby's death. Then, in the 1690's, he slips from sight far more completely even than Ogilby.

I have often felt, as I leafed through manuscripts or turned the pages of some book, that Ogilby hovered just offstage, as he must often have stood, watching his dramatic productions. Like the skilled producer-director that he was, however, he rarely appeared, either in person or through reference. It is my hope that, with this effort at integrating the many facets of his life, he may emerge in his own right as a figure of some importance in his time. Once fully identified, he may even be found in unsuspected company and gain acknowledgment in places hitherto unsearched.

Index